MARGIN OF ERROR

Pollsters and the Manipulation of Canadian Politics

CLAIRE HOY

KEY PORTER BOOKS

To Lydia, Zachary, Clayton and Scarlet . . . my own perfect sample

Canadian Cataloguing in Publication Data

Hoy, Claire

　Margin of error

ISBN 1-55013-172-9

1. Canada — Politics and government — Public opinion.
2. Public opinion — Canada.　3. Press and politics — Canada.
I. Title.

HN110.Z9P84 1989	320.971	C89-094095-9

Key Porter Books Limited
70 The Esplanade
Toronto, Ontario
M5E 1R2

Typesetting: Alphabets
Design: Marie Bartholomew
Printed and bound in Canada

89 90 91 92 93 6 5 4 3 2 1

Contents

Preface

Peter Mansbridge doesn't know this. But in a way, he's responsible for this book.

There I was, sitting comfortably in my third-floor loft during the November 1988 federal election campaign watching "The National" when Mansbridge announced the results of the latest CBC election poll.

It had the Liberals, who until a week earlier were being written off completely, leading in Atlantic Canada, winning in Quebec, ahead in Ontario, but losing in the West.

What this meant, he proudly announced, was a Tory minority government.

I couldn't believe it. It made no sense, at least not with the information he'd offered the viewers. I told Mansbridge that, too. Mind you, since he was in his Toronto studio and I was in my Ottawa home, he likely didn't hear me yelling at my TV set. Just as well. I wasn't polite.

But it did give me the idea. It struck me then, at that very moment, that a book on the use and abuse and history of polling and pollsters in this country was overdue.

I've long been suspicious about their claims of scientific precision. I've often been outraged by the media treatment of them, the tendency to accept their findings uncritically, and their power to lead journalists and politicians, like dogs on a leash, through the issues of the day.

On the other hand, polls, properly conducted and carefully reported, can be a useful tool for journalists, politicians and the public.

The subject of public-opinion polls and the reporting of them has been debated in political circles for years, but despite the remarkable growth in both the number of polls and the influence they wield, nobody had really tried to bring it all together in a book. This is what I've tried to do here.

Naturally, I didn't do it alone. Many people helped.

First, the pollsters. I want to thank them, both the national and regional pollsters who gave freely and generously of their time for personal interviews. Decima's Allan Gregg, who in the past has been accessible, was the only pollster who refused to co-operate. He wouldn't even acknowledge several telephone and fax messages. But there you have it.

Many others also afforded me interviews: politicians, political aides, several journalists and academics.

I want also to thank head librarian, Erik Spicer, and his professional staff for once again sharing the wonders of the Library of Parliament with me. Without their help, it would not have been possible to collect the details necessary to make this project worthwhile. Thanks also to the staff at the National Archives for help in tracing the wartime origins of polling in Canada.

And, of course, my wife Lydia Huber for her help in researching, filing and compiling much of the data, and for her tireless support and encouragement.

Special thanks also to a few journalists who went to considerable lengths to help out: Jim Meek in Halifax, Francis Russell in Winnipeg, Jamie Lamb in Vancouver and Stevie Cameron in Toronto.

Enjoy. And God bless.

1

The New God of Politics

On July 20, 1988, when Liberal leader John Turner walked into the media studio at 150 Wellington Street, across the road from Parliament Hill, he had two things in his briefcase.

One was a copy of a suprisingly bold statement announcing his intention to let the unelected, Liberal-dominated Senate block passage of Brian Mulroney's Canada–United States free-trade deal until after an election.

"Let the people decide," said Turner.

In some respects, they already had, because the other document Turner carried contained the results of two recent public-opinion polls, worth about $200,000, by Liberal pollster Martin Goldfarb, commissioned despite the $6-million party debt.

One poll was a detailed, national in-home survey on basic Canadian attitudes toward the parties and the issues.

The other, more to the point, was a secret Goldfarb poll of the views of Quebeckers on one specific issue: did they feel Mulroney should have an election before completing the deal with Ronald Reagan and, if so, would they favour a plan to have the Senate withhold approval until after the people had spoken?

"We polled exclusively in Quebec for this one," says John Webster, the party's 1988 campaign director, "because we made the assumption that the strongest negative response to the gambit would be in Quebec on the basis that that's where support for free trade was high.

"Basically, the public's attitude in Quebec, no matter what their view was on free trade, was, they favoured an election," Webster says. "There was widespread support for the idea, so we did it."

And it worked.

Even though many resented what they saw as unwarranted interference in the electoral system by the appointed Senate, the move at least established that Turner was not only able finally to control his own caucus, but indeed had suddenly found the courage to make a decision based on heartfelt principle rather than on political expediency. The public was unaware that private polls, not overriding principles, had governed the seemingly bold policy decision.

Free trade, of course, would become the dominant issue of the election campaign. Ever since Mulroney had reversed himself after the 1984 election, announcing his support of free trade after having savagely denigrated the idea during his 1983 campaign for the party leadership, Turner and NDP leader Ed Broadbent had been competing with each other to be seen as the main opponent of the deal. Turner in particular needed something, anything, to salvage the remnants of his own tattered public image and his fractured party, yet until what party insiders called the "Senate gambit," he had not managed to coalesce anything around him and his party other than the sorry spectacle of a once-great party in decline.

The Senate gambit stalled, at least for a time, the anti-Turner sentiment from both within and without the party, forced Mulroney's hand, and brought on an election a few weeks later. But more significantly, it stole the free-trade issue from the NDP, much to the chagrin of big labour, ultimately catapulting Turner ahead of Broadbent and launching him on what he called the "fight of my life," a desperate gamble that not only saved face for the beleaguered Liberal chieftain, but damn near made him prime minister again.

Sadly, like so many motives for action of our modern political leaders, Turner's apparent "principles" were based on computerized data, and the derring-do was more illusionary than real. Turner knew he had massive public support before he made his move.

Despite this support, Turner's Quebec lieutenant, Raymond Garneau, who would end up losing his own seat in November, cynically told reporters as he walked into a Liberal strategy meeting in Montreal two days later, on July 22, 1988, "We're taking a risk in Quebec, but I'm prepared to fight an election on that."

He wouldn't have been so brave had the numbers been bad, but at the time Garneau knew that about two-thirds of Quebeckers who had been polled privately before Turner's dramatic move in fact supported the Liberal ploy. And the Liberals knew that, despite all their high-road rhetoric of principle and conviction, had the poll gone the other way, they wouldn't have done it.

This is not to suggest that Turner didn't genuinely see free trade as a threat to Canadian sovereignty, or to our social safety net, and indeed to many of our traditional industries, only that his strategy was dictated directly by his partisan pollster.

In late August, a regular Gallup poll seeking Canadian opinion on Turner's "Senate gambit" showed what his own polls had already told him in advance: 52 percent of 1,046 Canadians interviewed in their homes said he had done the right thing.

Perhaps he had. Perhaps not. But the point here is that he had been led less by conviction than by the simple expediency of what his pollster discovered that people wanted. Goldfarb, not guts, had divined the route. Such is the paramountcy of today's political pollsters that they've become, in effect, partisan Pied Pipers playing their tunes on the "scientific" instruments of random samples, clusters, margins of error, and weighting, enticing our political "leaders," like the rats of Hamelin, into an unseemly parade to the polls and beyond.

Turner, of course, was not the only marcher.

Broadbent's entire campaign strategy, which ultimately failed, was not predicated on the standard damn-the-torpedoes ideology of the socialists. Instead, it was powered by the party's modest polling machine, ironically a Made-in-the-U.S.A. model, that decreed that the NDP was weak on the economy and had best focus on issues of the heart — on Broadbent's personal popularity, on social services, and on the environment. In the process, the NDP not only missed a golden opportunity to beat the Liberals, but opened a gap between themselves and labour leaders. Labour, after all, had spent considerable time and money, fighting free trade during the two years leading up to the election, only to have their efforts betrayed in the crunch by their fellow travellers, not because Broadbent suddenly saw the light and endorsed Mulroney's scheme, but because his offshore pollster convinced him that the issue was a non-starter for a party seen to be weak on economic issues.

Unfortunately for the NDP, the public was interested in the economy, particularly in free trade. Broadbent had misjudged this interest to the point that the words "free trade" didn't cross his lips in his opening statement the day Mulroney called a November 21 election, leaving Turner with the opportunity to capitalize on the momentum he'd manufactured through his Senate gambit and claim the over-whelming campaign issue as his own. Broadbent would never recover. The NDP finished in its customary third-place slot, a particu-larly bitter pill in light of the party's genuine efforts to launch its first real coast-to-coast campaign to match the pre-campaign expectations stemming from record standings in the public-opinion polls.

Rather than sink or swim with traditional party ideology, Broad-bent went with the numbers, outdated numbers at that since the cam-paign strategy was devised at least six months before the election call. And in opting for power over principle, and losing both, the NDP had sacrificed its soul. Hence, it didn't get to celebrate the traditional moral victory it had always savoured in defeat, soothed by the knowledge that it had at least kept its virtue intact, even if the major-ity of voters had once again been led astray by the seductive promises of money and power made by the other two parties.

Within months of losing, both Turner and Broadbent announced their resignations, but at least Turner was able to save some face with the claim he had taken over a party that was on the way down and was leaving it when it was on the way up, and he'd done it by sticking to his principles. That wasn't entirely true, of course, but his cam-paign performance had been such that he was able to make the claim without too much embarrassment. As for Broadbent, his thirteen years of tireless slugging had brought the party's popular vote from 18 percent of the electorate to 20 percent, hardly enough to justify his campaign decisions. Broadbent was left in the position of the veteran baseball pitcher who had survived against stronger teams by sticking to his basic fastball, only to be finally knocked off the mound, and out of the game, when he resorted to spitballs and assorted junk pitches in a desperate bid for one final shot at a World Series ring.

As for Mulroney, he too turned to the polling gods to guide his timing and temperament, emerging from the firmament seven weeks later as the first Conservative this century to win back-to-back majority governments.

Just after the Liberals' Senate gambit, Mulroney, more poll con-scious than any prime minister in our history, seized upon a $90,000 Angus Reid poll done at public expense for the federal Finance department. Reid had surveyed 1,505 people by telephone between July 19 and 29, asking them to rate the relative importance they gave to nineteen different issues, and found that Canadians were demanding stronger anti-pollution laws, cleaner water, better housing, and programs to deal with illiteracy.

In the weeks before the election call, on October 1, Mulroney announced a $110-million national literacy program, a $110-million five-year clean-up plan for the St. Lawrence River, and a $196-million joint federal-provincial program to clean up Halifax harbour. In a September 15 cabinet shuffle, just days after receiving the final report from the Reid poll, Mulroney named Brampton MP John McDermid as the first federal minister of state for Housing, normally an area of provincial responsibility.

In July, then Health Minister Jake Epp had introduced a $6.4-billion child-care program, a mixture of public and private spending designed to create an additional 200,000 subsidized child-care spaces over the next seven years. The bill was passed in the Commons on September 26, but was still under study in the Senate when Mulroney dissolved Parliament and announced the November 21 election. The controversial program, criticized by nearly every group involved in the field, had an uncanny likeness to the findings of a poll done for Health and Welfare by Decima Research, the Tory's party pollster.

Indeed, in an October 7 campaign speech to the Women's Health Research Institute in Winnipeg, Mulroney reintroduced the plan, blaming "the unelected Liberals in the Senate [who] chose not to approve the Canada Child Care Act before the election was called." He didn't mention that he had called the election just two days after the bill had gone to the Senate.

Nor did he say, for all his talk in that speech about "our approach to national leadership," that the "leadership" in this instance had come directly from the June 1987 Decima poll, portions of which he cited almost word for word in his speech.

The poll had found: "The overriding imperative for day-care policy seen by Canadians is the need for flexibility and the provision of support by government for different forms of daycare, both formal and informal." Mulroney repeated that theme in his speech, saying, 'It is a Canada-wide program that is flexible enough to encompass regional differences and community preferences. Our approach is to provide genuine national leadership ... to offer choices to individual families, and to allow you and your communities to decide within that framework which of those choices is best for your personal circumstances."

Day-care activists had attacked the plan for providing so much money to those not in dire need through tax credits and for proposing to fund both commercial and non-profit day-care. Yet that's exactly what the Decima poll found Canadians wanted. Decima's executive summary said: "A majority of Canadians (63%) believe that all day-care centres should receive government financial support, not just government or non-profit centres. Just over half of the population (52%) feel parents should receive financial assistance, whether they spend it on formal or informal day-care services."

In his campaign speech, Mulroney parroted this finding, saying, "Our child-care program is not hung up on whether the service is delivered under public or private sponsorship: our sole concern is for quality day-care for children."

The depth of Mulroney's commitment to day-care was quickly demonstrated after the election, when the Tories' spring budget heralded a full-scale retreat from the campaign promises on the issue. No matter. The polls had served their purpose, the Tories had won, and, however the universe was unfolding, Mulroney felt he could ultimately reconstruct it again as he had after sinking to record lows in public opinion after his 1984 win.

And so it goes. Politicians and pollsters insist for the most part we are not being governed by polls. Polls, they say, are used by governments simply to discover the best way to deliver services, not to dictate which services will be delivered, and how. Yet, as public and partisan spending on polls continues to mount, the evidence shows that today's successful political "leader" is, by definition, the first person with the results of the latest poll in his back pocket. Methodology has replaced ideology as the new god of politics.

This process was not discovered by Mulroney. It has been evolving for the past couple of decades, as polls and pollsters have become increasingly important in party circles. With even the NDP trying to go with the flow, the three parties, which used to stand for dramatically different political principles and feel honour-bound to stick at least to some of them, have become relatively indistinguishable from one another. Rather than standing firm on opting out of NATO, for example, the NDP, frightened by polls that showed the policy to be unpopular, has waffled and weaseled to a position where it says it would get out of NATO, but not for a while. Leaders in the previous decade would not have succumbed to the numbers the way the current crop does, even though they had them.

Those who worship at the altar of public-opinion polls ask, what's wrong with finding out what the public wants and giving it to them? After all, the public pays the freight.

One response is that the essence of parliamentary democracy is that we elect politicians to lead, to take risks, to stand for something more than the latest popular sentiment or the collective public wisdom, which may be based more on short-term emotional or outright ignorance than on anything else.

When Mulroney first ran in 1984 he did not mention free trade once during the campaign. Indeed, the electorate, if they'd thought about it at all, justifiably assumed he opposed the concept since he had done just that a year earlier. Yet, when he first announced his change of heart, polls showed the idea to be popular, and it remained that way for the next couple of years. Public support for the deal began to slip only when people learned more about it, demonstrating another danger of giving unquestioning credence to opinions that have not only been created artificially by the very act of the pollster asking the question, but measure the views of people who often have no idea what the issue means and, until they were asked, rarely thought about it.

The escalation of polling has changed our political process drastically. The old-time political insiders, often serving the party out of genuine conviction, have been replaced by the technocrats, the men and machines with the latest tabulations. Even the ordinary MP and the majority of the cabinet ministers have become less a factor in the political process than they once were, thanks at least partially to the overpowering influence of polls. After all, who cares what the member from downtown Regina thinks, or what his constituents are telling him, when such opinions are matched against the might of the concrete numbers provided by the party pollster? Who can hope to compete against computer printouts, or convince colleagues in the face of such evidence to pursue an important principle if the numbers are unpleasant?

Political polling, of course, represents but a tiny fraction of public-opinion survey work done in this country. Few corporations of any size try to market their products without first hiring a pollster to measure public attitudes.

While market research, as it's called, is certainly more precise and painstaking than the political or issue polling done for various media outlets, it's the public polling people hear about, and that's primarily what this book concerns itself with.

It is not just political parties who have endorsed the sanctity of these numbers, however. Government departments, lobby groups, and the major media outlets have moved into the polling game with a vengeance. Just as polling results direct the politicians, the media, who often decry that trend, are now themselves regularly guided by the polls. Whether they commission their own — which has become the prestigious thing to do — or rely on other polls, the media regularly look to the results to decide not only what issues or persons to cover, but what approach to take. Media polls, in addition to helping the media manufacture their own news, enjoy the distinction of being the only area where journalists are routinely uncritical. Again, like the backbench MP or veteran party worker, the experienced journalist can't argue a case in the face of contrary polling numbers; therefore, even the greenest cub reporter becomes an instant pundit simply by waving the numbers at a camera or typing them into a word processor. This way, everybody becomes an expert, and the personal high that journalists derive from such expertise too often smothers their professional instincts to probe beneath the surface and determine just how representative a particular set of numbers is.

Polls are extremely perplexing. Certainly they have a legitimate place in the process, although more and more people are pushing for election-time bans. But they have become larger than life itself in many ways, often portrayed as absolute, take-it-to-the-bank indicators of what is about to happen, rather than simply as imperfect measures of how people felt, at one particular time, about something they may or may not have understood or cared about.

This might not even be that bad if we could be sure that the polls are as scientifically precise as pollsters and their disciples claim. But, as we will see throughout this book, we can't be sure of that. The only certainty is that, for the moment at least, pollsters will continue to become rich, and their findings will dictate to the captain and crew of the ship of state just exactly which course to steer, not necessarily because it's the right one, or even the best one, but because more poll respondents picked that course as their favourite.

2

In the Beginning

Mackenzie King had enough to worry about in the fall of 1941 without having to cope with an American psychologist-statistician, Dr. George Gallup, setting up shop in Canada and upsetting the delicate French–English tensions of the time.

The war in Europe was not going well, and pressure was mounting from both King's English-speaking ministers, who wanted him to rescind his oft-repeated promise that he would never resort to conscription, and his French-speaking ministers, who were threatening to resign if he did recant.

King, grandson of William Lyon Mackenzie, the "little rebel" of Upper Canada, knew firsthand the devastation conscription had wrought on the aging Sir Wilfrid Laurier's Liberals in the bitter 1917 election. Then, Sir Robert Borden's Conservative–Nationalist coalition ran on its Military Service Act, designed to guarantee fresh Canadian troops to fight with the British in the First World War.

King, a former Laurier minister, had shown even then why he would become known as "wily Willy." He declined Laurier's invitation to campaign across the country over the racially charged conscription issue, but at the same time rejected Borden's plan, running in the Ontario riding of York North as both a loyal Liberal and a proponent of a strong war effort. Two years later, he became Liberal leader.

Conscription was so traumatic for the Liberals it spawned what author Christina McCall-Newman describes in her book *Grits* as that party's major shibboleth: "You stick with Quebec no matter what, and should you quarrel with French-Canadian Liberals, never do so in public."

King was sticking with Quebec no matter what in 1939 when Hitler's armies were beginning their bloody assault on Europe, and King told the Commons bluntly that "as long as this government may be in power no such measure [conscription] will be enacted."

Conscription for overseas service was anathema to Quebeckers, who saw the war as more England's fight than their own. But with the war effort floundering, King's English-speaking ministers were flexing their muscles, and King was planning an April 1942 plebiscite asking for permission to relieve himself of his previous promises never to enact conscription.

It was in this political hothouse, in November 1941, that the Gallup organization announced it had signed up twenty-seven subscribing newspapers and would soon begin regular national surveys out of a downtown Toronto office. The Gallup organization had been born in Princeton, N.J., in 1935 and already had branches in England and Australia. One of its chief reasons for expanding into Canada at the time was that more than one-third of Gallup's U.S. newspaper subscribers had cancelled the service because of problems with the firm's 1940 presidential polls.

The Liberal government was not amused by this development, particularly when it learned that Gallup wanted to do a national survey on Canadian attitudes toward conscription and publish the results in newspapers across the country.

Montreal MP Brooke Claxton, who would later serve as Health and Defence minister and become a key figure in the party's 1945 election, sent a letter, dated November 21, 1941, to legendary Ottawa bureaucrat Norman Robertson, then under-secretary of state, External Affairs, asking if "steps might be taken to urge Dr. Gallup not to step into Canada with this subject [conscription] at this time." Claxton had dismissed polls as being "only trial and error . . . the result of such a poll in Canada might be misleading and unfortunate today." Robertson replied, "My own feeling is that such polls accurately run and fairly administered can be useful," but, he added, "it would be the better part of wisdom" for Gallup to avoid a public poll on conscription at the moment.

At the time, External Affairs, Finance, and the Prime Minister's Office were small and closely knit and all located in the East Block of the

Parliament Buildings, creating a daily working relationship that would be impossible today, given the current size and complexity of government. As a result of Claxton's complaint then, Saul Rae, father of current Ontario NDP leader Bob Rae, was dispatched by Robertson to visit the King Street West headquarters of Gallup, known formally as the Canadian Institute of Public Opinion (CIPO).

Saul Rae, just beginning his distinguished diplomatic career, had done his doctoral thesis under Gallup at Princeton, and the two men had co-authored a 1940 book, *The Pulse of Democracy*, which was to make Gallup the leading spokesman in the field and soon a household name in many parts of the world.

Institutionalized public-opinion polling was still in its infancy then. The first major example of using "scientific" methodology was Elmo Roper's July 1935 *Fortune* magazine poll on a variety of social and political issues in the United States. In October, Gallup began his syndicated service to thirty-five newspapers, flushed by his success in using his statistical sampling methods to help his mother-in-law campaign for an Iowa legislative position. The next year, former vacuum cleaner salesman Archibald Crossley opened his polling firm Crossley, Incorporated, with offices in Princeton and New York City. Crossley, a Princeton graduate, at one time was assistant research director for the Literary Digest poll. He became famous in the U.S. during the 1930s and 1940s for his regular Cooperative Analysis of Broadcasting, which set the standard for which radio stars and programs would survive and which wouldn't, the forerunner of the A.C. Neilson rating system for television.

Gallup published his first poll October 20, 1935, the result of a combination of personal interviews and mail questionnaires "from thousands of voters in every state in the union," conducted between September 10 and 15, promising to report the trend of public opinion on one major issue a week. This Depression-time poll uncovered some starkly conservative attitudes, with 60 percent of those asked saying government spending on relief was "too great," 31 percent saying it was "about right," and only 9 percent saying it was "too little."

Before the advent of "scientific" sampling, American newspapers and magazines used various methods, primarily straw polls, in their insatiable need to discover who was going to win an election before voting day arrived. Straw polls made no attempt to make sure the sample was representative of the population at large, but simply involved asking readers or groups of assembled people what they thought about a particular issue or candidate.

The first known straw poll was conducted by the *Harrisburg Pennsylvanian* on July 24, 1824, and it showed Andrew Jackson far ahead of John Quincy Adams, 335 to 169, in the presidential race, with Henry Clay at 19 and William H. Crawford at 9. The next month, the *Raleigh Star* polled 4,256 voters at various political meetings in North Carolina and found Jackson to be far ahead. Adams would win the presidency that year, making Jackson wait another four years before becoming the country's seventh president.

In 1833, General Charles H. Taylor, editor of the *Boston Globe*, dispatched reporters to carefully selected voting precincts, a system still used by television networks today, particularly when doing exit polls in an effort to get a jump on the official count.

In 1904, the *New York Herald* polled 30,000 voters in New York City, and four years later it collaborated with the *Cincinnati Enquirer*, *Chicago Record-Herald*, *St. Louis Republic*, *Boston Globe*, and *Los Angeles Times*, in predicting the 1908 and, later, the 1912 presidential elections with only limited success.

The *Farm Journal* began presidential predictions in 1912, and the *Literary Digest*, an upscale publication much like Canada's *Saturday Night* magazine, which was for a time the leader in the field, conducted its first postcard poll among its subscribers in five states. In 1916, *Literary Digest* mailed 11 million ballots to telephone owners, in 1920 it sent 16.5 million to telephone and automobile owners, and in 1928 it increased postcard distribution to 18 million. In all cases, Republican strength was overestimated because people able to afford phones and cars then, and hence receiving the ballots, tended to favour Republicans. In 1932, the *Digest* mailed out 20 million ballots, and 3 million were marked and returned, giving the magazine its best year for accuracy, a margin of error of just 0.9 percent, which it described as "almost magical accuracy."

The magic wouldn't last. In 1936, after Gallup, Roper, and Crossley entered the field with their new sampling methods, the *Digest* mailed out 10 million postcards. The results, which the editor boasted were "neither weighted, adjusted nor interpreted," gave Alf Landon a commanding lead (57.1 to 42.9 percent) over Franklin Delano Roosevelt. The electorate, however, gave FDR a landslide, with 62.5 percent of the vote, making the *Digest*'s 19.6 percentage-point error the largest ever registered in a national poll in a presidential election. In the meantime, Roper, Gallup, and Crossley had all shown Roosevelt winning handily, although even Gallup underestimated the win by 6.8 percent. Still, the *Digest* experience illustrated the point that asking large numbers of people predominantly from one socio-economic group produces results that do not reflect the attitudes of the public at large. The *Digest*, in fact, would soon go out of business, and modern polling, based on the scientific laws of probability, would begin its ascendancy as a result of that 1936 presidential race.

Even though Gallup had suffered some problems in the 1940 presidential race, his organization and the new methodology he and others were using had gathered enough public recognition and credibility, and as a result, subscribers, to allow him to expand into Canada. By using the newspapers to spread the polling gospel, and hence, as self-promotion, Gallup was the first pollster to recognize the value of the publicity that numbers could generate.

Saul Rae was the logical person to discuss the current domestic difficulties with the CIPO officials on behalf of the government, since he was the only External Affairs official who understood the new survey techniques and, having studied at Princeton, he knew all but one of the senior staffers of the Canadian organization.

In a lengthy report to Norman Robertson, Rae said the CIPO had 150 interviewers across the country, 40 of them in Quebec. He said a preliminary, unpublished poll had shown 38 percent felt conscription was "the most important issue" facing Canadians, well ahead of price controls and intensifying the war effort. To the question "If you were asked to vote in the next few weeks on the question of selective service for overseas duty, would you vote for it, or against it?" 60 percent were in favour, 30 percent against, and 10 percent undecided.

Rae cautioned Gallup officials about Canada's "complex racial, religious and political structure," and that because of Canada's war effort it was "essential that, in the national interest, no material should be supplied in Canada for the use of the Hitler propaganda machine." A July 1942 Gallup, for example, asking Canadians to name "the greatest man living in the world today," showed that Hitler was chosen by 19 percent of French-speaking respondents, and by 2 percent of English-speakers. Respondents were evenly split on Roosevelt (27 percent French, 25 percent English), and Churchill was chosen by 38 percent of English Canadians and 23 percent of French Canadians. This was just the sort of finding the government didn't want publicized, and Rae bluntly warned the CIPO that they would be wise to avoid "issues vital to the effective functioning of the Canadian war effort, such as . . . conscription for overseas service . . . otherwise [the CIPO] might find itself involved in bitter controversies before it had had the opportunity to demonstrate its usefulness to the Canadian public."

Rae reported that CIPO editor John K. Tibby had "fully appreciated the importance of not publishing opinion studies of issues such as conscription until the research staff were fully satisfied that the polling techniques were thoroughly reliable." Tibby said it had been a "mistake" not to approach Ottawa before announcing its Canadian affiliate, "but his [Tibby's] chief defense was that the newspaper editors had suggested that Ottawa should be avoided," wrote Rae.

It wasn't that the Liberal government didn't want to know public opinion on conscription. Rather, they didn't want the public to be reminded how badly French and English opinion was split on the issue, and they especially didn't want newspapers publishing results of a conscription poll before the April 27, 1942, plebiscite. The plebiscite was troublesome enough. It showed that 64 percent of Canadians voted in favour of releasing King from his promise never to introduce conscription. In Quebec, however, the vote was 27 to 73 against, while the rest of Canada voted 88 to 12 in favour. The two solitudes had never been more solidified.

The CIPO had wisely avoided the issue, as Rae had requested, but after the plebiscite Rae was again dispatched by the government to begin tortuous discussions with CIPO boss Arthur Porter, whom he knew from Princeton, to conduct a secret poll of Quebeckers on their attitudes toward the war.

Brooke Claxton, who had previously dismissed the newfangled polling methods as "trial and error," suddenly championed the hiring of the CIPO for a secret poll in his home province. In a June 1942 confidential memo to Robertson, responding to Claxton's request to invite Porter to discuss such a poll, Rae said if either the government or the Liberal party were to pay for this poll and the financing to be discovered by the public, it could lead to "considerable difficulties."

Gallup was already running its regular newspaper poll on public issues in Canada and doing polls for the Wartime Prices and Trade Board and the National Finance Committee on attitudes toward such things as sugar- and gas-rationing. But since rationing was widely accepted as necessary by the public, these issues were not controversial.

Conscription was another matter. Conscription for overseas service would not come until the end of 1944, but after the plebiscite King introduced Bill 80, a law providing for mandatory domestic service. That was seen as the thin edge of the wedge by conscription opponents, and King's Quebec lieutenant, Works minister P.J.A. Cardin, resigned, hundreds of Quebec municipal councils passed resolutions against the bill, and when Montreal mayor Camillien Houde complained, on August 12, 1942, that the national military registration was "unequivocally a measure of conscription," he was promptly seized and shipped off to internment, and his statement was censored.

Rae, pushing ahead with plans for a top-secret poll of Quebec, said the best way to avoid future political embarrassments would be to "quietly contact" Hadley Cantril of Princeton, who received an annual grant for special polls from the Rockefeller Foundation. "I feel sure he would be able to meet the expenses of our Quebec poll out of the Rockefeller funds and that he would make the results available to the Canadian government on a confidential basis.... It would give the Canadian government some useful information and would leave the poll free from the charge that it is government inspired" — even though it was, of course, government inspired.

Indeed, King himself would always maintain publicly he had little use for polls, but Claxton had been joined in pushing for a secret poll by Walter Turnbull, King's principal secretary, who would not likely be acting on his own hook, a clear indication that, despite his public sentiments, King was giving his personal stamp of approval to the project. In fact, the initial meeting with the CIPO's Porter and Princeton's Cantril was slated for Turnbull's East Block office on June 16, 1942. It turned out Porter couldn't make it, but Cantril attended, stepping off the train in Montreal for a meeting with Claxton before proceeding to Ottawa. Cantril's expenses, paid by the government, included two nights at the Chateau Laurier at $6 each, overnight accommodation in a Pullman car ($7.40), plus regular train fare and meals, amounting to $62.42, which wouldn't buy you a cup of coffee with a pollster today.

Ultimately, the Rockefeller Foundation idea was dropped, but the project wasn't. The CIPO actually set up a dummy organization, the Canadian Opinion Co., to do its secret wartime polling, while continuing its regular polls for its newspaper subscribers and various government boards and agencies. The CIPO simply added specific questions to the regular polls on touchy confidential issues, passing those results on to the government, but withholding them from the newspapers. A bill for one of these polls obtained by the author through Access to Information from the National Archives shows the Canadian Opinion Co. charged the Wartime Information Board "to preparing, conducting, and analyzing field interviews." The invoice includes an unexplained item: "20% to c.i.p.o.," Gallup's commission for completing the work.

An August 20, 1942, letter from Porter to Robertson concerning the confidential survey of French Canadians says some of the information was published in Gallup subscribers' newspapers, but "much of it, for obvious reasons, would not be suitable for release in the press. We trust that you will be good enough to keep the enclosed information strictly confidential." They were.

In September 1942, Rae sent a memo to his boss, future prime minister Lester Pearson, with a copy to Claxton, about the methodology used for the secret survey called "Quebec and the Present War." It involved one hundred "intensive interviews," in various parts of the province. Rather than standard question-and-answer techniques, however, the pollsters elicited their responses "in the course of long conversations." The results were not encouraging for King. Of 57 people asked if Canada would be endangerd by the fall of England, 48 said "no," 9 "yes."

Of 72 people asked if Quebec was controlled by English Canada, 68 said "yes," only 4, "no." Of 66 people asked if French Canadians were treated as equals in Canada, 63 said "no," 3 had no opinion — nobody said "yes." Of 65 responses to "Why does Canada want conscription?" 33 said, because "they are against French Canada," 14 said, "to defend England," and only 18 said, "to win the war." Of 72 people asked if conscription was forthcoming, 67 said "yes," only 5 said "no." Two years later, their predictions, and worst fears, came true.

Rae told Pearson that the survey showed that the "most urgent" question to deal with was "our counter-propaganda. Canada, and in particular Quebec, has long been the target for an extensive barrage of German or German-inspired propaganda aimed at creating dissension between French- and English-speaking Canada." (One of the more persistent rumours uncovered by the Wartime Information Board, for example, was the false story that German sailors were coming ashore at night along the St. Lawrence and being fed by Quebec farmers.) Rae said data from the survey would be a useful tool in devising strategies to deal with this problem, the first such use of survey data by the Canadian government.

As a result of the poll, Rae offered what he called his "tentative conclusions":

French Canada should be convinced:

1) that conscription is not to punish French Canadians;
2) that it is not for England;
3) that the U.S. has conscription;
4) that acceptance, if necessary, will retain for them the good will of the rest of Canada and the U.S.

And so, polling had suddenly advanced from the days of straw polls. No longer was it essentially an object of curiosity designed to hype election interest and sell papers; now, polling had become a tool to be used by government to elicit public opinion and use it as an aid in setting policy. However, it would be nearly two decades before the political parties got involved in a substantive way with the techniques devised by Gallup and others.

Paul Martin, former cabinet minister and government leader in the Senate, had been elected to the Commons from Essex East in 1935 and elevated to King's cabinet in 1945, the first year Gallup polled a Canadian federal election, predicting the Liberals would win with 39 percent of the vote, just 2 percent less than they actually got.

Martin was introduced to George Gallup at Princeton by Rae during the war. "I don't think I'd even heard of polling at that time," he says.

"In the beginning, few people had any confidence in polling, but as time went on, and Gallup gained respectability, people started to think there may be something in this.

"But Gallup would not approve of what's going on now. I remember him saying to me that it has to be done sparingly in order to be effective. There are far too many polls now, and they're too costly."

While Martin has personally witnessed the astounding transformation of polls and pollsters from objects of ridicule at worst, and curiosity at best, from figures on the fringes of politics to near-gods, absolute necessities who often set the political agenda, this status wasn't achieved without some embarrassing growing pains.

In the late 1940s, for example, there was a popular parlour joke that asked the question: "Do you believe in the polls?" The answer was, "Certainly I do, just like President Dewey."

The reference, of course, was to the 1948 U.S. presidential election, where all three major pollsters — Gallup, Crossley, and Roper — had Dewey comfortably beating Harry S Truman. Gallup had it 49.5 to 44.5; Crossley, 49.9 to 44.8; and Roper, 52.2 to 37.1, all with Dewey on top. The electorate didn't agree. They gave Truman a fairly comfortable 49.5-to-45.1 win over Dewey, an event that jolted the pollsters into making substantial changes in their methodology.

Their big mistake was to stop polling ten days before the vote. Their sampling methods had led to an imbalance, weighted toward higher- and middle-income voters who were more likely to be Republicans, and they had made little effort to determine whether poll respondents would actually be voting, a major polling conundrum to this day. The experience also prompted them to study trends, rather than just draw conclusions from a single poll at any given time.

It happened that George Gallup had scheduled a speech to a political audience the day after his embarrassment. He began by telling what may be an apocryphal tale to illustrate the point that he expected a tough audience.

He said that, because he travelled so much, his wife, stuck home with the kids, had been nagging him to take her along. He'd resisted, saying it would be no fun for her to be alone while he was out working all day. But she persisted, and finally he took her to New York. When he returned to the Plaza Hotel after a long workday, he wanted to order room service, but she said the concierge had raved about a French restaurant nearby. He balked, but again she insisted, so off they went. When they arrived at the restaurant, the coat-check girl said, "Hi, George. How are you tonight?" His wife gave him an icy glare. The *maitre d'* approached, saying, "Good evening, Dr. Gallup, your usual table I presume," by which time his wife was getting really edgy. Just as they sat down, the flower girl handed Mrs. Gallup a rose, saying, "This time it's on me, George."

That was it. His wife jumped up, rushed out of the restaurant, and leapt into a cab. Gallup ran out after her and got into the cab just as it was pulling away. The couple began arguing in the back seat, and the cabbie turned around and said, "Hi, George. I see you've got another tough one on your hands tonight."

In fact, Gallup and the other pollsters had a tough one on their hands for years after the 1948 debacle. Many subscribing newspapers cancelled their contracts, and it took a long time for the pollsters to regain public confidence to the point where major politicians would make use of their services.

The 1957 Canadian election didn't help. The mighty Liberals had been in power since 1935, and Gallup's pre-election poll showed them fourteen points ahead, easily romping back into office. When the ballots were counted on June 10, however, John Diefenbaker's Tories had won a minority government. The media had put so much stock in Gallup, that *Maclean's* magazine's editorial, written before voting day but published the day after the election, said, "For better or worse, we Canadians have once more elected one of the most powerful governments ever created by the free will of a free electorate." Not exactly. But Diefenbaker loved it. He had the editorial framed and hung over his bed. At his first news conference as prime minister, he greeted *Maclean's* Ottawa editor Blair Fraser with, "Good morning . . . Prophet."

Diefenbaker, of course, would always maintain that polls are for dogs, a view that obviously overstated the shortcomings of the survey techniques. That attitude, however, has been replaced among politicians by an opposite and equally extreme view, that polls not only measure attitudes with the same precision as a tool-and-die maker uses in casting a die, but can replace the mythical crystal-ball gazer with hard scientific proof of the outcome of future actions.

The truth, as usual, lies somewhere between Diefenbaker's unchecked contempt for polls and the current deification of them and, more recently, of the pollsters themselves. Still, given the two extremes, Diefenbaker's view was closer to the the mark — and better for democracy.

3

Coming of Age

As is true of most things Canadian, partisan political polling began in the United States — during the 1960 presidential election, to be precise. That's where both John F. Kennedy and Richard Nixon brought polling into the modern political age, elevating their own partisan pollsters to key advisers and using their detailed numbers to determine which issues to hit, how to hit them, and, more ominously, how to manipulate the public.

Kennedy hired Lou Harris and Nixon retained Claude Robinson, a former Gallup partner who had opened his own company, Opinion Research Corp. Since then, every presidential candidate has employed a full-time pollster, and the practice has spread to every level of government and, more recently, to lobby groups of every description.

During the 1950s, the federal parties had done limited partisan polling, but it wasn't until after the Kennedy–Nixon battle that it really began to be considered essential in Canadian political life.

Maurice Sauvé, who had used polling to help Liberal Jean Lesage win the 1960 Quebec election, was guest speaker at the annual meeting of the Ontario Liberal Party in London. In the audience was Keith Davey, the quintessential back-room boy of Canadian politics, who had recently become enthralled with polls after reading Theodore White's detailed account of the 1960 election in *The Making of the President*.

Davey says, the book had "almost become a textbook for me," and when Sauvé spoke on the use Lesage made of polling, Davey made up his mind right then that the Liberals had to get in on the action in a big way.

So Davey approached Walter Gordon, who was national campaign-committee chairman for the party, and said they needed to hire a pollster. Davey had inherited a poll done by MacLaren Advertising. "They [the Liberals] had spent a lot of money, including this survey, but I didn't think it was very helpful."

Gordon agreed, and asked Davey who was the best in the business. "I said Lou Harris. So we got Harris in 1961."

Harris did extensive polling for the Liberals in the 1962 and 1963 elections, but after that he went into the private polling business and the Liberals hired Oliver Quayle, another American, for the 1965 and 1968 elections.

In his book *The Rainmaker*, Davey wrote, "There is no secret to winning elections, but too many academic journalists and politicians make it seem complicated. Most people knocking on doors during campaigns have a difficult time sorting out strategy from tactics. They become consumed with the tactical side of campaigning which, of course, is a very significant component. Far more important, however, is the overall strategic game plan. In the final analysis any campaign comes down to the major issue, whether it is a personality or a policy.... Having determined the best issue, then that becomes the issue of the campaign. Polling is extremely useful in making this determination."

This notion first occurred to Davey after reading about the 1960 U.S. presidential election where Harris had rated various issues in order of public concern and the Democrats had to go down to the seventh-rated issue to find the American people giving the Republican government a negative rating. The issue was a poor U.S. image abroad; so, armed with that information, Kennedy concentrated on it, and in that tight election it probably made the difference. It was the first major example of what has become commonplace, using polling data to exploit and manipulate, while at the same time allowing it to set the agenda for the campaign, and the Liberals were quick to adopt the technique.

Having lost the 1962 election, the Liberal party, as its polls showed, was sagging and could lose again in 1963. According to Harris, the polls showed that while Lester Pearson was admired, he was seen as indecisive, prompting Davey to invent the mid-campaign slogan, "Sixty Days of Decision." (It would have been a hundred days, but

Maryon Pearson, enthusiastically endorsing the idea, gushed, "Everyone will think of Napoleon when you talk about one hundred days.") Davey and the other party hacks didn't think the image fit, so they lopped forty days off the target-date for a new Canada.

"The net result was that we imperilled a new government," wrote Davey, "for it would be impossible to accomplish all that had been promised in just sixty days. But we also got the campaign a new start." They also got Diefenbaker out and Pearson in, with a minority government of his own.

Even then, the Liberals were spending between $50,000 and $75,000 on a national poll, and smaller amounts on provincial polls. Davey recalls picking Harris up at the Toronto airport to drive him to Queen's Park with news of a survey done for newly elected Ontario Liberal leader Andy Thompson. "We were just talking about these things, and I said to him, 'Lou, what do you say to a candidate if he is absolutely out to lunch, has no chance of winning, and should look for another line of work?'

"Lou turned to me and said, 'You're going to find out in about half an hour.'" Thompson didn't stick around long enough to contest an election. By 1966, he was gone.

In the summer of 1965, Quayle arrived in Ottawa with a poll that showed the Liberal lead over the Tories at less than half what Gallup had shown. Diefenbaker appeared to be making a come-back with the public, and Quayle advised the Liberals, "Go now and maybe get a majority, at worst a minority, or wait for several months and watch Diefenbaker actually win another election."

So they went. And they won. But there had been no particular need for an election, no overwhelming public issue — little but a hired American pollster telling them that this was the best time for them, if they were to hang on to power. On November 8, the Liberals won 131 seats; the Tories, 97; the NDP, 21; and 16 seats went to various splinter parties. It was the last election for both Pearson and Diefenbaker and the first for a Quebec intellectual named Pierre Trudeau, who went on to greater glories.

Davey didn't work the 1968 election — with Trudeaumania at its zenith, that outcome was never in doubt — but was resurrected right after 1972. "I remember having lunch with Quayle at the Inn on the Park in Toronto in early 1973 and I was prepared to express the view that it was time we used Canadian polling. Well, it became no contest, because it turned out that poor old Quayle, who is now deceased, had clearly become an alcoholic. Sad, but true."

Davey, of course, had somebody in mind at the time, a young Toronto pollster named Martin Goldfarb whom he'd met at the 1968 Liberal leadership convention. Goldfarb had been polling for Paul Hellyer. "After that convention, Marty and I became great personal as well as political friends. His brother, who's a chartered accountant, gave me a lot of very important valuable advice way back early on about my own personal affairs. So Marty and I became great friends, and I respect him to this day a great deal."

And, to this day, Goldfarb is still the Liberal pollster, even though it almost didn't happen. After the convention, Goldfarb wrote an article in *Maclean's*, which Davey recalls as "one of those traditional smart-ass things saying how Trudeau could be defeated by the Tories in the next election. It was all about how you market tomatoes, and politicians are the same." That created some difficulty for Davey. "Trudeau said, 'Wasn't that the guy with the tomatoes?' but we hired him and Goldfarb and Trudeau got along very well."

The Tories actually got into polling before the Liberals, although not in a major way. When George Drew was Ontario premier in the 1940s he had used Toronto researcher Vic Gruneau for some rudimentary political polling. Gruneau actually took over the Gallup organization in the spring of 1955 after one of the original owners, Wilf Sanders, left to become chief executive officer of the Canadian sector of J. Walter Thompson, then the world's largest advertising agency.

In 1953, after Drew had become federal Tory leader, his campaign chairman, Allister Grosart, hired McKim Advertising of Toronto to conduct an opinion poll. Veteran Tory operative Dalton Camp, in his book, *Gentlemen, Players and Politicians*, says Grosart was "determined that the issue in the election would be taxes; I was resolved that it should not be." McKim's questionnaire, which Camp describes as "preposterous," polled about 3,000 Canadians just before the 1953 budget, "when public interest in taxation was heightened," asking if people thought taxes were "too high." Naturally, most did. "Grossart was pleased with this result," wrote Camp. "I was indignant, suspecting that primitive research was being employed to advance poor strategy."

In the end, Grosart did use the poll to convince Drew that taxes should be their campaign issue. It didn't impress the voters, however. The Liberals won 170 to 51.

"When polling started, it wasn't taken all that seriously," says Camp now. "It was something equivalent to doing an enumeration. Interesting, but not critical. The system was such that we took only one poll, before the election of course. It was too expensive to do more. I used to run the national [Conservative] office for $30,000 a month in the mid-1960s. A poll then would cost $20,000. That was big money to me. They still are expensive."

Times change. Now it's the Tories who are far and away the biggest poll consumers. The party first began to get serious about polling in Ontario under premier John Robarts in the 1960s. The fat-cat Ontario Tories had been in power since 1943, had more money to spend than their federal cousins, and Robarts had begun to notice American hot-shot Robert Teeter, head of the political division of Market Opinion Research of Detroit, who had been making a name for himself polling for the Republican party. So the Ontario Tories hired him and were paying him between $10,000 and $15,000 a poll, big money then. Before long, Robert Stanfield hired him for some Nova Scotia polling (and would use him after he became federal Tory leader in both the 1972 and 1974 elections), and Duff Roblin's Manitoba Tories also gave Teeter work.

"In the late 1960s and early 1970s, he was acknowledged to be state of the art, the fastest gun in the business," says Senator Finlay MacDonald, Tory campaign chairman in 1972 and a veteran of dozens of federal and provincial campaigns. "He was the one who would do the so-called target ridings [now standard procedure], and used the term a 'national wave,' a big poll where they went out to the whole country and got back voter intentions. But they were expensive, and therefore not used often then.

"Before that, the stuff we used to do was totally unscientific and usually resented like hell by the candidate," MacDonald says. "If we had a candidate we were worried about, we started to find out, by whatever means — phone calls, different things like that — and inevitably the candidate would hear about it and come rushing in, irate as hell, and say 'What are you doing asking all those questions?' We'd say, we're just trying to be helpful, and he'd say, 'What's the matter? Do you know something I don't know?' It used to cause a little bit of tension. . . . We were just trying to see if he was in difficulty, and if he was, we'd put more resources in to help him."

The Tories, for the most part, didn't make nearly the use of polling that their political rivals did. One exception was Bill Davis in Ontario. The first thing he did when he won the leadership in 1971 was to hire Teeter for an extensive province-wide poll, which found that while about 80 percent of Ontarians knew who Davis was — he'd been Education minister for ten years — they didn't know much about him. Teeter believed first impressions would be difficult to change, so he recommended a lot of travelling around the province to meet people, something Davis and his Big Blue Machine operatives did with a vengeance, leading up to a fall election. Teeter also found that while Ontarians had great regard for John Robarts, who had just stepped down, they wanted the new man to do different things. This was a time when Canadian cities were bristling with excitement over the so-called citizens' movements, when advocacy groups were beginning to challenge the Establishment, and when such issues as environmental concern were in their infancy. Teeter said Davis needed a symbolic gesture to show himself as a man for the times, so the first attempt was a ban on logging in Quetico Provincial Park, which the Tories hoped would please the naturalists and delight what *Toronto Star* veteran Val Sears called the trendy "townhouse environmentalists" in Toronto. It didn't work. So, then, Davis stopped the controversial Spadina Expressway. That did work. And apart from the fact that Davis broke a contract with Metro Toronto to do it, and much of today's traffic chaos is a direct result, the decision certainly catapulted Davis into prominence as a modern "progressive."

In the mid-1970s, Teeter simply became too busy in the United States to bother with Canada. Teeter kept polling for the Republicans and, in 1988, was named by president-elect George Bush to co-chair his transition team. Bush also offered him the job as deputy-chief of staff in his administration, but Teeter declined.

Actually, Teeter's friendly departure suited the Tories at the time because they, like the Liberals before them, were having mild anxiety attacks about a foreigner telling them what Canadians were thinking. But the Tories still didn't have their own pollster and, in Ontario, Davis hired Goldfarb for a series of secret polls taken under the minority Tory government in the late 1970s, the findings of which directly affected government policy. Davis was forced by the opposition, in March 1980, to release twenty-two polls, which cost taxpayers $434,212. By his last term in office, in the early 1980s, Davis would be spending about $500,000 of taxpayers' money annually on polls. Responding to Liberal criticism in the legislature in 1980, Davis said he had made the polls public to demonstrate that "these were not the kind of polls that could be used for partisan purposes."

In fact, they were. They had recommended a hard line on the Parti Québécois sovereignty-association plan; a tough response to Alberta's pressure for higher oil prices; and no increase in income and property taxes — all followed slavishly by the Davis Tories. Indeed, when Davis denied the truth of this he used as an example newly appointed Consumer minister Frank Drea's instant announcement that there would be "no more topless waitresses" in Ontario. Davis said that announcement was made "within minutes of his swearing in . . . before he had a chance to read anything, let alone polls for his new ministry." Perhaps, but a ministry poll did show the public was strongly opposed to half-naked waitresses and wanted even more sex scissored from movies.

In a recent interview, Davis said the polls did sometimes "indicate the depth of feeling" about issues, but there were "very few issues where people who followed these matters closely wouldn't be within a point or two of what the polls disclosed in any event. I don't want to minimize polls, but I do think their importance in terms of policy considerations is exaggerated." Davis said he used them mostly as a "security blanket," to "reinforce what is already your point of view and help you feel better about it." He said party polls are different. There, "it's not as easy to measure with your own instincts, because people don't always level with you. They say you're doing well because they know that's what you want to hear, when in fact you may not be doing so well."

With Teeter off to greener Republican pastures in the United States, the federal Tories were temporarily left without a pollster to call their own. In the mid-1970s, a bright, long-haired Alberta student named Allan Gregg had moved to Ottawa to begin a post-graduate program in political science at Carleton University. Gregg went to some Liberal friends, looking for work, but found nothing, then approached Carleton history professor Richard Clippingdale, an active Conservative, who in turn put him on to Bill Neville, soon to become the party's caucus research director.

In his book *The Insiders*, John Sawatsky set the scene of the initial meeting between Gregg and Neville in the cafeteria of the Confederation Building. "If the locale was unusual for a job interview, so was the candidate. Gregg arrived without a tie, because he didn't own one, and his hair reached halfway down his back. He never apologized for his appearance. Indeed, he revelled in it and used it to grab attention. Being out of fashion was his cachet and reflected his personal culture; more than anything else in life, Allan Gregg really wanted to lead a rock band."

So he got a desk and an $11,000-a-year researcher's job for the summer of 1975 and stayed on for two days a week after returning to Carleton in the fall. The party was trying to make do with an in-house program run out of party president Michael Meighen's office by Ian Green, Meighen's executive assistant, who was using volunteers to place random calls on free long-distance phone lines belonging to the Commons. Through his research activity, Gregg eventually met Green, offered to help, and before long was drawing samples and helping design questionnaires. When Joe Clark won the leadership in 1976, Gregg ended up as Meighen's executive assistant, and by this time his polling had become more sophisticated and regular, enough to impress Lowell Murray, Clark's campaign director, who signed Gregg on in 1977 as the first member of his campaign team. From there, Gregg not only has grown to be the enduring Tory pollster, but has easily outdistanced Goldfarb and other "name" pollsters as Canada's answer to the Delphi oracle.

One thing Gregg had going for him was his powerful friends, especially in Ontario, where many of the major players in the Big Blue Machine, such as Norman Atkins and Hugh Segal, became his close friends and associates, representing a continuous link between the early heavy use of polling by the Ontario Tories and the current excesses by the federal party. Indeed, this same group, which formed around Davis, also was thick with Stanfield and, after a shaky start, moved in as a major back-room strategist for Brian Mulroney. When Mulroney wanted to dump Gregg after the 1984 election (he was upset with criticisms of him in a book Gregg co-authored called *Contenders* on the 1983 Tory leadership campaign) it was Atkins and the Ontario contingent, the old Davis connection, who rallied around and convinced Mulroney to stick with Gregg. In the early 1970s, Segal and Joe Clark worked together in Stanfield's office and, for a time, Segal dated Maureen McTeer before she began going out with Clark.

Meanwhile, back in the early 1960s, when the Liberals and Tories were getting into the polling game, the CCF–NDP were sanctimoniously denouncing the technique as an unfair intrusion into election campaigns. Several resolutions to ban polls were approved at NDP con-

ventions and, for years, NDP MPS presented private members' bills
seeking to have them banned.

In 1963, however, McGill political-science professor Michael
Oliver, who later became NDP president, went on to the University of
Rochester to grade a seminar on Canadian politics being put on by
political scientist Peter Regenstreif. The year before, Regenstreif had
met *Montreal Star* editor-in-chief George Ferguson through his friend
Mason Wade, who also taught at the University of Rochester. The
Star hired Regenstreif to interview between three hundred and four
hundred people across the country and write twelve articles on the
1962 federal election. Unlike Gallup and others, Regenstreif successfully predicted that the Tories would not win a majority because
of the emergence of the Social Credit in Quebec.

Naturally, when Oliver came down to grade Regenstreif's seminar
students, Regenstreif "got talking to him about how important polling for the NDP would be. Until then, they'd never done a poll." As a
result, Regenstreif agreed to do a poll for them in late 1964. "I did it
basically for expenses, about $10,000, I think it was. And I remember
early in 1965 going to their headquarters at 100 Argyle Street and they
were all there, David Lewis, Tommy Douglas, Stanley Knowles, and
they were pretty skeptical about the process.

"But I told them to get off some of the airy-fairy stuff they'd been
talking about and talk about bread-and-butter issues. They actually
did what I told them to do, and in 1965 they went from 12 percent to
18 percent of the vote," says Regenstreif.

Regenstreif also helped the Saskatchewan NDP in their unsuccessful
1964 election bid against Liberal Ross Thatcher. The federal Liberals
had dispatched MacLaren Advertising for an in-depth survey of attitudes to guide the party's strategy. As a result, Thatcher cooled his
violent attacks on the NDP and completely changed his position from
being an opponent of to being a proponent of Medicare. "The hoax
worked," wrote journalist Walter Stewart. "The Liberals won that
election, but it was a triumph of cynical manipulation, not politics."

As for Regenstreif, he didn't seem to display any particular party
loyalties. Besides his NDP efforts, he also worked for the Liberals in
both Manitoba and Alberta, for John Turner's losing leadership bid
against Trudeau, and for former Ontario Tory treasurer Darcy
McKeogh's failed leadership bid against Davis in 1971. For a time,
largely through his newspaper work with the *Montreal Star* and the
Toronto Star, Regenstreif became widely known. He was the first to

begin translating overall numbers into seats, a dicey practice in the Canadian system, which he eventually abandoned after several embarrassing seat projections.

Even now, the NDP doesn't have a particular party pollster the way the Liberals have Goldfarb and the Tories have Gregg. In 1988, for example, the party hired Washington pollster Vic Fingerhut, but his role was to analyse data collected by Access Survey Research, a subsidiary of Winnipeg pollster Angus Reid. The NDP also hired Sorecom of Montreal to do some Quebec-based polling between 1984 and 1988. "We're suspect of developing gurus," explains Bill Knight, who headed the party's 1988 campaign. "They become like medicine-men of the tribe, they know everything, or think they do. That creates problems we just don't want. We want the data so we can make our own judgments. . . . The most important ingredient in all this stuff is grey matter. Pollsters don't have a monopoly on that." True, but given their misreading of the electorate in 1988, some within the party are having second thoughts about the wisdom of allowing poll results to set the campaign strategy.

By the Trudeau era, polling had arrived in Canada as a permanent and increasingly costly fixture in the political landscape.

While Trudeau himself claimed he wasn't interested in polls — he appeared to treat them with the same disdain he showed for journalists — his loyal cadre of back-room boys was crazy about them.

Davey insists that Trudeau "never looked at the numbers. The numbers were looked at by us, and we would tell Trudeau about them. We would certainly get into them in great detail, Jim Coutts and Tom Axworthy in particular, but I can honestly say, and I'm not trying to gild the lily, Trudeau did not live and die by the polls at all. . . . He began to accept some of the survey information. He was particularly interested in survey information about him. He liked to know what he could do to improve his image, how he could improve his style. But what he wouldn't do was take policy decisions based on the data from the surveys."

Oh really? Then others did it for him, which amounts to the same thing since major policy positions wouldn't be taken without his knowledge. Which brings us to 1974, and certainly the most cynical Canadian use of polling up until that time. The minority Liberal government had been defeated on May 8, 1974, over John Turner's budget, a vote it wanted to lose because Goldfarb's polls showed the party would win a majority if it held an election then.

In his book, Davey explains: "The most basic tool in establishing a strategic game plan today is political polling." Goldfarb had discovered that inflation was overwhelmingly the major issue of concern for Canadians, hardly surprising since double-digit inflation was ravaging the land, and Stanfield, a politician of unusual principle, felt obligated to say what he would do about it — impose wage-and-price controls — if he became prime minister.

The Liberals, however, felt no compulson to be honest about their intentions, but they were happy Stanfield was, since his scheme proved to be so unpopular with the public. Since Goldfarb's polls showed them that nine out of ten Canadians thought they hadn't been handling the inflation issue well, the Grits didn't want to fight an election on that issue.

"The Tories should have tried to make the opposite case, but instead of talking about the problem of inflation and making it their issue, they offered their solution," wrote Davey. "Any solution they offered would have been a critical strategic mistake, but this one took the form of a highly-contentious wage and price freeze. Pierre Elliott Trudeau had a field-day with his 'Zap! You're frozen!' — a phrase he used repeatedly. Everywhere he went, he warned Canadians of what the freeze would do to aspiring wage earners and struggling small businessmen."

And so, with their strategy determined by the polls, the subterfuge complete, the Liberals defeated Stanfield and his unpopular wage-and-price control solution. But a year later, having run successfully against controls, Trudeau imposed the wage freeze himself.

This cynical action did not, of course, make Trudeau Canada's favourite pin-up boy at the time (and he would pay for it in 1979), but the Liberal strategists didn't care. They had won, and they were arrogant enough to believe they could win the next time. That's all that mattered. After all, they were Canada's natural governing party and they deserved to win.

But even legendary Liberal cockiness began to wane slightly by May 1976 when a Gallup poll put Trudeau's popularity at a record low, finding 49 percent of respondents saying they didn't like the way he was doing his job, just two weeks before his eighth anniversary as prime minister. It seemed the more we got to know him, the more we disliked him. Joe Clark, the new Tory leader, had another problem. A Gallup poll two months after he became leader showed only 60 percent of Canadians asked even knew who he was. "Joe Who?" was more than a cutting headline invented by the *Toronto Star*.

With Trudeau trailing badly in public opinion, the Liberals were desperately seeking an issue that could restore public confidence in their man. Any issue would do, but thanks to René Lévesque, they landed a dilly.

When Lévesque's separatist Parti Québécois defeated Robert Bourassa's Liberals in 1976, Trudeau's fortunes instantly began to improve. By July 1977, for example, Gallup had the Grits demolishing the Tories, 51 to 24, as most Canadians felt Trudeau, a Quebecker, was more capable of keeping Canada together than was Clark, an Albertan.

As a result, the Liberals paid Goldfarb $100,000 for a poll in 1977 and it confirmed the common wisdom, that Canadians were edgy about Lévesque and trusted Trudeau's instincts on this issue more than they did Clark's. Goldfarb, Davey, et al. wanted Trudeau to exploit public fears over national unity and call an election, but Trudeau, ironically, felt it would look too crass, even for them, to have an election a year before it was customary.

Again, the next year, Goldfarb completed a $100,000 party poll, but this time there were some major problems, particularly in Toronto, and Trudeau wouldn't pull the plug. Upon hearing of a Gallup poll in November 1978 putting the Tories ahead (42 to 37) for the first time since January 1967, Trudeau, who usually had nothing to say about polls, quipped to reporters, 'It's pretty damn lucky I didn't call a general election.... It shows I know something about politics, eh?"

As it turned out, he didn't know everything. His decision not to run, taken mainly because of the poor polling results (which he and his apologists claim didn't influence his actions), left him in the impossible position of trying to do what no other Canadian prime minister had ever done — win an eleventh-hour election. He didn't succeed, and for a time it appeared the Trudeau era was over. It wasn't.

In the midst of this heightened use of party polling, two other major developments were unfolding — the dramatic increase in polling by government departments, boards, and agencies, and the entry of major media outlets into the polling field.

Goldfarb, in addition to being the party pollster, was a major beneficiary of government polls at the time, and some of his non-partisan work was criticized for appearing to be conveniently designed to promote a partisan cause rather than to assist government departments in an objective, non-partisan fashion.

Of all the issues that triggered Trudeau's passion over the years, none was as important to him as the political and linguistic evolution of Quebec. In 1977, then, after Lévesque's victory, and at a time when Goldfarb was commissioned to do a party poll, he also completed four polls for various federal departments, including one for the secretary of state on what Canadians felt about federal bilingualism programs.

It was that poll, however, that generated a heated controversy in Quebec, with academics and pollsters accusing Goldfarb of pushing the federal view at the time to the detriment of Lévesque's separatist position, rather than remaining neutral and objective. Goldfarb's findings showed that support for separatism was dropping, the direct opposite finding to that of a poll taken around the same time by Montreal's Centre de Recherches sur l'Opinion Publique (CROP) and published in the French-language Le Devoir.

It's but one example where the distinction between partisan polling and legitimate government polling was grievously blurred, a particularly difficult distinction to make when the partisan pollster and the non-partisan pollster are the same person, in this case Goldfarb.

At the same time, media outlets had decided to plunge into the polling business with a vengeance. Gallup polls, of course, had always been carried in subscribing newspapers, but until the mid-1970s the television networks, which had been satisfied to report those polls, too came to recognize the publicity and prestige value of having their own polls to report.

In 1979, when Trudeau could no longer delay and called a May 22 election, the media charged into the fray and produced a series of conflicting results. In late April, for example, Gallup put the Liberals ahead 43 to 38, while a CBC poll, conducted by Carleton University sociologists and its journalism school, had the Tories ahead 40.2 to 38.4 percent. Then another Gallup, released three days before the vote, had the Tories and Liberals tied, while CTV, two days before the election, released a poll by Thompson, Lightstone and Company Ltd. that showed the "undecided, won't vote or not talking" category was winning, chalking up 40 percent, with the Liberals and Tories at 24 percent each. None of the polls proved to be particularly accurate, since Clark won a minority government, 136 to 114 seats, with 26 New Democrats and 6 Socreds, even though the Liberals had won the popular vote, 40 to 36 percent. This illustrates yet another difficulty with polling in Canada, as opposed to in the United States where polling originated and better suits the system. There, global numbers are more relevant because the presidential candidates win or lose on the popular vote. In Canada, of course, the system of riding-by-riding representation means that it is not unusual for a party to win the most seats while losing the popular vote. Pollsters have devised computer models to get around this problem internally, but the highly publicized media polls, which have grown to influence voting patterns, generally report only the overall numbers.

In any event, after Clark won in 1979 he foolishly announced he would govern as if he had a majority. Well, he didn't have a majority, an obvious fact that came crashing home to him on December 13, 1979, with the defeat of Finance minister John Crosbie's budget, which featured and eighteen-cent-per-gallon excise tax on gasoline, and spoke of "short-term pain for long-term gain." Even though the polls, public and private, showed the Liberals well ahead, Trudeau had announced he was quitting and the Liberals had set March 28–30 for a leadership convention. The Tories gambled that, despite favourable polls, the Liberals wouldn't force an election when they were leaderless. One of the anti-Clark lines of the time was, "Why not? The Tories don't have a leader either." In any event, the gamble failed, the budget was defeated, February 18 was set for election day, and Trudeau, like Lazarus, returned from the partisan dead to win 147 seats, leaving Clark with 103 and Broadbent with 32.

The Liberals had won 44 percent of the vote; the Tories, 33; and the NDP, 19.8. In what had become the public-polling sweepstakes, CTV's Thompson, Lightstone poll came closest, finding 43 percent of its respondents favoured the Liberals; 33, the Tories; and 22, the NDP. It was a telephone poll of 2,000 households, taken February 13–15, compared to Gallup's in-house survey of 2,055 homes, taken February 12–13, that overestimated Liberal strength by four points, underestimating the Tories by five, and overestimating the NDP by about four. The final CBC-Carleton poll, which phoned 2,507 households two weeks before election day, had it Liberals, 47; Conservatives, 30; and NDP, 19. On an open-line radio show in Charlottetown, on February 5, the day after the CBC-Carleton poll gave Trudeau a seventeen-point lead, Clark said the poll was more of a problem for the CBC than for him because it didn't correspond with other polls.

He also agreed with a caller who said polls should be prohibited because they are misleading and influence voters.

Another major war of the pollsters broke out, this time in Quebec, over the May 20 referendum on sovereignty-association. As always happens when numerous polls are done, it was difficult to know which poll to believe. There are many reasons for this. For one thing, polls aren't always comparable. They may have been done at different times, using different methods (one may have been a phone poll, the other in-home interviews), the questions may be worded differently and asked in a different order, and the non-sampling errors aren't likely to match either. In addition, the fact that relatively similar polls often produce drastically different results should be kept in mind when you hear people talking about the precise "science" of polling. It isn't that precise.

The referendum, of course, was a battle over two distinct views of Quebec — Lévesque's view that it could be essentially an independent nation, albeit with strong links to Canada; and Trudeau's view that Quebec could be strengthened within Confederation to correct what he and most Quebeckers perceived as historic injustices against them.

While political leaders across the land and Qubec Liberal leader Claude Ryan fought hard for the federalist side, it essentially became a battle of wills between two wilful men. The federal Liberals pulled out all of their big guns to stop Lévesque from winning the referendum. Trudeau himself campaigned tirelessly, as did Lévesque, leading up to the vote. Many saw the fate of Canada itself hanging on the strength of a simple "oui" or "non," and the pollsters, both public and private, were a major part of the action.

In late April, a CTV poll had the "yes" side of René Lévesque well in the lead, 45 to 31, with 24 percent still undecided. If the undecideds were factored in the same proportion as were the committed voters — a common, but highly questionable polling assumption — the result was 59 to 41, a runaway victory for Lévesque. But another poll, conducted two days earlier, for the Institut Québécois d'Opinion Publique (IQOP) for the weekly *Dimanche-Matin* newspaper, gave the "yes" side 41.2 and the federalist "no" forces 40.9, with 17.9 percent undecided.

At the same time, the weekly French-language business newspaper *Finance* reported that it had obtained an internal PQ poll showing 61 percent of francophones would vote "yes." There were no further details given. The IQOP poll, which sampled 761 voters, found 48.8 percent of francophones planning to vote "yes" and 73.2 percent of English and other non-French groups planning to vote "no."

A week later, CROP conducted a CBC poll that showed 47 percent of their sample of Canadians outside Quebec favoured talks with that province. However, the poll didn't specifically speak of negotiating sovereignty-association, an odd oversight since that was the issue in dispute, and Lévesque branded federalist politicians "liars" for claiming the poll supported their cause. He seemed to have a point.

Lévesque was at it again April 30 when he accused Gallup of manipulating a survey to make it appear that a majority of Canadians outside Quebec opposed negotiating sovereignty-association. When Gallup asked 1,516 respondents if Ottawa and the provinces should agree to negotiate sovereignty-association if Quebeckers voted "yes," 60 percent said the provinces should not, 27 percent said they should. As for the federal government negotiating, 55 percent said it should not and 32 percent said it should.

Lévesque said Gallup first asked people outside Quebec how they would advise Quebeckers to vote; 75 percent replied "no," only 13 percent said "yes." "Psychologically, they were all conditioned to give this second answer." Again, he had a point.

Another CROP poll, released May 9 by the CBC, had the federalist forces in the lead, 45.5 to 39.6, with 14.9 percent either undecided or not saying. The company began with a random sampling of 1,500 and found 856 people who would answer its telephone survey. On May 17, federalist leader Claude Ryan announced that a poll commissioned by three newspapers showed the "no" side winning 57 to 43. In addition, there were other media polls with various results by Goldfarb, IQOP, and McGill University sociology professors Maurice Pinard and Richard Hamilton.

On May 11, IQOP had the separatists losing 37 to 40, but a week later reported them winning 40.4 to 36.5. CROP's last poll came up with 45.5 to 39.6 for the "no" side, while Pinard–Hamilton had it 49 to 37 for the federalists just four days before the vote. Factoring out the undecideds, Pinard–Hamilton had it 57 to 43, well within the margin of error for the actual vote itself, which saw the federalists winning 59.5 to 40.5. A post-mortem by Andrew Phillips in the Montreal *Gazette* found some intriguing factors. Pinard and Hamilton, for example, placed the referendum question in the middle of a list of about forty questions, while iqop put it right up front. Unlike iqop, Pinard–Hamilton told their interviewers not to read the entire 114-word referendum over the phone because listeners' attention would flag or they would become confused. They also asked undecided voters some follow-up questions to find out which way they were leaning, something else iqop didn't do.

In April 1980, a month after Bill Davis had released a series of government-sponsored public-opinion surveys, NDP leader Ed Broadbent went after Trudeau to release his. Trudeau refused, although he did say, "I certainly agree that no partisan survey should be made by any party in office with public funds," apparently forgetting the controversial Goldfarb polls from three years earlier.

During their short term in office, Clark's Tories had commissioned Gregg's firm, Decima Research, to do polls for the departments of Energy, Mines and Resources; Multiculturalism; and Federal-Provincial Relations. They weren't made public either, something that had no impact whatsoever on Clark's insistence that the Liberal polls should be released.

In October, both opposition parties again attacked the Liberals for refusing to release the results of publicly funded polls, and finally, on October 10, then Justice minister Jean Chrétien announced they would release 129 of the 141 polls taken by the government since March 1979 and costing taxpayers $5.2 million. Chrétien said the remaining 12 polls would be released after the government finished analysing them. One of those was a $61,000 Goldfarb poll for the Canadian Unity Information Office on constitutional reform and energy matters. Chrétien said that if it were made public at that time it might reveal energy policy before the government had a chance to state it, a tacit admission of the important role of polls in setting government policy.

Among the polls released was a highly partisan one by Tory pollster Allan Gregg's Decima firm, a $101,845 effort commissioned at public expense when Clark was prime minister, trying to discover why ethnic voters were attracted more to the Liberals than to the Conservatives. Respondents were asked clearly political questions, such as what was their opinion of the federal Liberals and Conservatives, who were their political role models, what ethnic media did they listen to, if the government should be promoting ethnic diversity.

Another poll by Decima while Clark was in power asked, "How would you describe the attitude of the federal government under Mr. Clark toward the people of Quebec?" — a question more blatantly political in nature than anything found in the Liberal polls.

Still, that didn't stop Clark from accusing the Liberals of using public funds for partisan gain.

"We all know that these days extensive use is made of public-opinion polls," he said in the Commons, "not simply to determine what the public is thinking on a particular question but to determine what kind of appeals the public might be vulnerable to, what kind of fears or apprehensions might exist in the public mind or public psyche that would allow a particular kind of presentation made by a government."

Clark was certainly in a unique position to know what "extensive use" governments were making of polls at public expense, but he was hardly in a position to lecture the Liberals about it. In politics, however, sophistry is rarely a deterrent to unbridled bursts of sanctimony.

4

Welcome to the 1980s

For some Canadians, it was a dream come true; for others, their worst nightmare. But there he was, Pierre Trudeau, the most maddening, pleasing, perplexing, loved, hated, worshipped, vilified, vulgar, sophisticated, stubborn, passionate, obnoxious, arrogant, frivolous, brilliant politician this country has ever produced. What was he doing there? It was a time-warp, a real-life back-to-the-future drama, as he struck his familiar mocking, bantam-rooster pose, standing unerringly erect, as defiant in victory as he had been in defeat. It was late, and he'd just swept into power and into the crowded, sweaty, smoke-drenched room and jumped, sprightly, onto a small platform in the ballroom of Ottawa's Château Laurier Hotel. It was February 18, 1980. Trudeau, who should have been a memory of the 1960s and 1970s, glared out at the world and shouted, "Welcome to the 1980s!"

The decade would not prove to be as welcome for the Liberals as preceding decades had been. In fact, within four years of Trudeau's miraculous return to the throne, the party would be devastated by Brian Mulroney, the Quebec lawyer-businessman who had never held elected office until he took over the Conservative leadership; the Trudeau era would dramatically end and Mulroney's begin.

Good times were certainly in store for the growing army of Canadian pollsters worming their way into public consciousness with their fat contracts and widespread publicity.

The 1980s is a decade in which media polling has become an epidemic; in which polling has become not just a political tool, an early-warning guidance system, but an occasional substitute for policy itself; in which democracy itself was undermined by the pervasive influence of polls and pollsters who, for all practical purposes, replaced elected representatives, including cabinet ministers, and traditional political strategists as the major determinants of political action. On the strength of their computer printouts, pollsters came to be viewed as sainted public oracles, supposedly capable not only of probing our innermost thoughts and feelings, but of predicting our future actions as well.

With polls and pollsters competing for recognition, and poll-users in the media doing the same thing, examples of abuse mushroomed, and wildly conflicting poll results became commonplace. Yet the media consistently treated pollsters with an awestruck wonderment not afforded any other group in society, a serious disservice both to themselves and to their audiences.

While "Government by Goldfarb" became the calling-card of the Trudeau era, no prime minister in our history has ever been so enthralled by polls and so influenced by them as Mulroney.

Polls have become a perplexing reality in the political process; still a legitimate, albeit imperfect, measure of public attitudes, they are afforded an unhealthy level of credence in the affairs of state by political players and the public alike.

The Tories, of course, didn't start it. They just escalated a process begun by the Liberals. In 1980–81, for example, the government spent more selling its policies, programs, and politics than any private company in Canada spent hawking its products. With a 1980–81 advertising budget of $50 million — much of it built around the findings of several million dollars' worth of public-opinion polls — Madison Avenue had truly arrived on Parliament Hill.

Within weeks of regaining power, the Liberals hired Goldfarb and Sorecom, for $76,200, to find out what Canadians thought about constitutional reform and energy, the two major political issues of Trudeau's final term.

Actually, Canadians hadn't thought much about the constitution, but they had thought a lot about energy. Either way, it wasn't good news for the Liberals. To the extent that Canadians cared at all, it seems, they did not support unilateral patriation of the constitution. And they definitely had little confidence in the Liberals' ability to resolve the domestic and international energy battles.

No problem. Armed with its perceived strengths and weakness, culled from the poll data, and undeterred by shame, the Liberal government launched a $4.9-million advertising blitz, in August 1980, to coax Canadians, using their own tax dollars, to accept the wisdom of Liberal aspirations. You remember, don't you? Those commercials showing Canada geese flying over a pond, with someone humming "O Canada," that were designed to send us all into a patriotic frenzy and demand that Trudeau get on the next flight to Westminster and bring the constitution back with him? Well, we ended up with a constitution, which didn't excite the masses, and the National Energy Program, which did.

Having long ago discovered their expertise in cynical manipulation, the Liberals, in 1981, put their skills to the test, trying to pull off a political manoeuvre that, even by their standards, was considered crass. Goldfarb was right in the thick of it. Liberal MP Peter Stollery, after a decade of stunningly inconsequential representation of the downtown Toronto riding of Spadina, was looking for an even easier ride on the public weal. What could be easier than the Senate? Nothing apparently, for in early 1981 Davey and Stollery had breakfast at Toronto's Park Plaza Hotel, where Davey offered Stollery a Senate appointment if he could help Jim Coutts get the Liberal nomination in the subsequent by-election. At the time, Goldfarb said the Liberals had a seemingly insurmountable lead of two-to-one over the combined opposition in that riding, numbers that convinced them to cut the deal and call an August 17 by-election.

In one of those rare occasions that restores lost faith in democracy, Spadina voters, desensitized as they were to Liberal chicanery, none the less couldn't swallow this naked display of vote vulgarity, and chose a sour, radical New Democrat named Dan Heap by 176 votes over Coutts. Davey, in his book *The Rainmaker*, blames the loss on assorted disasters: record interest rates, high unemployment, and even Trudeau's exotic trek through Africa. He even blames Stollery's ineffective election machine: "In the final analysis too many Portuguese stayed home and too many Italians did not bother to vote." Apparently it didn't occur to Davey that, despite what Goldfarb's early "scientific" wisdom had shown, the voters in Spadina were simply disgusted with the way the Liberals conducted their affairs. Three years later, it would become devastatingly clear that this feeling was widespread, a sort of national nausea, not one confined to voters in a single riding. The only cure was to flush the Liberals right out of the political system and begin again.

Clearly the Liberals had suffered from a faulty belief in the predictive powers of polls. Coutts wouldn't be the only victim of such misplaced optimism. In Ontario, three weeks before Bill Davis won his final election, NDP leader Michael Cassidy was demonstrating his need for remedial poll-reading lessons, interpreting the results of a *Toronto Star*–Goldfarb poll as good news for him and bad news for the provincial Liberals. The poll gave the long-ruling Tories 54 percent, with the Liberals at 27 and the NDP at 18. Cassidy announced this was good because a previous Goldfarb poll had put the NDP at 14, so the increase of four points showed that his party would keep its fourteen Metro Toronto seats (it lost four of them) and win more seats province-wide than ever before (it won twenty-one, down twelve from the previous election).

One intriguing aspect of polls, or at least of the reporting of them, is that journalists tend to ignore precedents. It doesn't seem to matter whether a pollster's previous work was good or bad. What counts is that the pollster is announcing some fresh numbers, period. On March 12, 1981, for example, McGill sociologist Maurice Pinard, whose polls had accurately reflected the outcomes of the 1976 Quebec election and the 1980 Quebec referendum, told University of Montreal communications students that the Parti Québécois would likely lose the April election because of the polarizations created in that referendum vote. Pinard said that "unless the Union Nationale does [vote-splitting] miracles, the PQ will be defeated." Two weeks later, when the PQ was winning a poll commissioned for *Le Soleil* and the Montreal *Gazette* by Pinard, he explained that the shifting polarizations were helping the PQ and they were benefiting from the continuing popularity of René Lévesque, as if Lévesque hadn't been popular two weeks earlier. But Pinard wasn't finished yet. By the next week, he'd gone full circle, saying the PQ was "moving to a sure victory" and could win 87 of the National Assembly's 122 seats. It actually won 80, a big-enough win for Pinard to be seen by the media as having called it again. Yet in reporting his final comments, journalists ignored the fact that Pinard had been all over the map in the preceding few weeks, a generosity that only a pollster would ever be shown.

About this time, another insidious use, or misuse, of polls began to emerge in the political system. Alberta's premier Peter Lougheed, generously seen by reporters as a man of great principle, was unhappy with a poll conducted by the Calgary-based Opinion Centre for the *Calgary Herald* and *Edmonton Journal*, showing that 55 percent of Albertans supported his energy and constitutional positions. So he did what any egocentric politician would do, he bought his own poll, tacking a few questions onto a Gallup omnibus, to discover that 68 percent of Albertans supported his constitutional stance. The first poll had asked whether respondents "approved" or "disapproved" of policies, but Gallup asked them to "support" or "oppose." Thus, an Albertan could have disapproved of Lougheed's stand, but still supported its thrust. "It reconfirms what we thought," said Lougheed. "We believe there are a number of Albertans who do support us, but want us to take a stronger position."

During fiscal 1980–1, Lougheed's government spent $330,509 on thirty-one polls, including $4,100 to survey Albertans' attitudes toward spear fishing, $1,650 to survey people who held sturgeon-fishing licences, $3,000 to test reaction to a government TV ad, $200 on a goose-hunter-success questionnaire, and $34,550 to evaluate the Stamp Around Alberta program.

Clearly, Lougheed had become a believer. And having found how responses can be manipulated simply by skewing questions, Lougheed convinced the so-called Gang of Eight — the eight premiers opposed to Trudeau's constitutional package (all but Ontario and New Brunswick) — to hook onto another Gallup omnibus to demonstrate support for their side. Respondents were never asked directly whether or not they supported federal plans. Instead, they were asked if they thought Trudeau should meet the premiers to reach an agreement (88 percent said "yes,"); if they believed all changes except for an amending formula should be made in Canada (90 percent did); and, if they thought "the federal government's action to patriate the BNA Act without the agreement of all provinces is going to divide or unite all Canadians." Sixty percent said it would divide us, but André Blais, a University of Montreal political scientist, called that question "pretty biased. The question sets the ground by leading people to express their support for agreement and discussion, and then asks if the federal government is being divisive. That's useless and biased."

Jean-Pierre Nadeau of the Institut Québécois d'Opinion Publique (IQOP) was even more direct. "It seems like a funny kind of poll. It looks as if Gallup arranged questions to suit the ideas of its clients."

This was not the only time that sort of thing would happen with the Gallup omnibus, as that organization allows clients not only to have questions asked, but to write the questions themselves. It also provides a graphic example of how politicians had discovered that polls could now be used for much more than measuring attitudes; they could actually be structured to advance a partisan point of view and still be given a high amount of public credibility by the media.

The lack of caution by the media in reporting polls, which became widespread later in the decade, was just beginning to be commonplace in the early 1980s. In October 1981, for example, the regular monthly Gallup put Clark's Tories at 39 percent among decided voters, one point ahead of the Liberals, the first time the Tories were ahead of the Liberals in more than two years. The NDP had 20. Remarkably, a Canadian Press "news" story, distributed to newspapers and broadcast outlets across the country, concluded that the Conservatives, with their one-point lead, "could easily win an election, possibly even obtaining a majority of seats in the Commons, with support divided among the three parties that way." A story displaying such appalling ignorance of any other field would never have been sent across the wires, let alone published in a host of newspapers from coast to coast. Anybody with even the slightest knowledge of polling error would know that a one-point difference is meaningless, but the fact that Canada's national wire service chose to ignore that demonstrates how far polls had come to be seen as exact measures of public attitudes. There has been little discernible improvement in the intervening years.

Polls were also becoming more of a factor in setting government policy at this time, even though politicians insisted, as they still do, that they first arrive at a position and simply use polls to help determine the best way to present it to the public.

Goldfarb's annual report, sold to clients for $14,000 a copy just two months before the spring 1982 federal budget, bore a striking resemblance to government policy actions. Goldfarb wrote, "There is a desire to see some measure of punishment of the civil service because it is not giving the public what Canadians consider value for their money." In the budget, picking up on that theme, the Liberals introduced a two-year plan to keep pay increases down to 6 and 5 percent for 500,000 federal employees, stripping them of all collective-bargaining rights and breaking dozens of negotiated contracts in the process.

The growing power and sophistication of political polling was not restricted to the federal arena. In November 1982, Montreal *Gazette* journalist Claude Arpin wrote a detailed two-part series, outlining the spending of $20 million for about two hundred polls by the PQ since they had won power in 1976. It was sparked by the resignation of Marcel Giner, a brilliant, Algerian-born bureaucrat who had introduced public-opinion polling as part of the day-to-day operations of the PQ government.

Giner resigned over his complaints about the "unethical" use of his scientific expertise. He argued that the PQ — supposedly a party of high principle — was using his polls and others for partisan gain. One example was the government's decision to get tough with its public servants during the 1982 negotiations. Apart from its separatist sentiments, of course, the PQ supposedly paralleled the NDP in terms of its ideological output, and as such had gained wide support from that province's powerful labour movement. But during those tough economic times Quebeckers, like other Canadians, began to resent the relatively secure and well-paid jobs of public servants. Armed with an $85,000 poll by IQOP, ordered by the Secrétariat des Conférences Socio-économiques, a politically charged group within Lévesque's office, the PQ ordered a series of Draconian measures against the public service, a politically popular move but an obvious betrayal of what the party supposedly stood for.

Canadians were soon able to witness yet another use of polling as a political weapon in a political civil war, which broke out within the Conservative party itself. Joe Clark, who had won the leadership in 1976, then won the 1979 election and lost in 1980, had never been popular with large sections of his own party. At the February 1981 Tory convention one-third of the party delegates had voted for a leadership convention, and the next convention was set for January 28, 1983, in Winnipeg.

Like elections, leadership battles provide tremendous opportunities for pollsters to display their clout in helping determine the outcome of events. It is one thing for a politician to offer his public support or critique of another politician, but it is quite another matter to be able to wave survey numbers around to "prove" whichever case he's trying to make.

Just a few weeks before the Winnipeg convention, the rabidly right-wing National Citizens' Coalition, no friend of Clark, who they saw (quite properly) as a pink Tory, commissioned a poll by AJF Associates of New York, conveniently showing the federal Tories would fare better against Trudeau with Lougheed as leader instead of

Clark, a poll that was widely cited by Clark's opponents at that time.

The exercise sparked a plethora of media polls, ranging from a Southam News–Carleton Journalism poll on January 14, 1983, showing that 76.7 percent of committed delegates opposed a leadership convention, to polls commissioned by a group of Bill Davis supporters, showing that their man would crush Trudeau, and beat a Turner-led Liberal party, while Clark, of course, would lose. That poll, commissioned by Davis aides, was a direct effort to pressure their man into seeking the leadership. It didn't work, but it did represent yet another use of polling to affect the political process.

After Clark did not improve his standings in Winnipeg and decided to step aside, pollsters were again busy in the intervening months leading up to the June 1983 leadership convention.

One of those polls, a Gallup commissioned by Brian Mulroney, prompted Canadian Gallup president Frank Kielty to admit that numbers showing Mulroney closing fast on Clark could be highly inaccurate. "It's unwise to attach precision to the results that came out of the poll," said Kielty, which didn't stop journalists from doing it and didn't resolve the question of why Gallup would allow its name to be used for such obvious partisan purposes by a major contender in a leadership race. Despite Kielty's protestations about his own company's poll, a front-page, four-column *Globe and Mail* headline proclaimed: "Mulroney Gains In New Poll," while the Montreal *Gazette*, also taken in, said, "Mulroney Is Closing Gap: Poll," just the sort of publicity a candidate would kill for to build momentum going into the convention.

The whole thing got so silly that Carleton journalism professor Joe Scanlon, in an *Ottawa Citizen* article after the convention, wrote, "The criticism aimed at the accuracy of political polling after the Conservative convention in Winnipeg [where Carleton's poll was embarrassingly bad] should not be repeated this time." Why not? Well, wrote Scanlon, "while the pollsters were wrong about the outcome of the final ballot — they picked Clark to squeak by Mulroney — they were right about almost everything else." Actually, they weren't. But even if they had been, choosing Clark to beat Mulroney is surely the only pick that matters.

But whatever the pollsters thought, the sorry leadership of Clark had ended, and the boy from Baie-Comeau, as he loved to call himself, was now in charge. Within three months of Mulroney's winning the leadership, Gallup put him at a record high 62 percent, with the Liberals languishing at 23, a record low, focusing attention on the appropriateness of Trudeau's continued occupation of the country's top job.

While the public, it seemed, had had enough of Trudeau, a group of PET's pals — Coutts, Axworthy, and Davey, in particular — leaked three polls, two by Goldfarb and one by CROP, all of which gave the Liberals more support than had Gallup. The idea of the leak was to spark a groundswell of support for Trudeau and to convince him to stay. It did neither. He quit after a late-night walk in a snowstorm on February 29.

A month later, in what the media appropriately called "a shocker," Gallup reported the leaderless Liberals were now ahead, at 46 percent, with the Tories plunging to 40, the first time since August 1981 that the Liberals had passed the Tories. Predictably, Goldfarb said the figures "are not far off our own mapping." Just as predictably, Ian McKinnon of Decima said he didn't believe the "volatile swings" from Gallup. And Tory campaign co-chairman Norman Atkins, hoping to calm the nervous troops, told the party's caucus that Decima showed the Tories at 53, with the Liberals at 39. Gallup official Clara Hatton admitted that the turn-about was so stunning the company went back and rechecked its figures. "We think it's correct," she said. One would hope.

All this feverish polling activity wasn't lost on the Liberals when they gathered to anoint the new Messiah at the Ottawa Civic Centre in mid-June. A CTV–Goldfarb poll released June 15, the day before the voting, gave Turner a 47 to 38 lead over Chrétien. Goldfarb was also a major player in a bizarre convention battle between the Turner and Chrétien polls, which had delegates shaking their heads, wondering what to believe.

For several days, Chrétien aide Eddie Goldenberg had been spreading rumours among journalists that their polls showed Chrétien would beat Mulroney, while Turner would lose to him. Chrétien's big weakness, of course, was the perception by delegates that, although they liked him, he couldn't win an election. Turner, not nearly as well liked, none the less was seen as a winner. On Friday, June 15, the day before the vote, *Toronto Star* reporter Bob Hepburn ran into Goldenberg, and again the Chrétien aide claimed to have the numbers showing his man would fare better than Turner against Mulroney.

"I started pressing him on his claim," says Hepburn. "I told Eddie I wanted to see the polls. I wasn't going to write about them without seeing them. So, that evening, Eddie walked in and gestured to me to see him underneath the seats in the auditorium in a 'secret' spot where we were seen by every journalist in the place. Anyway, Eddie hands me this poll. He had a sheaf full of them and was waving them around for whoever wanted them."

Sure enough, it was a Goldfarb poll, and it said that, under Chrétien, the Liberals would win 45 to 43, while, under Turner, the Tories would win 45 to 42. The survey, conducted earlier that week, had been commissioned by wealthy Ottawa developer Robert Campeau. Goldfarb at first denied he'd conducted the survey, but ninety minutes later he returned to confess to reporters he had conducted the poll after all.

News of the Chrétien poll spread rapidly around the convention floor — especially when pro-Chrétien delegates were waving placards with the numbers on them — and Turner's people were eager to counter with a poll of their own, one conducted by Angus Reid showing Turner would beat Mulroney 45 to 43, while Chrétien would be slaughtered 52 to 35.

"I remember specifically we went to Reid," says Hepburn, "and we said, 'Chrétien's people gave us these numbers.' Reid was sitting in the stands, and he pulled out a pen and a piece of paper and scribbled down some numbers. I said, 'Come on, where's your material,' but that's all he had, just some handwritten numbers on a piece of paper. A lot of people, me included, felt Angus Reid's credibility went down that day."

Indeed, for the next year, Reid and Goldfarb would be involved in a bizarre call to arms, a partisan cold war where both men were supposedly coming to the aid of the party but, in fact, were fighting for the job of official Grit soothsayer.

Goldfarb, of course, had been the Liberal pollster since the early 1970s. Reid wanted the job, and said so publicly. The two men had never been close. Reid's first contact with Goldfarb had been in 1977, and unfriendly. Reid was teaching research at the University of Winnipeg and he and a colleague, David Walker (now a Winnipeg MP, but at one time Reid's partner), were friends with Lloyd Axworthy, then the only Liberal in the Manitoba legislature. Axworthy was thinking of jumping into the federal arena, "and he dropped by the house one night and asked me have a look at a poll that this guy I had never heard of, named Marty Goldfarb, had done," says Reid.

"The poll concluded Lloyd shouldn't run. I was an arrogant young professor at the time — I guess I haven't changed that much — but I wasn't impressed, so I got on the phone and it was my very first contact with Martin Goldfarb. It was a conference call, and he said, 'Listen, kid, leave it to the pros. We know what we're doing.' In a sense, bug off.

"I remember flying to Toronto that night . . . and I thought, my god, with that kind of attitude, I think there's room for somebody else in the business. So I've always credited Marty with getting me into this business," says Reid.

A week after Turner won the leadership, he convened a dinner at the Château Laurier with Keith Davey, Bill Lee, and John Payne to establish a kitchen cabinet for the new prime minister. Part of the evening was spent arguing over who should be the party pollster, with Davey pushing for his pal Goldfarb and Lee arguing the party should break from the old Trudeau gang and bring in Reid.

A week later, Davey and Tom Axworthy were summoned to Turner's Château Laurier suite to hear Goldfarb argue for a quick election. In *The Rainmaker*, Davey writes, "It was a remarkable evening. Turner, shortly to be sworn in as prime minister, was feisty, profane and aggressive. Goldfarb was respectful, but obviously surprised by Turner's directness and Bill Lee's subtle quizzing about his professionalism. The Goldfarb study had been commissioned to double-check Angus Reid, the Winnipeg pollster who would be reporting to the leader the following morning."

Goldfarb favoured an early election. So did Reid. The two men had done polls for the party right after the convention, showing the Liberals comfortably ahead, especially in Quebec where they had a thirty-nine-point lead, prompting MP André Maltais to say, "There is not one safe seat in Quebec for the Conservatives." Maltais, MP for Manicouagan, would lose his seat to a Conservative named Brian Mulroney. So would most of his Liberal colleagues, in Quebec and elsewhere.

But at the time, incredibly, both pollsters and all the party officials were seduced by the excitement of the immediate polling numbers. They had forgotten, apparently, that trends are what count. With a few exceptions, the Tories had consistently run ahead of the Liberals since after the last election, and anybody with a rudimentary understanding of polls knows party popularity always shoots up right after all the publicity surrounding a leadership convention.

Turner had no organization to speak of, not enough money to mount a good campaign, and would turn his back on the chance to be seen flitting around the country, being prime-ministerial, accompanying the Queen and the Pope, both of whom had scheduled Canadian tours. All Turner had was a desire to run, and polls and pollsters telling him to strike.

Reid was hired to do the daily tracking. He did abut 20,000 interviews during the course of the campaign and charged $350,000. "There was no doubt that I had an interest after the Liberal leadership of becoming the Liberal-party pollster," Reid says. "There was also no doubt that, during the 1984 campaign, Marty himself billed the Liberal party for about $500,000 for his strategy studies."

David Walker says Reid was disgusted at a mid-campaign meeting when Goldfarb presented Lee with a standard research report of 1,400 interviews. "Reid was writing down the market value on a piece of paper, maybe $100,000 at most, and Lee said 'How much is this Marty?' Goldfarb looked him straight in the eye, and said, '$250,000.' So they paid him. It's incredible how easy it is for these guys [party pollsters] to do that," says Walker.

The campaign, of course, was a disaster. A late-June Gallup gave the Liberals an eleven-point lead over the Tories, with 49 percent decided voters, far more than either Goldfarb or Reid had found. Reid had them six points ahead; Goldfarb, two points.

Turner, shopping around for his own riding at the time, had decided to return to his roots in British Columbia and, he hoped, fly the Liberal flag in Western Canada where the party under Trudeau had become a four-letter word. The *Vancouver Sun* hired Marktrend to poll 1,200 people in three Vancouver ridings, concluding that Turner would lose in Capilano, be in a tight race in North Vancouver–Burnaby, but enjoy a clear lead in Vancouver Quadra, 41.3 to 28.5 over the incumbent Tory Bill Clarke. He chose Quadra.

The bubble burst quickly. Less than a week into the campaign, a Southam–Carleton Journalism poll put the Liberals at 45, with the Tories coming on quickly at 42.5. The NDP had only 9.5. The undecided was at 26 percent.

While Turner's Liberals were flailing away, Ed Broadbent's New Democrats were having their own problems with pollsters. They'd fired Regina pollster Larry Ellis who had predicted the party would lose more than half of its twenty-five seats in Western Canada, a position he said was culled from the results of seven polls. Broadbent accused Ellis of having "a personal axe to grind" with the NDP, an over-reaction that led to a barrage of questions from reporters demanding to see the polling figures Broadbent claimed refuted those from Ellis. The NDP poll, by Michael Morgan and Associates of Vancouver, sampled only six hundred people, with a margin of error of plus or minus six, and was conducted in late May and early June, at least ten days before Turner became Liberal leader. Even then, it showed that, in the thirty-one ridings then held by the NDP, Tory support was ahead, 27.9 to 26.6, with the Liberals at 15.5, and 30 percent undecided. The poll did not "flatly contradict" the Ellis findings, as Broadbent had claimed.

The Liberals got some good news on July 30, when the *Globe* published its *Globe*-CROP poll (conducted by Michael Adams and Donna Dasko of Environics, and Yvan Corbeil of CROP), giving Turner a ten-point lead. Another poll, taken by Thompson, Lightstone of Toronto for CTV in the last week of July, had the Tories winning 45 to 36, the first indication of the impact of Mulroney's win over Turner in the televised leadership debates, although the poll had an unusually high 38 percent undecided. A Southam–Carleton Journalism poll, August 1–7, had the Tories winning 51 to 32, and the August 9–11 Gallup had Tories, 46; Liberals, 32; NDP, 18; a sixteen-point Liberal drop in Gallup in one month.

A CBC poll of 2,661 Canadians taken by Market Facts of Canada Ltd. between August 4 and 12, and broadcast August 20, predicted "a strong, possibly massive majority government." It showed the Tories at 49, Liberals at 32, and NDP at 18, with the Tories winning in every region and every province. That prompted Davey to complain publicly that the polls were out of date, but, "I don't argue for a moment that the polls are not debilitating. They certainly are. They are very morale-destroying. They are very tough to take." Davey had been brought in to run the sagging campaign in early August after Bill Lee left in disgust and, although he told Canadian Press in late August that private party polls showed the Liberals in better shape than the public polls indicated, he wrote in his book that, over breakfast with Turner at 24 Sussex Drive, on August 4, Turner had said the party was a couple of points behind, and Davey replied, "I think you should understand that we are ten points behind and falling away fast." It got worse. A Southam–Carleton Journalism poll published on August 25 put the Tories at 56.5, with the Liberals at 27 and the NDP at 15.

All of this was simply too much for Geills Turner, who blasted media organizations for conducting "biased" polls. "I think it's quite clear that the CTV network is supporting the Conservatives," she said. "I'm not saying it's biased, I'm saying their political philosophy has always supported the Conservative party. The *Globe and Mail* is supporting the Conservative party. Southam News is known to be supporting the Conservative party." She said a recent poll commissioned by Global TV and CKVU-TV in Vancouver, showing Tory Bill Clarke leading Turner in Vancouver Quadra 53 to 20, with the NDP second, at 23, was a case in point. Officials for all the media organizations flatly denied any bias.

Gallup, which had been all over the map, finally settled down for its final poll, published September 1, putting the Tories at 50, the Liberals at 28, and the NDP at 19, which is exactly where the electorate put them on September 4.

Once the Tories achieved power, Mulroney's obsession with polls quickly became apparent. Between January 1984 and December 1987, the federal government, most of that time under the Tories, commissioned 799 confidential polls, roughly four per week. The total cost was impossible to determine, since the work is contracted out to private firms, which keep their fees confidential, but a Montreal *Gazette* investigation at the time determined that taxpayers had spent $5 million for just 61 of them, so the total cost could have hit $64 million.

The Tories were clearly using polls to test policies on focus groups and indeed to get a feel for public reaction before introducing any major legislation.

In 1987, four months before Defence minister Perrin Beatty introduced his defence white paper, for example, Decima Research Ltd. was paid $140,000 for a survey to "explore the public's awareness, understanding and perceptions of the Department of National Defence and defence issues." A month before the Tories introduced tougher immigration laws, Angus Reid conducted a $98,770 survey on Canadian attitudes toward immigration. There was a $50,000

Decima poll on "public attitudes towards child care" six months before Health minister Jake Epp introduced his day-care program, and two surveys by the Toronto firm of Ruston, Tomany and Associates Ltd., one for $79,000, the other for $76,000, before the Finance department brought out its Canada Savings Bonds in 1987.

Even the government became concerned enough about the expense of polling to set up a central clearing-house for polls in the spring of 1986, operated jointly by Statistics Canada and the co-ordinator of public-opinion research, Supply and Services. Since then, all departmental polls must pass through this system, essentially an effort to cut survey costs by weeding out duplicate polls. In the past year, this system has approved $4.8 million in eighty separate contracts, slightly less than government spent in 1987. But that doesn't tell nearly the whole story. It doesn't count the political polling by the PMO, or polls commissioned by cabinet ministers or their staff. Best estimates of current total federal spending on polling and other public-opinion research, including focus groups and Statistics Canada survey work, is about $100 million a year.

There is no end in sight. Two days after the 1984 federal election, the *Vancouver Sun* published an interview with several polling experts, predicting that campaign polling had reached its peak. University of British Columbia political scientist Donald Blake said that, with major polls on average every two weeks throughout the campaign, "I can't see much more than that next time. . . . It's probable that the level of polling we have now, or at least the level of reporting of it, is as extensive as it will ever be."

It doubled in 1988.

5

Showdown

It began in confusion, a perfect setting for Abbott and Costello's famous "Who's on First" comedy routine. Nobody seemed to know who was on first, second, or third.

During the previous four years, the Conservatives had hit a record high (60) in the Gallup, and a record low (22); the NDP, a record high for them (44), grabbing the lead in the public-opinion polls (several of them) for the first time in party history; and the Liberals, well, they were up and down and in and out, but somehow hanging in there, with a leader who consistently rated below "none of the above" for choice as prime minister.

Some of the old polling "truths" weren't working. For example, month-to-month numbers don't mean that much; what matters is the trend and the average over several months. Perhaps, but if you look at the ten-month average in Gallup leading up to the election, the Liberals should have been comfortably ahead, averaging 37, compared to the Tories at 31, and the NDP at 30. Clearly the trend over the previous two years showed the Tories coming back, but then, when a government hits 22 on the thumbs-down scale, where else can they go but up?

The first Gallup, February 3–6, 1988, amid reports that Michel Côté had been fired as Supply and Services minister over a $250,000 personal loan that violated conflict-of-interest guidelines, had the Liberals up five points, to 41; the NDP unchanged, at 31; and the Tories down three, to 27. An Angus Reid poll for Southam News and the *Toronto Star*, February 17–23, found a virtual dead heat: Liberals and NDP, 33; Conservatives, 32. The only thing that wasn't close was the approval ratings of the three leaders, with Turner at 34, Mulroney at

36, and Broadbent in the stratosphere, with 63. That would prove to be critical to the kind of campaign the NDP would run. Rather than relying on its typical team approach, the party decided early on, too early as it turned out, to focus on Broadbent's personal popularity, hoping that would be enough, combined with the unpopularity of the other two, to convince Canadians to overcome their historical reluctance to support the socialists. It wasn't enough.

By early March, Gallup had the Liberals falling to 37; the NDP up two points, to 33; and the Tories up one, to 28. Environics, March 7–24, had it Liberals, 40; NDP, 30; and Conservatives, 29; and a Reid poll, March 17–21, had the Tories and NDP tied for first, with 34; and the Liberals in third, with 30, further cementing deeply held Liberal suspicions that Reid never gave them a break.

The media began writing stories about the confusion. Donna Dasko, vice-president of Environics, told *Ottawa Citizen* reporter Paul Gessell, "This is not a good situation for the polling industry. One of them has to be wrong." Not necessarily, only if you ascribe a scientific precision to polling, which isn't really justified. The common media practice of comparing polls, while interesting, isn't terribly valid. You're not comparing the same animals. For example, Gallup used in-home interviews. So did Environics, although they used phone interviews in their previous three surveys. Reid used the phone. What's more, the surveys were not taken at the same time of the month, and their non-sampling errors could never match.

And the questions were different. Not by much, but it doesn't take much to get a different response. Reid asks, "Thinking of how you feel right now, which party would you be most likely to support if a federal election were held tomorrow?" And, of course, he asks that question after the leadership question. Every other pollster puts party preference first, then leadership. Gallup's standard question is, "If a federal election were held today, which party's candidate do you think you would favor?" Environics asks, "If a Canadian federal election were held today, which one of the following parties would you vote for?" They then list the three major parties, and follow up on the undecided with, "Perhaps you have not yet made up your mind; is there nevertheless a party you might be inclined to support?" Hence, Environics had 15 percent undecided, compared to 21 for Reid and 27 for Gallup.

At first blush, the questions appear to be the same. But they're not. Gallup asks which "party's candidate" do you "think" you would favour, compared to Reid's "which party" would you be "most likely" to support and Environics's listing the parties and asking which "would you vote for." The difference between being asked about a "party" and being asked about a "party's candidate" could be significant. Many voters may not like the party, or more particularly the party leader, but may think the local candidate is great. And eliciting from someone that he or she is "most likely" to support a party doesn't mean that person *will* support that party. As for listing the three parties, that too could alter results, since, believe it or not, many Canadians can't even name the three parties, let alone tell you anything about them.

There are other problems, too. Donald Monk, president of Canadian Facts Ltd., by far Canada's largest market-research firm, says, "I used to have a rule that if a question had more than seventeen words it was bad." Monk points to recent studies showing a high rate of functional illiteracy in the country, and says, "A lot of surveys tend to assume knowledge that isn't there. You'll get answers to questions, but whether they understand it or not is certainly an open question.

"A fairly substantial section of the population has never listened to the news. They buy a paper to read the sports page, that sort of thing. They have zero interest in the political world. Even after Bill Davis had been premier for ten years, many people in Ontario still didn't know who he was.

"Anyway, if nobody in Canada changed their voting preference between period one and period two, and a hundred surveys were done, they are still going to vary. . . . That's why it's better to look at the trend information, except you can't do that at the red-hot time of an election."

Another major factor helping to explain wild swings in polling numbers is a process political scientists call "dealignment," essentially a decline of party identity, the loss of faith in political efficacy, and the rise of swing voters. For decades, people would generally vote the way their parents voted. Bill Davis tells stories of when he was a young man in Brampton, Ontario, and there was one barbershop where Tories went and one where Liberals went. It was the same for everything — lawyers, funeral homes, butchers, bakers, and candlestick-makers. In Atlantic Canada, these traditional party loyalties are still strong, but in most other areas they are breaking down. What that means, then, is that a single event — an act, a speech, whatever — could have a significant impact on a poll. People are doing more shopping around, and if they happen to walk into the Liberal store one week only to discover a gang of Liberals is trying to get Turner to quit, then they're liable to walk down the street to the Tory or the NDP store.

In April, Tory pollster Allan Gregg, asked about the confusion over the polls, said, "I'm upset because public-opinion polling puts shoes on my kids' feet. It confounds the political process, it confounds the consumer of the polls and puts public-opinion polling in disrepute because what people say is . . . 'They [pollsters] just make these things up.'" Of course, Gregg was secure in the knowledge that whether or not his polls contributed to the confusion, nobody would know except for a small group of senior Tories.

In any event, the Liberals jumped into the lead again in May. The May 11 Gallup had them at 39; the NDP, 31; and the Tories, 28. A May 18–24 Reid had Liberals, 37; Tories, 31; and NDP, 30, primarily as a result of an eleven-point increase in Quebec, the epicentre of an internal party revolt against Turner.

In June, Lac-Saint-Jean Conservative MP Clément Côté resigned to allow Tory star Lucien Bouchard to run in a June 20 by-election. A week before the election — and ten days after Gallup had shown a ten-point Tory drop in one month in Quebec — a poll, by a local firm, of 397 eligible voters had Bouchard trailing Liberal Pierre Gimaiel 23 to 21, with the NDP at 6, and 43 percent undecided. In fact, Bouchard won easily, with 55 percent of the popular vote, compared to 35 for the Liberal and only 10 for the NDPer. That should have sent a message to the NDP, but it didn't. Largely because of strong polling numbers in Quebec, the NDP was gearing up for an election to concentrate much of its time and resources to win ridings in that province — the party has never won a seat there, although it had one for a while when an MP crossed the floor to its side. This poll-driven Quebec push not only came up empty in the campaign, but it had affected the party's position on major issues, such as Meech Lake, where it tried to pander to Quebec and lost some of its traditional support. The push also accounted for Broadbent's mid-campaign embarrassment when a group of Quebec NDP candidates took a hard line on French-only linguistic rights in the province, and Broadbent tried to explain it away as a "nuance," to avoid undermining the support he still thought he had in Quebec.

By mid-August, Gallup was predicting a Tory minority, even though their numbers had the Liberals ahead 35 to 34 in popular vote, with the NDP at 30. Gallup vice-president Lorne Bozinoff, who would go on to say many silly things in the election, predicted the expected campaign "will indeed be a genuine, three-way confrontation." That's what Broadbent thought, too. In any event, Bozinoff explained his Tory-minority prediction, based on a computer model, by saying that the Tories had a sizeable lead in the Prairies and "significant support across other regions." Gallup felt the redistribution added ridings that are more traditionally Conservative. The problem with this sort of analysis, which more and more pollsters seem inclined to indulge in, is that it defies good sense. Granted, the Tories may have been strong in the Prairies — although breaking down a relatively small region means a much greater margin of error — and anyway, what the Tories were doing in Alberta can't be compared to what they were doing in Saskatchewan and Manitoba, yet all three provinces are lumped together as "the Prairies." It may be convenient to make them a homogeneous political unit, but they are far from that. What's more, Gallup had the Grits comfortably ahead in the two largest provinces, Quebec and Ontario, and just one point back of the Tories in B.C., the third-largest province. Despite this, Bozinoff claimed the Tories would win 130 seats; the Liberals, 115; and the NDP, 50. It made no sense. Not with his numbers.

It got worse. In the regular September poll, Bozinoff translated a 37-to-33 Tory lead (with the NDP at 27) into a comfortable Tory majority of 166 seats, leaving 85 for the Liberals and 44 for the NDP. No party since the Second World War had won a majority with 37 percent of the popular vote. Several won more of the vote and still had a minority, namely the 1957 Tories, with 39 percent; 1963 Liberals, with 41 percent; 1972 Liberals, with 39 percent, enough to just beat the Tories by two seats; and the 1979 Liberals, who got 40 percent of the vote but actually lost the election to Joe Clark's Tories (136 to 114) who had only 36 percent of the vote. None of that made Bozinoff's seat projections impossible, mind you, just far-fetched.

But Bozinoff fetched even farther beyond common sense in Gallup's first post-debate poll (no, not the infamous rogue poll, that came the next week) taken October 26–9. Gallup found almost identical numbers — Tories, 38; Liberals, 32; NDP, 27 — to the aforementioned September poll. Yet even though the Tories were up a point, Bozinoff had them dropping 12 seats from his earlier projection, to 154, a narrow majority. The Liberals, although down a point from that September poll, magically gained 17 seats, leaving only 29 for the poor NDP, a drop of 15 seats, even though their vote was identical (27 percent) in both polls.

It didn't do wonders for Gallup's reputation. Part of the problem could have been the company's decision to do weekly election polls for the first time. Indeed, the weekend the election was called, Gallup broke from their traditional in-home interview routine and conducted a phone poll, released just as the parties were heading out to the hustings. Reid was also doing weekly hits for Southam, and Michael Marzolini's Insight Canada (the brash newcomer who proved the most reliable) was actually doing daily rolling polls for CTV, the same kind of thing the parties themselves were doing to keep abreast of rapidly changing moods.

Peter Dwyer, vice-president of research for PIR Communications Ltd. of Halifax, says the problem with weekly campaign polls is that quality control suffers and therefore the results are not as reliable. "The crucial concern in polling is to ensure sampling is done randomly," says Dwyer. Normally, that means using the Census enumeration areas, drawing a proportionate number of households from each area, and having a computer dial randomly generated phone numbers. What happens during elections, says Dwyer, is that because of time constraints, where polls must be done in two or three days, pollsters will drop call-backs and in-house screening. According to proper polling methodology, pollsters should make four call-backs to a respondent before choosing another name in order to keep the sample's randomness as pure as possible. That doesn't just mean four calls on the same day. It means at least one call-back on four consecutive days, trying to reach the respondent. "If you've only got two days to turn around your poll, you can't do that," says Dwyer.

While the election grabbed the headlines, of course, a Gallup released in early September, based on 911 in-home interviews with adults across the country in July, indicated people had other things on their minds. It also suggested there may be more than political differences separating New Democrats from the two old-line parties. New Democrats, alas, don't do it as often. The survey found that declared Tory and Liberal supporters had sexual intercourse twice a week, while New Democrat supporters, apparently too busy saving the world, had sex on average just once a week.

Whatever the Tories were doing, it seemed to be working, as they began to put some distance between themselves and their political opponents in September. Environics had the Tories ahead in the popular vote for the first time in thirty months, perhaps the reward for more than $12.5 billion in megaprojects promised since May, such things as a $400-million contribution to the heavy-oil up-grader in Lloyd-minster, Saskatchewan, and a $1-billion grant and $1.6-billion loan guarantee for the $5.2-billion Hibernia development off St. John's, Newfoundland.

In any event, the Environics poll of 1,485 eligible voters, August 22 to September 6, showed the Tories at 37, the Liberals at 33, and the NDP at 25. The next week, Gallup had the Tories ahead for the first time in seventeen months, with 37 percent, compared with 33 for the Liberals and 27 for the NDP.

On September 27, the rabidly pro-Tory *Toronto Sun* reported that Mulroney "will easily win a majority government and the NDP will make historic gains at the expense of the Liberals." This hot news came from Decima's internal Tory polls, predicting the Tories would win 160 seats. And the final pre-campaign poll, a Southam–Angus Reid survey taken September 22–7, had the Tories at 40 percent, with the Liberals collapsing to third place, at 26, while the NDP moved up to 31.

The scene was set. And polling set the agenda, not only for the party leaders themselves, but for the media coverage to boot. By the end of the campaign, there would be 26 published national polls, up from 12 in 1984, about 4 a week on average, plus at least 250 local and regional polls published in every part of the country in newspapers and magazines and on radio and television stations. That doesn't count the party polls, of course. Indeed, one of the more scandalous oversights in the Canada Elections Act is that it doesn't count party polls as a campaign expense, even though the Tories spent about $5 million; the Liberals, well over $600,000; and the NDP, $300,000, on polling and related research during the campaign period. In addition, all three parties spent hundreds of thousands of dollars on polling in the period leading up to the campaign, and the taxpayers chipped in another $2 million or so for polls commissioned as government contracts but, in fact, used by the Tories for partisan purposes.

For the Tories, the only expenditure matching their massive polling operation was their media advertising campaign. But advertising counts as an election expense. Polling doesn't.

In 1985, two days after John Fraser resigned as Fisheries minister in the tainted-tuna affair, Marcel Masse, the Tories' Quebec lieutenant, also resigned after hearing that the RCMP were investigating him for alleged election-spending irregularities. At the heart of the matter was whether Masse had deliberately counselled his former employer, Lavalin Inc. of Montreal, to pay a volunteer campaign worker, Marthe Lefebvre, $2,235.68 so that the payment would not be part of campaign expenses every candidate must file with Elections Canada.

It turned out that Masse had not broken any laws because the definition of expenses was so vague. As a result of the controversy, however, chief electoral officer Jean-Marc Hamel commissioned the Toronto law firm of Borden and Elliot to offer a legal opinion on the act. In a March 3, 1988, letter to Hamel, Toronto lawyer E.A. Ayers wrote that the definition of election expenses is "so troublesome, cumbersome and ambiguous" it is "virtually impossible" to determine what constitutes an improper return. "In our opinion, the entire definition of election expenses is fraught with so many difficulties and is so vague and so uncertain in so many respects that if it is the wish of Parliament that rigid controls be maintained on election spending, it must be amended."

The Tories did promise to do just that. Indeed, a bill aimed at cleaning up some of the problems was introduced in June 1987, but it died on the order paper. The big problem is that the parties like the vagueness of the definition. The act defines election expenses as those "for the purpose of promoting, or opposing directly and during an election, a particular registered party or the election of a particular candidate."

One major legal problem hinges on the word "directly." Would that include the cost of renting a coffee machine in campaign headquarters for use by campaign workers, for example? Lawyers don't really know. What they do know, however, is that it doesn't cover the cost of polling, despite the massive use parties make of it. Elections Canada legal counsel Yvon Tarte says polling "is not considered a direct promotion of a candidate" under the act. It does, of course, have a direct effect on things that are considered expenses. For example, part of the Tory advertising budget was spent buying time on afternoon soap operas because Allan Gregg's polling determined that was an audience the Tories could reach effectively. "On a $45,000 spending limit, you had some people spending $50,000 on additional campaigning that wasn't covered," says Tarte.

The act sets a spending ceiling for each party (in 1988 it was about $7.8 million) and for individual candidates. The parties get back 22.5 percent of this spending from the taxpayers, and, of course, individual contributions to campaign expenses are tax deductible. In 1984, for example, the Tories spent $6.4 million and were reimbursed about $1.4 million; the Liberals spent $6.3 million and got back just under $1.4 million; and the NDP spent $4.7 million and received just over $1 million.

The definition of election expenses goes back to 1974 when the spending law first came into play. At the time, polling was not a big expense. Although it has mushroomed dramatically over the years, even the amendments proposed by the Tories following a three-party agreement in the wake of the Masse affair did not include polling as an election expense.

Bill Knight, former NDP federal secretary, who ran the party's 1988 campaign, says it's possible the Tories could introduce a tougher elections act, perhaps to limit third-party advertising or maybe even to impose a ten-day ban on publishing polls during campaigns, "but we'd be whistling in the dark if we expected them to change the rules on expenses. If polling had counted, they would have to either cut polling, or cut 80 percent of their advertising. . . . I'd be very surprised to see them change that."

The Tories actually started getting serious about this election in 1986 when Senator Norman Atkins set up his strategy group, with pollster Allan Gregg as an important component. The Tories were organizing dry runs, an elaborate campaign school, and getting most of their literature and advertising work done (as were their two opponents) before the writs were dropped. Acting on a Gregg poll, Mulroney went out in early summer, on a pre-campaign run through the regions, promoting the theme "managed change," which Gregg had picked up as a perceived source of Tory strength. Gregg had been conducting weekly polls for the Tories throughout the summer, and during the campaign regularly polled fifty selected ridings, did national "rolling" polls of 500 samples a night, plus four national polls with samples of 1,500.

In mid-campaign, then Health minister Jake Epp told the *Winnipeg Free Press*, "We're doing a lot of polling. I'm getting figures every day, a running total every 24 hours. We're running a very scientific campaign. If you've got the money, you can do that." Especially if it doesn't count as campaign spending.

The Liberals, of course, didn't have the money, but they spent a bundle anyway. John Webster, Liberal national campaign director, says the party originally targeted $500,000 to poll twelve bell-wether ridings "but we found in the first part of the campaign it was a hopeless undertaking. In some ridings, it was meaningless. We were so far behind in some ridings, in Quebec especially, it wasn't telling us anything."

So they moved from that to a rolling sample, with Goldfarb polling about two hundred people a day even before the TV debate. "The most reliable and detailed stuff is your rolling polls," Webster says. "It allows the standard questions on issues, but you can also substitute questions on a short-term basis. When costing of our programs became an issue, for example, we were able to change the questions. It also allows for cumulative totals and a bar graph on a three- to five-day spin, which is really quite helpful."

Webster says the party didn't do national samples "because we knew the media would be doing a ton of them. Our polls enabled us to measure the rolling samples against the national media samples."

Like the Tories, the Liberals did some specialty polls, such as the one on the night of both televised debates. "We did well in both debates, although it was a clearer win in the data after the English debate. We got data back in the third hour while the debate was still going on," Webster says. "But we didn't do the numbers the Tories did. Harry Near [Conservative operations director] told us they knew what kind of gum the people were chewing watching the debate."

The Liberals also had an in-house computer model for seat projections from every poll. "We found that, combined with Marty's own projections, we were within five or six seats."

Webster says the Tories were clearly on an upward trend when the election was called and "our Senate gambit was designed to kick-start the leadership numbers. We were faced with low leadership numbers contrasted to a good share of party-preference numbers, so we hoped the Senate gambit would increase those leadership numbers. It helped some."

Knight says the NDP had built a substantial database of polling material since 1984, mainly through Sorecom and Access Survey Research (a wholly owned subsidiary of Angus Reid, which did the actual campaign field-work). "We knew we had fundamentally changed our base since 1984. Traditionally, it was in the 11-to-13 percent range and we could get our vote up to 19 percent. But we'd developed a base of about 20 percent.

"What was tough on us was that, as free trade became a more

salient issue, people started heading back to their partisan base. Ironically, so did our people, so by the time of the debate we'd overextended our market grab in terms of being able to service it by at least nine to eleven points."

Knight says one of the dangers of polling is that it can give you a "deadly information overload" and it can become "too reactive. If polling shows you're weak in a certain spot, you have a tendency to say, 'Well, we're weak here. Let's back away.' That was the case with us on the question of managing the economy."

Knight says political parties "tend to get consumed by their weaknesses. Think of the Grits. They tried to devour their leader because the polls showed he was weak. But while everyone else was reading the polls, Turner went out and read a history book. That's how he positioned himself so well on the free-trade debate. He didn't just look at numbers, he looked at history."

The NDP was sampling about two hundred people a night on Monday-through-Thursday polls, plus doing some separate polling in Quebec where it had staked so much of its resources in an effort to break through. American pollster Vic Fingerhut helped party officials write the questionnaires and analyse the results. "His role was as an adviser," says Knight. "I think Vic's stuff was absolutely dead on."

Not everyone agreed. In fact, the bitter internal split on election strategy went back to February 3, when, at NDP headquarters on Slater Street in downtown Ottawa, a meeting between senior party officials and senior Canadian Labor Congress (CLC) officials developed into a shouting match because the party had decided, even back then, it couldn't win a free-trade showdown. Instead, the party officials argued that their polling showed they should concentrate on Mulroney's lack of credibility, something else they didn't do. The union people were furious. The CLC and several union affiliates had fought a long, pitched battle against free trade and weren't happy with the notion of soft-peddling it now that an election was expected. But, for the good of the party, orders went out to cool the criticism to avoid driving a wedge between labour and the party. The resentment simmered for months, reaching the boiling-point, and going public, when it became obvious in mid-campaign that the strategy was a poor one, although there were many private complaints flowing from labour to the party, particularly after Broadbent's opening campaign statement didn't even mention the words "free trade," let alone signal to the country that he saw it as a major issue. "And then they wonder why our people vote Liberal," says one labour leader. "We bust our guts, and our bank accounts, to fight this bloody deal, and they say, lay off it. Worse, the advice comes from an American pollster, for god's sake."

While the leader, of course, has always been important to the NDP, as he has to all parties, it tended to pride itself on the fact that its campaigns were more issue-oriented, more ideological, and therefore less of a leadership cult — yes, less American-style — than those of the Tories and Liberals. Not this time. Ed was the medium and the message. And it was all based on his high standings in the polls. So, too, was the rest of the NDP campaign, the decision to begin with a soft approach, almost prime-ministerial, riding above it all, avoiding the normal campaign blood and guts. The NDP believed its polls. Unfortunately, the party was operating on polls that were six months to a year out of date. Things had changed. The Tories had made a comeback. The Liberals, despite Turner's personal disasters, were strong. And no matter how many star-brights they wished upon, they were not going anywhere in Quebec.

On a post-campaign CBC radio program, campaign organizer Robin Sears said, "We attempted to move in marketing terms from a niche marketer into a national brand name without examining what the costs and consequences of that would be. . . . Our resources were smaller . . . and our anticipation of the ferocity of the attack which would be launched against us was naive."

And so, Fingerhut took much of the blame. Knight says he doesn't deserve it because, unlike Gregg, who has direct access to Mulroney, "all our stuff is filtered. It went through the grist-mill of party people, campaign people, and union people." Maybe so, but that didn't stop the angry recriminations both during and after the campaign. The irony is that with fifty-three seats, the NDP had never won more. But it was the expectations of greatness that did them in; expectations fuelled directly by public-opinion polls; expectations that prompted Broadbent to go on and on about this being "the first three-way election in Canadian history"; expectations that prompted Broadbent to muse aloud in mid-campaign about how wonderful Canada would be if we had a polarized, two-party system, without the Liberals.

"That hurt us, no doubt," says Knight. "But it didn't come from the polls. Quite the reverse. I think that came from the hopes, dreams, that New Democrats have been perpetually caught up in, the notion that without the Liberals we could.

"But our polling has consistently shown that if you scratch every Canadian deeply enough, you'll find a Grit. They're the most resilient, the Coca-Cola of Canadian politics. They're the sleeping giant, a formidable foe. We knew that. And we knew right away we had a problem when Ed said that."

After the campaign, Canadian Auto Workers president Bob White, having bitten his tongue for months, openly accused the party's brains-trust of handing the free-trade issue to Turner. In a no-nonsense, seven-page letter, White, the closest thing to a god in the union movement, delivered a stinging rebuke of the campaign: "Many canvassers told me they couldn't believe our ads, or daily events dealing with other issues, while at the door people were talking about free trade." Maybe Fingerhut and other senior strategists should have pulled themselves away from their sophisticated databanks and knocked on some doors with labour. Defeated Toronto MP Lynn McDonald says, "We had the most passionless, cold, empty campaign.... People kept joking about this whole fairness-for-average-Canadians stuff. We were being told that it was going to get us votes, but nobody in caucus believed that.... The whole thing was absolutely meaningless."

In a post-campaign interview with Linda Diebel of the *Toronto Star*, Fingerhut said he read the psyche of Canadian voters properly when he advised the J DP to play down free trade. "My assumption was that free trade would be part of the election campaign, but only one part. We wanted to broaden the base because we didn't want this campaign to be fought on one issue."

Fingerhut's argument was that the NDP was not believable on economic issues. Best to stick to the "soft" issues, which is what they did, and leave the "hard" issues to the big boys — tough strategy when you're trying to convince Canadians you're in the same league as the other two parties.

For Turner, of course, free trade was the campaign. Even though it hurt him by the end — "He started to sound like a one-note Johnny," says Webster — his performance on that issue, the passion he displayed, particularly during the TV debates, is what ultimately kept him from an electoral nuking.

"The original idea on trade, which Marty suggested in a strategic survey before the election," says Webster, "was to be used to harass the trust and credibility of Mulroney because Canadians did not believe the guy. Our numbers showed us that. Trade was supposed to be used to raise doubts about Brian Mulroney, as opposed to trade itself.

"And the second front on the credibility issue was the national sales tax. We tried some other issues in the beginning, but they didn't catch on. At the end, when we wanted to switch to the sales tax, the leader refused to give other speeches except his free-trade core speech, the 'cause of his life' speech.

"So the Tories came out with their heavy guns," says Webster. "Mulroney called Turner a liar. We should have called Mulroney a liar. But he [Turner] didn't want to do that. I think the public was looking to him to answer back, and he didn't. He didn't feel comfortable getting into that kind of a fight."

It didn't bother the Tories, although for the first half of the campaign they didn't have to fight. All Mulroney had to do was show up, the perfect political package, complete with a blue ribbon, just floating from one photo op to another, a political Fred Astaire, dancing endlessly on the political stage, within sight of the cameras, but far enough away that those grubby journalists whose companies paid hundreds of dollars a day for the privilege of a ticket couldn't get close enough to ask a question, or do anything that could trigger Mulroney's famous Irish temper. His choreographers knew, from bitter experience, that Mulroney says it best when he says nothing, or at least, as little as possible, all of it carefully scripted.

This bubble phase of the campaign may have upset the journalists, but it didn't seem to offend the public. The Gallup on October 3 gave Mulroney a ten-point lead over Turner. Two days later, Reid had the Tories at 45 and the Liberals in last place, at 26, one behind the NDP. The next day, Insight on CTV gave the Tories 46, a nineteen-point bulge over Turner. And so it went. The October 10 Gallup had it Tories, 43; Liberals, 32; NDP, 26. The next day, Environics had it Tories, 42; NDP, 29; and Liberals, 25. Then came another Insight poll, on October 14, with the Tories at 46, still nineteen points ahead of Turner. The first CBC poll, October 16, had the Tories heading for a clear majority at 42, with the NDP at 29, and John Turner, sore back and all, limping along at 25. On October 24, the final poll before the TV debate, Gallup had the Tories home and dry at 40, with the Liberals at 29 and the NDP at 28.

It was pretty heady stuff, enough to prompt Mulroney to confidently predict he was headed for yet another massive victory. At an October 10 Montreal rally, Mulroney said he felt the "same sense I have felt all week, the sense of 1984." The only problem the Tories seemed to have was keeping the troops from getting too cocky. In an October 13 speech in Toronto, where the Tories had not expected to be leading public-opinion polls, Finance minister Michael Wilson told his campaign workers to keep working. "Don't pay any attention to those numbers that we're reading in the papers," he said.

While Mulroney was crowing, and Broadbent was speaking of a two-party system, the Liberals were firing verbal rockets at each other. Turner had campaigned well since the opening gun, but few noticed. They did notice the polls, and they noticed whenever Turner slipped up, but he didn't get much help from his "friends" either. In mid-October, former Liberal president Iona Campagnolo mused aloud that the party could be on the road to oblivion. About the same time, Martin Goldfarb and Tom Axworthy published a book, *Marching to a Different Drummer*, that was widely characterized as yet another attack on Turner. In fact, it wasn't. But the timing was really stupid, and the two authors, who weren't exactly political neophytes, must have known what the reaction would be. "Their book itself didn't say anything," says Webster. "But the coverage of the book contributed to the question of disloyalty and confusion which seemed to be enveloping the campaign at that time."

And, as often happens when it seems things couldn't possibly get worse, they did. The CBC's Peter Mansbridge, stepping out of his normal news-reader role to give the story more clout, reported that a group of key Liberals had plotted a coup to oust Turner in mid-campaign. The story, with little supporting evidence and not a single clip from anyone involved, none the less skilfully mixed innuendo, technique, coincidence, and even a dollop of fact to give the distinct impression that a regular meeting of the campaign team and a subsequent memo to the leader were considerably more than that. Worse, the follow-up stories about the "coup" made the story even stronger, despite denials from all the accused plotters.

In the book *Election*, written by three well-known partisans — Liberal Michael Kirby, Tory Hugh Segal, and New Democrat Gerald Caplan — Kirby, a partner with Goldfarb, and chairman of the Liberal strategy committee, essentially argues there was some truth and some fiction to the report, and even that some of the truth was taken badly out of context.

Webster, still angry about the story, says, "I was never even called by the CBC. They never talked to me before they accused me of being part of this." Webster said part of the memo sent to Turner contained the polling data "without editorial comment. All the famous Kirby memo did was provide a summary of the data we had collected. People didn't want to believe what the data said at that point because it was so devastating."

In any event, it didn't help. Nor did the October 20 results of the party's internal polling on the twelve bell-wether ridings, showing losses of between three and five points in a week in most of them, particularly in Halifax, Toronto, Montreal, and Vancouver. The only good news in the numbers was in Moncton and St. Boniface. Everywhere else, it was disastrous.

In an October 21 *Globe* column headlined "Pop Go The Liberals," journalist Jeffrey Simpson wrote, "A once proud party is disintegrating before the eyes of the Canadian public. The evidence of internal disarray and searing internal enmity is everywhere apparent." It certainly was.

The same day, Webster, Segal, and Knight taped CTV's "Question Period," to be broadcast October 23, with Pamela Wallin. Webster says they were handed the latest Insight poll, before it was broadcast — pollsters will tip you off in advance — and while Segal gloated about the Tory numbers, Webster's only defence was to wait and see, things will improve. "The debates will obviously have quite an impact as I believe will the advertising campaign," said Webster. "So we are looking ahead." Even Webster didn't foresee the impact the debates would have on the campaign.

With the possible exception of the *Toronto Sun*, every major news outlet in the country reported Turner as the clear winner of the debates. So did all the polls.

The final two pre-debate polls not only had the Liberals miles behind the Tories, but showed them mired in last place. The October 21 Insight for CTV had Mulroney comfortably ahead, at 43 percent of decided voters, the NDP at 30, and Turner's tattered troops at 25. A Gallup, published October 24, the day of the first, French-language debate, had it Tories, 40; NDP, 29; Grits, 28.

Then the earth moved. Not permanently, but long enough to end Broadbent's hopes of finishing second, and strong enough to send shockwaves through the Tory campaign and, perhaps more importantly, into the Canadian business establishment, which consequently launched the most vigorous, most expensive campaign against Turner — or, at least, *for* free trade — that this country had ever seen. For it was on free trade, the issue Broadbent had missed, that Turner made his most telling points, accusing Mulroney of having "sold us out."

Right after the debate, Mansbridge went to two "undecided" voters the CBC had standing by in a Winnipeg studio. Both said they believed Turner had won the debate, hands down. Mansbridge, looking curiously peeved, then turned to David Halton, the CBC's chief political correspondent and, before allowing him to say anything, warned him not to "fall into the trap" of picking winners and losers. At CTV, the normally opinionated Craig Oliver was uncharacteristically fuzzy during his immediate reaction to the debate. Neither network had been particularly hesitant about expressing itself when the Tories appeared to be waltzing to a win, but even if the networks were reluctant to pick a winner, a host of post-debate polls showed the general public had no qualms about doing so.

An immediate post-debate Insight poll for CTV asked the question "Who won?" and 59 percent of eligible voters who responded said, Turner. Mulroney got 16; Broadbent, 11. Among undecided voters, Turner did even better, getting the nod from 66 percent, compared to 10 percent for Broadbent and just 7 percent for Mulroney.

On Friday, October 28, three days after the English-language debate, the *Globe*–Environics poll had the Tories and Liberals tied at 32 percent, with the NDP trailing at 28, a stunning reversal. A key point here, not well explained by the *Globe* at the time, was that this poll was actually a panel, not a random sample of voters. The paper did explain, in a sidebar on the inside page, that the 811 respondents interviewed for their post-debate impressions were originally part of the *Globe*–Environics poll in early September. Panels are, of course, a legitimate technique, but they shouldn't be compared to your standard random surveys simply because the respondents are not randomly, but specifically selected by the pollster.

On October 29, the born-again Grits had vaulted into a first-place tie with the Tories in a Southam–Angus Reid poll of 1,502 Canadians surveyed one and two days after the debates. Both parties stood at 35 percent of the decided voters, the NDP at 28, prompting Reid to say the election is "now a new ballgame. . . . It appears that while there was a Tory surge in August through to early October, the concrete really hadn't set regarding the commitment of voters towards the Tories. And now things have come unglued." Ah, hindsight. Before this, Reid and the other pollsters were confidently predicting a Tory majority.

Other things were changing too. Two weeks earlier, a *Globe*–

Environics poll put support for the free-trade deal at 44 percent, a gain of seven points since June. Opponents were at 42 percent, up two points. The October 29 Reid, however, showed 54 percent opposed to the deal, with 35 percent in support. A July Reid poll had both sides at 42 percent.

On Hallowe'en, Gallup got into the post-debate sweepstakes, but their poll, taken four days after the debates, had the Tories down six points but still winning 38 to 32, with the NDP at 28. And the CTV–Insight poll had the Liberals ahead 39 to 35, with the NDP dropping back to 23.

The turn-around in the polls led to some silly excesses in the media. The *Vancouver Sun*, for example, did its own computer projections based on the Reid poll and concluded that the Tories "are facing a shut-out in Toronto, Saskatchewan and Prince Edward Island." Closer to home, the *Toronto Sun* said the Liberals would likely elect three members: Turner in Quadra, James Hatton in North Vancouver, and Tex Enemark in Vancouver Centre. Indeed, some newspapers even began writing stories about a possible Liberal cabinet, touting Enemark as a sure bet. The problem was, he finished third, and it turns out the national survey on which this projection was based had three respondents in Vancouver Centre, a huge downtown riding with more than 80,000 eligible voters.

The polls also signalled a change in Tory campaign tactics. Mulroney shifted from predictions of a majority and assorted partisan sloganeering to direct frontal assaults on both Turner and Broadbent. Tory panic reached the stage where even a relatively honest politician, Michael Wilson, accused Turner and Broadbent of spreading "lies . . . [and] sowing fear" about free trade, this in the same speech in which Wilson told his business audience that, without the deal, the Auto Pact might die. They also trotted out free-trade negotiator Simon Reisman to fight for the deal — although he spent more time fighting with and insulting anyone who dared express an opposing view — and former chief justice Emmett Hall, whose royal commission on Medicare had led to the establishment of the national health-care system, to say the Liberals and New Democrats were wrong in suggesting that the deal would hurt Medicare. Reisman's intervention, his bully-boy tactics, probably lost as many votes as it gained. Hall, however, helped the Tory cause.

At the same time, of course, the party advertising campaigns had already clicked in, and the Liberal ads — particularly one showing the Canada–U.S. boundary line being erased by the free-trade deal — had far more impact than did the Tory and NDP ads.

The polls, of course, kept coming. The *Globe*–Environics poll had the Liberals winning 37 to 31, with the NDP at 26. Another poll, conducted by John Yerxa Research Inc. for the *Edmonton Sun* and *Calgary Sun*, found that even in Alberta, of all places, only 40 percent of those asked supported free trade, while 39 percent opposed it. The Alberta Tories launched a $500,000 advertising campaign of their own aimed at convincing undecided Albertans that the deal was good for them, whether they realized it or not.

Amid this feverish activity, however, nobody anticipated what came next — the November 7 Gallup. Suddenly, the Liberals had leapt to 43 percent of decided voters, a twelve-point lead over the Tories, with the NDP at 22 percent, and 10 percent still undecided. It was an unprecedented turn-around, just two weeks before election day, and Gallup said it would mean 170 Liberal seats, compared to 91 for the Tories and 34 for the NDP. The biggest change was in Quebec, where, a week earlier, the Liberals had trailed the Tories by fourteen points and suddenly were ahead by nine points. Gallup vice-president Lorne Bozinoff wrote in the release accompanying the poll, "It appears plausible to argue that the recent campaigning by popular favourite son Jean Chrétien has served to boost Liberal support in Quebec." This was Bozinoff's first federal election as a pollster, and his lack of experience was beginning to show. How did he know what impact Chrétien was having? He hadn't asked that question in his poll. And if Chrétien had that much political potency in Quebec, where did it go on November 21? After all, he campaigned right up until voting day.

Bozinoff also wrote, "Never in the 46 years that Gallup has been monitoring Canadian federal elections has a party experienced a similar mid-campaign reversal in support." He might have also added that never in their forty-six years had Gallup monitored a Canadian federal election on a weekly basis.

All the other pollsters dismissed it as a bad poll, a rogue. Conservative campaign official John Tory says, it was "just silly. We knew from our own polling that we were never anything close to twelve points behind. It was just so ridiculous, we knew it couldn't be true. To me the story is what happened to Gallup in that election. Whether it's had any impact on their private-sector business, which is really where these guys make their money, I don't know. But if I was a private-sector client I'd say, 'Geez, this guy comes out and produces a poll like that, so wildly inaccurate ...' I'd wonder whether he's going to do the same when I'm testing my new car models."

Bozinoff says the poll had no effect on his private-sector business. "I don't think anybody mentioned it to me at all.... Our private clients are a little more sophisticated than that."

Even though the Tories didn't believe the poll, they knew that, with the Gallup name attached to it, many people would. Pollsters claim they go to great lengths to secure their numbers before publication, but Tory and officials from other parties confirm that the companies give them the numbers before they make them public. In the case of this Gallup, that allowed the Tories to react immediately.

"My experience tends to suggest that the more time you leave bad news out there without responding, the more it tends to sink in," says Tory. "It gives people a chance to get depressed about it or start to believe it. In this case, what we did was we got on the phone that night to people across the country and said, 'Look, there is a Gallup poll coming out tomorrow.' You know what it's like if somebody tells you a bit of bad news ahead of time. Sometimes, when it comes out, it doesn't seem as bad because you're prepared for it, you've had twelve hours to think about it and rationalize it. So we did that.

"Secondly, we got a memo put together, which we sent out on our electronic mail system the next morning so that literally within half an hour of most people hearing the news in the morning, when they came to work there would be a memo up in all the campaign head-quarters for the workers and all the campaign managers and candidates to see, saying this poll is not consistent with our own research, it's not consistent with any other polls we have seen published. The memo said, 'Carry on, we've got the right strategy, we're on the right track, don't pay any attention to this.'

"It also allowed us to decide what we were doing in terms of the PM's reaction. There wasn't any doubt there. He just said he didn't believe it, it doesn't square with our polls, and that's what he went out and said to the press the next day. But it gave him time to collect his thoughts," says Tory.

Despite the controversy, Bozinoff defended the poll. He said because it was published on a Monday, it was considered the first poll of that week, "but it wasn't, it was the last poll of the previous week and we were being compared with other polls done that week."

Bozinoff said, the worst thing for pollsters is the dreaded "V" word — volatility. "You heard that a dozen times. This campaign was volatile . . . unlike most Canadian campaigns. The public was faced with an emotional issue, a nationalistic issue, a series of choices they didn't really like, so that reduced their loyalty or any kind of tie to one of the parties."

On October 31, with the post-debate turn-around in fortunes, the Liberals stepped up their daily polling activity, shifting to nightly rolling polls for the rest of the campaign in Ontario and Quebec — with 150 interviews in each province — shooting the answers straight into a computer so they'd be keypunched and tabulated and ready for study the next morning.

Not all Liberals were happy with the polling. One issue that came up late in the campaign and took some momentum away from Turner was the question of how much his campaign promises would cost and who would pay. Acting on advice from Goldfarb and Kirby that the numbers showed the issue wasn't hurting them, Turner delayed for several days. In the meantime, regardless of what else he was saying, the media concentrated on the costing issue. They'd ignored it earlier in the campaign, but now that the polls suggested Turner had a chance to win, the question of costing became important.

One veteran Liberal organizer, speaking after the campaign on the understanding that he wouldn't be named, said, "Kirby kept insisting the data showed the costing issue wasn't hurting us. But all our candidates were telling us they were getting it at the door. People, quite legitimately, wanted to know how we were going to pay for our promises. That's what took away our momentum. It put us on the defensive again."

Indeed, some concerned Liberals were sending memos to the party hierarchy, suggesting they pick a date to announce the costing. "But they didn't, and it really hurt us. If we'd announced it beforehand we wouldn't have had reporters asking the leader about it every day for two weeks.

"Our polling was really pathetic," he said. "I'm not into conspiratorial things, but why did Goldfarb publish his book in the middle of the campaign and why did Kirby act the way he did, that stuff comparing business to the Ku Klux Klan, for heaven's sake? Before the Mansbridge story broke, Kirby certainly told all those [senior party] guys that the figures were hard, that the Tories were rising and the Liberals collapsing, and there was nothing anybody could do to turn them around. Well, he was shown wrong a week later."

The polls, of course, continued.

Mulroney, who normally had little to say about polls, told journalists outside a cabinet-making plant in Hull, Quebec, that Tory polling results "indicate an entirely different conclusion, a tight race that is getting even tighter. I'm very satisfied with the way our campaign is going. We're closing the gap on a daily basis and I'm well pleased with that. I can assure you that ours show something quite different.... We have every reason to be confident and we are."

Mulroney did not say what the Decima polls showed, but one insider says that, at the time of the Gallup, the Tory polls showed the Liberals three points ahead. "That's the worst it ever got for us, but we weren't particularly spooked by it. The distribution was good, even if the global numbers weren't. And we knew it was temporary and we had all those business guys coming out, guns blazing. Together, we were out to destroy Turner's credibility. We did a damn good job, I think."

As for Turner, who usually was even quieter on the subject of the polls than was Mulroney, he said he didn't need any polls to know he was going to win. "We don't need polls to know Canadians are responding to us in rejecting this trade deal.... I don't see any polls.... I know the country as well as anybody. We're going to win. We're going to form a government."

The poll-fed euphoria didn't last long. A *Globe*-Environics poll, published on November 10, showed the Tories just two points behind (35 to 37) and the NDP at 24 among decided voters, a virtual tie eleven days before the election. The pollsters concluded that "the parties are so close that seat projections suggest a minority government, but do not indicate which party could form it." And then, along came Reid, as he often has at the brightest moments for the Liberals, to announce that the Tories were ahead in his poll, 39 to 35, with the NDP at 24, and 22 percent undecided. Reid, who just a few weeks earlier was confidently predicting a healthy Tory majority, said it was now too close to call. "It's sort of like a person in a used car lot. There's a lot of indecision on which of the three you want to go with."

Yet another poll, this one a CTV–Insight effort, had the Tories and Grits at 39 apiece, with the NDP slipping to 20. Insight Canada president Michael Marzolini, somewhat precipitately, said the Liberal vote "has acquired a new backbone and now rivals the PC support in firmness. This is the third consecutive weekly poll that has placed the Liberals leading or tied for first place. Despite some recent PC gains, time and a steady performance has served to solidify Liberal voter-intent.

"Until this week the Liberal vote was soft, and in danger of disappearing overnight." What it all means, he said, was Canadians will wake up November 22 with a minority government. We didn't. It seems the Liberal vote wasn't that hard after all.

On November 14, with one week to go, Gallup had the Liberals and Tories tied at 35, with the NDP at 26 and only 8 percent undecided. Undaunted by their other absurd claims in the campaign, Gallup went on to say this would mean 141 Tory seats, 112 for the Liberals, and 42 for the NDP. This sort of seat projection can be done with some accuracy when parties are using rolling samples, but it becomes a mug's game when it's based on 1,026 personal interviews across the country. Bozinoff, incidentally, argued that, since only 19 percent of those asked who would make the best prime minister picked Turner (down 3 percent from the previous week), that shows "upon closer reflection, long-seated questions concerning Mr. Turner have resurfaced in the electorate." That may have been the case, but his numbers didn't show that. A 3 percent shift is well within the margin of error and, therefore, as he should know, meaningless.

The Tories were so concerned about the polls that on November 17 their campaign headquarters actually sent out a formal press release on polls, claiming "mounting evidence of momentum" from an analysis of media polls during the previous two weeks. "Most dramatic change was reported by Gallup, whose poll on November 7 reported the Liberals in front with the support of 43 percent of decided voters. . . . But, one week later, Liberal support had fallen eight points, to 35." This is the same poll the Tories dismissed out of hand at the time. Now they were using it as evidence they had the momentum.

On November 18, a poll by Sorecom of 1,170 Quebeckers put the Tories in front 44 to 36, with 17 for the NDP, and 18 percent undecided. Sorecom polling director Soucy Gagne said this would mean 50 to 54 Quebec seats for the Tories, 20 to 23 for the Liberals, and 1 or 2 for the NDP. Sorecom wasn't even close, as three days later the NDP was shut out — although they had one close call — with just 14 percent of the Quebec vote; the Liberals got 30 percent of the vote and 12 of the seats, and the Tories won 53 percent of Quebeckers' votes and 63 of their seats, well outside Sorecom's projections.

Finally, on the eve of the vote, we had the three final election polls. Gallup had it Tories, 40; Liberals, 35; NDP, 22. According to Reid, it was Tories, 41; Liberals, 33; NDP, 23. And Insight called it Tories, 43;

Liberals, 32; NDP, 20, which is exactly how the voters went two days later.

By the end of the campaign, all the public pollsters, their reputations shaken by their roller-coaster results, were using larger samples than they were at the beginning, hoping to cut down the margin of error and get a better reading at the same time. Gallup, true to form for this campaign, mixed its methodology in the same survey, a questionable practice, conducting 2,097 in-home interviews and 1,970 telephone interviews, and combining the results. They set the margin of error at plus or minus 3 percent, down a percentage point from the standard Gallup sample, and said they believed the survey was the largest public-opinion poll ever published in Canada. Perhaps it was, but it didn't help that much. The fact that no party in this century had won a majority with 40 percent of the vote did not dissuade Bozinoff from projecting a comfortable majority of 162 Tory, 97 Liberal, and 36 NDP seats. He underestimated both the NDP and the Tories by 7 seats, and gave the Liberals an extra 14. Despite that, Gallup was still within their margin of error. That should tell you not to take polls too literally. It's an interesting and influential activity, but it's not a perfect science, even when it's done properly.

6

The "Science" of Sampling

To Malcolm Muggeridge, the use of public-opinion polls in our time is akin to the Roman practice of killing a chicken, throwing its innards on the ground, and reading the future from the patterns created.

Winston Churchill once said, "There is nothing more dangerous than to live in the temperamental atmosphere of a Gallup poll, always taking one's temperature."

And there was John Diefenbaker's disdainful quip about polls being for dogs.

Naturally, they were entitled to their opinions. Indeed, according to the pollsters, everybody is entitled, which is why they spend their time trying to find out what those opinions are, that plus the fact it's one of Canada's greatest growth industries and, for some, a quick road to fame and fortune.

The fictional Sherlock Holmes, while not a pollster, certainly had an abiding interest in discovering why people act the way they do. In *The Sign of the Four*, Holmes noticed that small groups of people could be used to predict the actions of a larger group.

"While the individual man is an insoluble puzzle," he said, "in the aggregate he becomes a mathematical certainty."

Holmes overstated the exactness of the "science," as pollsters and their devotees continue to do. But there is no doubt that polling relatively small numbers of people, done properly, can measure the views of a larger population better than any other method we know of.

At first blush, this makes no sense. How can the views of 1,000 out of 26 million Canadians represent anything more than the views of the 1,000 people who were polled? Gallup used a spoon-and-soup analogy to say that, with proper stirring, a cook can taste one spoonful and tell how the entire pot of soup is doing. True, the population at large is more diverse than a pot of soup, but if pollsters study the various ingredients that go into the population soup, structure their questions properly, follow a specific recipe of data collection, and let it simmer before serving, then the laws of probability as set out by Johann Bernoulli in 1713 do work.

Until late 1943, the Dominion Bureau of Statistics (now called Statistics Canada) collected all its data through old-fashioned enumeration methods — going to everybody's house and asking. By 1948, however, the Statistics Act was amended "to authorize the collection of statistics by means of sampling." A 1952 Bureau document notes: "[sampling] permits surveys to be made much more quickly and with a fraction of the staff required for complete enumeration, yet it can yield results well within the margin of error necessary for practical purposes; indeed when properly applied, this method is frequently capable of furnishing data of a higher quality than can be obtained by ordinary enumeration."

How do they do it? Well, in a 1983 Statistics Canada manual called *Survey Sampling*, the first thing is to define just what a survey is. Actually, there are two kinds. *Descriptive surveys* primarily estimate certain characteristics or attributes of a population, such as average income of farmers, or the percentage of unemployed persons, or how much money an industry spends on research and development.

Analytical surveys, however, are intended more to explain than to describe. These surveys are less common than descriptive ones, but are more than ever in vogue with party pollsters eager to tell their employers not only who and what, but why people are attracted to or turned off by a particular program or politician. In most cases, descriptive surveys are needed before an analytical survey is undertaken.

The first task in planning a survey is to decide just what it is you want to know. Sounds simple, but it's not always. Take, for example, a survey of "housing conditions of the poor." Does "housing conditions" mean the type of dwelling, its age, and/or its location? What does "poor" mean? Does it mean a person's income, his debts, both? Is there a standard of comparison, and if so, what is it? Is a family of three, earning $20,000 a year, but living mortgage-free in a Prince Edward Island village, poorer than, say, a Toronto man with a wife and one child, earning $30,000 a year but paying a monthly rent of $1,200?

Take a simple question, such as, "Do you own a car?" Well, sociologist Stanley Presser, of the National Science Foundation in Washington, wrote, "That sounds like a simple question. But is it really? What does 'you' mean? Suppose a wife is answering the poll, and the car is registered in her husband's name. How is she supposed to answer? What does 'own' mean? What if the car is on a long-time lease? What does 'car' mean? What if they have one of those new little vans or a four-wheel-drive vehicle? My God, that sounds like a simple question! You can imagine how diverse the factors become in a more complicated one."

Whatever the questions, whatever the information sought, the pollster must have sorted out the implications before making the first phone call or knocking on the first door.

The pollster must also develop a *sample plan*, which contains three basic elements: *sample design*, basically what a sample consists of and how it is to be obtained; *estimation procedures*, which show how estimates of the population characteristics are going to be constructed from the sample; and *estimates of precision*, which essentially are procedures to measure sampling error.

The sample design describes the target and survey population, the frame, the survey units, the size of the sample, and the sample-selection methods. When pollsters speak of the "population," or "universe," they mean the aggregate or collection of units to which the survey applies. It could be people, or a collection of schools, households, trees, whatever is being studied. Once that has been decided, units within the population must be determined by their age, size, or whatever other features identify them. Then, geographic boundaries, such as municipal, provincial, regional, must be drafted.

A *survey frame* comes next. In the Census, for example, the frame consists of area units called Enumeration Areas (EA's), commonly used by pollsters and readily identifiable on maps and in the field. The frame can simply be a telephone book or computer printout, anything that lists the elements to be covered in the survey population.

The *size of the sample* must also be decided. Among other things, with national surveys costing $40 to $50 a person, the size is a major determinant of the cost of the survey. A popular misconception holds that the size of a sample must increase in proportion to the size of the population. Not true. To best illustrate this, Gallup uses just over 1,000 to test public opinion in the United States, with its 260 million people, and uses the same sample size in Canada, which is one-tenth the size. If it didn't work that way, either we could have a sample of 100 in Canada, which obviously wouldn't tell you anything, or Gallup would have to sample 10,000 in the United States, which would cost a fortune and give you only marginally better results. However, if you wanted a comparable survey of, say, Toronto, you would have to poll the same number of people there as you did in your national survey in order for it to be statistically correct. Pollsters don't do that because it would be too expensive.

Surveys, of course, are not perfect. Thus, every pollster must contend with sampling errors and non-sampling errors. *Sampling error* is an unavoidable error attributed to studying a fraction of the population rather than the whole. The size of this error generally diminishes as the sample size increases, but such things as different population characteristics, sample design, and estimation methods also affect the error.

Non-sampling errors are also unavoidable. Basically human errors, they can arise from respondents who don't answer the questions truthfully — twenty years ago, for example, the U.S. Census Bureau studied the voting habits of Americans and found that 10 million more eligible voters said they voted than actually did vote. Non-sampling errors can also include an interviewer checking off the wrong box by mistake or a computer operator punching in the wrong response. Whatever the cause, you can't do a survey without some error, and there are mathematical equations called *sampling variance* and *coefficient of variation* to determine the size of these errors and adjust the results accordingly. Thus, we end up with what you will recognize as, say, a "95 percent confidence interval," which simply means if the sampling is repeated indefinitely it will be right 95 times out of 100. That's the theory anyway.

Even before they get down to what questions they're going to ask, however, pollsters sometimes conduct *focus groups* where they pay selected people $25 to $50 to sit in a room with another couple dozen people for two hours, being led through specific issues by a moderator, reacting to the issues and to each other. This technique isn't used all the time, mainly because of the cost, but certainly the political parties use it extensively in the period leading up to election campaigns, to get a feel for the public mood and specifically for reactions to their leader and/or party advertising or their opponent's leader and/or advertising.

Pollsters use two basic types of sampling methods: probability sampling and non-probability sampling. *Probability sampling* simply means that if you are surveying, say, voter intentions, your sample is chosen at random, giving everybody the same statistical opportunity of being polled. It means selecting from random numbers, available in published tables or generated by computer algorithms. *Non-probability sampling*, while less statistically accurate, is usually cheaper and more convenient. It depends on assumptions that there is an even or random distribution of characteristics of the population being surveyed.

Within these two broad categories, of course, there are a host of variations. *Simple random sampling* (srs) means selecting a predetermined sample size so that each unit has an equal chance of being included in the sample. There are two wrinkles in this category, srs *with replacement* and srs *without replacement*. All that means is that "with" replacement allows a unit to be selected on more than one draw, while "without" means once a unit has been selected it cannot be selected again.

Systematic sampling, more frequently used than srs, simply means selecting units from a list at specific intervals, following a random start. srs leaves the selection of a sample entirely to chance; *stratified sampling* does not. It involves the division of a population into relatively homogeneous groups called "strata" and the selection of samples independently within each of those strata. Say, for example, you wanted to find out how many Canadians smoked cigarettes. The sample would represent both men and women and take into account known data about the differences in smoking patterns among various age groups. By using this data to restrict the survey to more relevant groups, systematic sampling offers a better representation.

Another commonly used technique is called *cluster sampling*, where pollsters will survey city blocks or dwellings, rather than the population at large. It isn't as accurate as simple random samples but it reduces costs by clustering a sample into compact groups.

Then there's *multi-stage sampling*. Say you wanted to survey people in their homes to measure opinion on a new bookmobile service being offered by the city council. The first stage might be city blocks or groups of city blocks, followed by a second stage consisting of dwellings prepared for selected city blocks, and, finally, the third stage, where you interview people from a list of people living within the selected dwellings.

Multi-stage sampling differs from *multi-phase sampling*, however, in that the latter uses information collected from a large preliminary sample, plus more data from subsamples of the entire sample. The Canada Health Survey is an example of multi-phase sampling. It first collects information dealing with general health habits, such as smoking, nutrition, and exercise, then moves into physical measures that require such things as blood tests and blood-pressure readings, which obviously couldn't be done by the interviewer at the door.

While pollsters want you to think that all this probability sampling is highly "scientific," the Statistics Canada manual says, "the use of this term, often wrongly, lends credence to the results of a sample survey. While a probability sample does have a well-founded theoretical basis, it can nevertheless yield poor results."

Non-probability sampling techniques also have their own subcategories. *Haphazard sampling*, for example, is what television reporters do in man-on-the-street interviews. Another method, *sampling of volunteers*, involves certain medical or psychological experiments where it would not be practical to select people randomly. *Judgment sampling* is used for selecting units based on a set of assumptions about the population. It's used widely to select focus groups and to administer pre-test questionnaires, for example.

Finally, *quota sampling* is common in opinion and market-research surveys. It means quotas are calculated from existing data, such as age groups and sex, and interviewers are given instructions telling them how many interviews they must have with men, women, various age groups, etc.

This system, commonly used by the political pollsters, is cheaper than a probability sample, easier to administer, and quick. Unfortunately, it doesn't permit sampling errors to be estimated, and interviewers can't always fill their quotas within each group.

Once the sampling design is complete, and the interviewers are back in the office with their field-work, then the pollster must worry about *weighting*, which essentially involves relating the sample back to the population as a whole. If, for example, your survey is short on men, as reflected in the overall population, then the pollster weights the sample so that it comes out proportionally.

In a 1985 interview, Decima's Allan Gregg said Canada is a difficult country to poll accurately because "there are really five regions, not one nation." Only 9 percent of Canadians live in Atlantic Canada, for example, and a national sample of 1,000 would mean only 90 respondents for the entire region, too small to count on accuracy. "I poll 200 in Atlantic Canada and then depress the figures to make a national calculation," said Gregg. "Never weight up. . . . Always weight down."

Telephone polls are often done by a system called *random-digit dialling* where no directories are used, but telephone numbers are simply selected at random from known working exchanges and area codes. It doesn't rely then on telephone books, which are quickly out of date and don't contain unlisted numbers. The disadvantage of the system is that up to 80 percent of the numbers dialled are either non-working numbers or ineligible organizations and businesses. However, this percentage has been substantially reduced in many polls by a system developed in 1978 of clustering phone numbers. Another method, often used by Michael Adams at Environics, is to select numbers from a telephone directory and add a constant number to the last digit. If your constant is 2, then 555–6640 would become 555–6642. The purpose is to give the 10 percent of numbers that are unlisted a chance at selection.

But just getting somebody on the telephone isn't the end of it. After all, not everyone in the household is equally likely to answer the phone. For example, women are three times more likely to answer than are men, and older people are more likely to answer than are younger adults. The interviewer can ask to speak to the person who had the most recent birthday, or the one with the next birthday, or the oldest male, youngest female, whatever technique the pollster decides upon to avoid bias and make the sample as random as possible.

In their regular monthly polls, Gallup still sticks to the *in-home interview* style, although they abandoned that practice for some of their election-campaign polls because of time and cost restraints. That too can create sticky problems in the training and selection of interviewers. What happens, for example, if an East Indian interviewer shows up on a doorstep in small-town Alberta? Polling officials admit it's a problem. The same problem can hamper phone interviews, when certain accents in the wrong areas of the country can prompt respondents to hang up rather than answer the questions.

Most pollsters usually use telephone surveys, although there are exceptions for special, in-depth work. Pollsters don't like to use telephone questionnaires that take longer than thirty minutes to answer, for example, since most people aren't prepared to devote more than a half-hour to it and, if it does go on, they'll sometimes hang up, having wasted both their own time and the pollster's.

One of the most serious problems skewing surveys is the *non-response error* resulting either from people who refused to answer or from those who simply were not located. Non-response is usually greater in telephone surveys than in face-to-face surveys, but it's becoming a major bugaboo for pollsters. Part of the reason, certainly, is the large number of polls being done. People are simply getting tired of them or, in places like Toronto, where the non-response problem is becoming acute, they've just been called too often or feel they're too busy to spend thirty minutes to an hour on the phone with a stranger.

Halifax pollster Don Mills says that, with the twenty-six public polls in the last federal election, plus at least four times that many private polls, "it is making it more difficult to gather information. It is twice as hard in Toronto to get somebody to answer a poll than it is in Atlantic Canada. We are seeing more and more resistance from the public in even participating in polls in the first place."

Pollsters claim they get to speak to at least 60 percent of the respondents chosen by whatever sampling method they use. But interviews with students and others working the phones for them tell a different story.

One nineteen-year-old University of Toronto student who worked part time phoning for Gallup (at $6.50 an hour) said, "My average survey was 10 minutes in length. In a four-hour stretch, you'd probably call a hundred and maybe get five or six to talk if you were lucky.

"Once a woman answered the phone and said, 'How dare you interrupt me! I'm making love with my husband in the bathtub.' I could hear the splash, splash, splash. I marked that down as a 'refuse.'"

Her friend, also nineteen, did the same thing for Decima, and said, "You always did better in rural areas or small towns. If you saw stacks and you had a chance to choose, you'd never choose Toronto.... People in Toronto will tell you to fuck off. I was so shocked. The first person I ever called told me to fuck off and I really thought I was going to cry. But they get polled so much here because most of the big companies are here and there's no long-distance charges."

Polling firms do have people working full time to check outgoing calls, but, oddly, they seem to believe that, just as sampling a small percentage of the population can measure attitudes, checking about 10 percent of their interviewers can catch all the cheaters. It's not the same thing. It's like the police catching speeders. Sure, they ticket the ones they nab, but the ones they don't catch are still speeding. Anyway, missing a representative opinion is no big deal if you get it elsewhere. But missing somebody faking an interview can, and does, skew the results. The interviewers know the odds of getting caught aren't great, so many take the chance. "All the girls admitted they faked call-backs [return calls]," said the part-time Gallup researcher. "I hated calling people back."

Another error factor seldom discussed is the problems caused by interviewers not sticking exactly to verbatim reading of their carefully crafted questionnaires. While pollsters go over the questionnaires in painful detail with the interviewers before beginning any poll, they can't always police things, such as different inflections among questioners or variations in the question's phrasing done by interviewers who simply get bored asking exactly the same question again and again.

How much of a difference could that make? Plenty. Researchers have discovered that even a tiny variation in the wording and context of a question can make a significant difference, what is called a *response bias*. Not only that, the answers to identical questions can vary between polls, depending on how the question is meshed with other questions.

A graphic illustration of these problems was seen in the spring of 1988 when three well-known public-polling companies — Angus Reid, Environics, and Gallup — released polls within a few weeks of one another and showed wildly different results. Gallup had the Liberals at 38 percent of the decided vote, the Tories at 31 percent, and the NDP at 30 percent. Reid had the Liberals dead last, at 30, thirteen points behind both the Tories and the NDP. Environics had still another version, with the Liberals ahead, at 40; the NDP second, with 30; and the Tories struggling, at 29.

Toronto Star columnist Carol Goar, writing on these discrepancies, pointed to four technical factors that could explain them, at least in part: Reid asks people which leader they like before asking which party they prefer; Gallup and Environics had conducted in-home interviews, while Reid's was a phone poll; Reid pushes uncommitted voters harder to determine if they are leaning to one of the parties, giving him an undecided total, usually between five and eight percentage points below the others; Environics takes its survey over a two-week period, while Reid and Gallup have a three- to four-day turnaround time; and, of course, statistical and human error must be taken into account.

Another constant problem with polling, or at least the reporting of polls, is that the numbers are routinely treated as if they're as precise, say, as the score of a baseball game. They're not. If a poll says the Tories had 42 percent of the decided voters, that number is not carved in stone. First, there's the margin of error to consider. If it's plus or minus four points, it can mean the Tories could be sitting anywhere from 38 percent, almost certainly a minority situation, to 46 percent, a landslide. Either way, the pollster could, and would, claim he was within his margin of error.

Worse, what pollsters never tell you is that the moment they drop the undecideds and don't knows from the poll and recalculate the decideds totals, the margin of error goes up another couple of points. The *margin of error*, remember, is a theoretical number based on a perfect poll. There is, of course, no perfect poll. It's simply an abstraction based on the notion that if you had one million red marbles and one million blue marbles in a huge vat and you take out 2,000 marbles at random, you would end up with 1,000 of each colour, plus or minus 2.2 percent. Unfortunately, people aren't as reliable as marbles.

Every time a pollster deviates from his overall sample into a sub-sample of any kind, the margin increases. Thus we have the absurd excesses of media polls breaking vote preferences down into provincial units in, say, Manitoba, where the national sample means that only about 54 Manitobans were asked and the margin of error for that result is 18, plus or minus. If it had the Tories at 40, they could be anywhere from 22 to 58. You don't need a poll to determine that bit of political intelligence.

National polls routinely report their results from Atlantic Canada, but what they don't tell you is that, in a national sample of 1,000, that means about 90 respondents come from Atlantic Canada, giving you a margin of error of about 11 percent.

Political scientist Hugh Whelan, in the 1972 edition of *Politics, Canada*, published a study of political polling in this country and argued that pollsters are guilty of deceit in reporting their error margins. He argues that the percentage should be weighed against the proportion of the vote it applies to instead of against the entire sample. In other words, if Gallup gave the Tories 40 and they got 44 percent in the election, Whelan argues, that's a 10 percent error (4 is one-tenth of 40), not a 4 percent error.

And journalist Walter Stewart, in his 1973 book *Divide and Con*, says, "[Anybody] could predict the outcome of any election just by repeating the totals from the last election, and be right (within the margin of error) most of the time." It's true.

Another problem with the reliability of polls is that even if their measure is right, and we don't really know that for sure, they're often measuring artificial opinions. People often view a poll in much the same way they viewed tests during their school days. They don't want to fail. So if a pollster calls and asks if they're concerned about the deficit, day-care, the environment, whatever, many people don't want to look like uncaring shmucks, even anonymously, and will express a concern about these things even though they may rarely, if ever, think about them.

The other trick pollsters use is to ask questions about something that was just in the news. It not only helps get more responses, but it makes for bigger headlines, and hence more publicity for the pollster.

In February 1989, for example, Winnipeg pollster Angus Reid discovered growing "concern" among Canadians over the deficit. Reid polled 1,002 adults between February 17 and 21, and found only 8 percent said the Tories should "not worry too much about reducing the deficit."

This prompted Reid to say, "For the first time in a long time, there is growing public sentiment that the deficit is getting too high and should be cut." Is there really that kind of sentiment? Do you know anybody wringing their hands over the deficit? Do you hear people discussing it over coffee, or on their way to work in the morning? Not likely.

But the important point here is that this measure of public "concern" over the deficit came in the wake of an avalanche of publicity about it. On January 30, for example, Brian Mulroney shuffled his cabinet, restructuring his cabinet-committee system to include a spending-control committee, telling reporters, "While we have been successful for the past four years in lowering the deficit . . . interest rates have been rising and we are expecting some difficulties on the fiscal side." That was just the opening shot. Over the next few weeks, Finance minister Michael Wilson made several speeches, warning of deficit-cutting measures, and Environment minister Lucien Bouchard inadvertently told a group of invited journalists of the government's plan to introduce "radical" spending cuts to lower the national debt.

The deficit-cutting campaign was quickly joined by a host of high-profile business groups, such as the Canadian Manufacturers' Association and the Canadian Chamber of Commerce. For the period leading up to the Reid poll, then, it was impossible to escape some news about deficits in the media. And so, while it's unlikely most Canadians would give the deficit much thought, or even know anything about it, Reid's poll came in the midst of a media blitz on the subject, undoubtedly affecting the overall level of "concern."

Former New Brunswick premier Richard Hatfield, no fan of the polls, said one of his major concerns is that there's an assumption when people are asked a question by a pollster that they know something about the topic. "It assumes a certain knowledge which most people don't have.

"Yet politicians have come to depend on them for everything. . . . I really think it's weakening political leadership. The whole purpose of poll reform is to demystify them and make them out to be what they are, the collective recounting of uninformed people at 8:30 on a Wednesday night."

That may be a bit harsh, but it does help to put the "science" of polling in perspective. It's certainly a useful tool, and often a reliable indicator of trends, but it's not in the category of the tablets from Mount Sinai.

A January 1989 Reid–Southam poll, for example, found that the approval rate for the Meech Lake Accord had dropped nationally from 51 to 32 percent since May 1987. The disapproval rate had gone up from 25 to 30 percent, and the "unsure" from 24 to 38 percent. Fine, except that a few days earlier Gallup had polled on Canadian perceptions of Meech Lake and discovered that only 6 percent of Canadians said they were "quite familiar" with the accord. If that's true, and people really don't know what the accord is about, then what's the point of measuring whether people approve or disapprove of it, let alone publishing those perceptions as the main, front-page story in newspapers across the country?

Pollsters often build a bias right into their questionnaire by the common device of listing options. For example, they'll ask a person to rate the importance of a series of issues facing the country, listing these issues for the respondents, many of which the person on the other end of the phone line probably never thought about, but feels obligated to respond to, to avoid sounding stupid or unconcerned about society.

University of Toronto political-science professor Nelson Wiseman says, "I would like to see more information, not about people's opinions, but about their knowledge." He cited a survey of 3,100 community-college students in Manitoba in 1984. Only 54 percent of them knew who was in power in their province. "So, asking people what they think about Meech Lake . . . what do they know about Meech Lake?"

Wiseman raises another point. Pollsters, in claiming great accuracy, point to their record of predicting elections. Assuming their record is as good as they say — which it really isn't — the fact remains that a few days before an election is probably the least typical time in society. After all, in a few days, 75 percent of Canadians are actually going to go out and vote, so they not only know about the election, but have given it some thought. "I think that the polls are very accurate in determining voter preference a week before [the election], but I have great doubts about using them for all kinds of other questions," says Wiseman.

Then there are a plethora of polls on questions that are downright silly. My personal favourite is the annual Gallup exercise of asking Canadians how much the various levels of government waste out of every tax dollar. On February 13, 1989, on its front page, the *Toronto Star* reported: "Canadians believe the federal government wastes on average 38 cents out of every tax dollar it takes in, according to a Gallup poll released today.

"Provincial and local governments fare slightly better, with respondents believing provinces waste an average of 33 cents of every tax dollar and municipalities waste 25 cents."

It went on to explain that this same poll in 1981 also pegged federal waste at 38 cents, while, in 1988, Canadians felt Ottawa wasted 37 cents of every dollar.

How would they know? How would anybody know? Finance minister Michael Wilson couldn't respond to that question in a meaningful way, and he's one of the few Canadians who at least knows how much the government spends, if not how much of that spending is wasted. Just what does "waste" mean? Well, that depends. Some people might think the entire defence budget is a waste, while others probably point to social spending as wasting tax dollars, and so on.

Why do pollsters do this sort of thing? Simple. Gallup vice-president Lorne Bozinoff says, bluntly, "A party pollster is judged to be a success if his party wins. I judge myself a success depending upon how close I am to the front page."

One quintessentially Canadian polling exercise that doesn't draw many headlines but claims a scientific purity and wields enormous influence in the world of academia is the regular post-election study to discover how Canadians voted, and why, commissioned by the Social Sciences and Humanities Research Council of Canada, called the National Election Study. The Council gave $470,000 to a four-member team of political scientists, led by Richard Johnston at the University of British Columbia, and including as participants André Blais of the University of Montreal, Jean Crete of Laval University, and Henry Brady of the University of Chicago.

The study is based on a forty-minute pre-election interview with 3,500 randomly selected voters across the country, followed by a post-election twenty-minute interview. Each respondent is asked to complete a written questionnaire. In the 1988 campaign, for the first time, the study included a daily mini-sample of seventy-eight interviews during the campaign by York University's Institute for Social Research.

The project began after the 1965 federal election, when Queen's University professor John Meisel conducted the research and published his findings. University of Toronto political-science professor Nelson Wiseman wrote a devastating critique of the program, using the 1974 election study as his focal point, in the *Journal of Canadian Studies*: "It is remarkable that although dozens of academic papers and books now rely on the survey data generated by these studies there has been little critical examination of the quality of the output and the assumptions underlying them."

Just under 40 percent of the total amount awarded by the Canada Council in 1974 for political-science research went to this single project. Wiseman concludes it wasn't worth it.

The 1974 study was based on a national sample of 2,562 voters in the three months following the July election. Wiseman said the principal investigators accepted the responses "at face value ... even though some of the most crucial statistics are contradicted by readily available alternative data — the official election results — or the actual behaviour, rather than the self-reported behaviour, of the respondents." For example, election returns showed 43 percent voted Liberal, yet the study sets the Liberal vote at 53.4 percent. In Newfoundland, the survey reported 80 percent voted in the election. Only 57 percent actually did. The survey, in fact, overreported voter turnout in every province, and Wiseman says similar distortions "between report and reality" exist in every other national election study. In 1972, for example, when the Liberals won by 109 seats to 107, and 39 percent of the vote to 35 percent for the Tories, the academic post-campaign study dutifully reported that 54.5 percent had voted Liberal and only 28.3 had voted Tory. The problem, says Wiseman, is that these faulty figures are then used to explain voting patterns. The political scientists attributed the 1974 Liberal victory to the impact of new voters and transient voters. According to their studies, the Liberal vote dropped a full percentage point betwen 1972 and 1974, when it actually rose by four points, from 39 to 43.

"The fact remains," wrote Wiseman, "that many voters misrepresented the partisan direction of their voting behaviour ... if there is so much confusion, distortion, invention, misrepresentation, and amnesia on the simple questions of turnout and reported vote, we must expect similar if not greater human failings in reporting more elusive matters such as people's party identification, interest in politics, etc."

This failing is, in fact, a common one conveniently overlooked in assessing polls. People don't always tell the truth. A 1973 U.S. experiment conducted by the National Opinion Research Center found that, in identical questions put thirty minutes apart, the partisan identification of 10 percent of the respondents changed. "A lot of people see surveys as a test," says Wiseman. "They don't want to flunk. They don't want to sound stupid. And they also want to sound like they're responsible citizens."

The 1974 study claimed "explicit attention has been given to providing regional subsamples of adequate size for meaningful analysis." In fact, wrote Wiseman, because the sample was a multi-staged, stratified, clustered one, "this meant sampling in only four federal constituencies in each of Manitoba, Saskatchewan, Newfoundland and New Brunswick. In Manitoba, for example, only 113 respondents were interviewed in 19 polling divisions, all in the southern part of the province." Wiseman said no one was interviewed in the northern portions of Quebec, Ontario, Manitoba, Saskatchewan, Alberta, British Columbia, or in the Yukon or Northwest Territories. But the study "offers a detailed analysis of how Canadians perceive the North without pointing out that no Northerners were surveyed."

The regional voting patterns in the study were even more skewed than the national numbers. In Quebec, despite a decent sample of 702 respondents, 70 percent of them told the survey they voted Liberal in 1974, but only 54 percent did. Even in Alberta, where the Liberals got 25 percent of the vote and won no seats, a plurality of survey respondents claimed to have voted for them.

The post-1979 election study, written during the Clark Conservative interregnum, noted the then-current comments from pundits on the "death of the Liberal party" and "a generation of Conservative governments." The principal investigators wrote, based on their extensive survey data, gathered at vast public expense, "We cannot state categorically that they [the pundits] are wrong." A few months later, the Liberals won a majority government.

Political polling, while amounting to several million dollars a year, is but a tiny fraction of approximately $350 million spent annually on polling and market research in Canada, most of that collecting data for private corporations. Indeed, Canadian Facts of Toronto is far and away Canada's biggest pollster, but because they stay away from the high-profile media game — they did the cbc's field-work, but the poll was not presented as a Canadian Facts poll — few people outside the market-research industry know who they are.

An editorial cartoon in the March 24, 1979, *Financial Post* depicted five corporate executives sitting around their boardroom table. The president, at the head of the table, was saying, "The PR boys have done a swell job for us. The awareness study shows 33% don't know what we do, 41% don't care, and the remainder are antagonistic toward us."

Just as political polling began to take off in the mid-1970s, so too did corporate polling, using the same techniques to sell a corporate image or product as politicians use to sell themselves. That 1979 *Financial Post* article, for example, contained descriptions of surveys done for a number of organizations ranging from the Canadian Pulp and Paper Association to the Mining Association of British Columbia, Canadian Cellulose Ltd., and the *Winnipeg Tribune*, which preceded a major revamping by a Martin Goldfarb poll. It didn't help, however, since the *Tribune* ultimately went out of business.

By 1986, the industry was billing between $200 million and $250 million a year. (Decima's Allan Gregg said polling for the Tory party then represented just 15 percent of the company's total billings.) A new breed of corporate managers and the advent of the information age fuelled the demand for both quantitative and qualitative research, and in 1984 alone, according to figures compiled by the Canadian Association of Marketing Research Organizations (CAMRO), the research business grew by 18 percent.

A typical survey costs at least $20,000, but many run up to $500,000, depending upon the size and complexity of the project. Environics, for example, was charging $13,800 a year for subscriptions to its syndicated national omnibus poll, and customers could add their own individual questions for a fee of from $650 to $1,200 for each question, the same technique Gallup uses to attract people who don't necessarily need a complete survey, but want the answers to one or two questions.

In February 1989, the *Globe*'s "Report on Business" section ran several lengthy articles describing how the Canadian hotel and travel industry uses extensive market-survey work to promote both "product differentiation" and "market segmentation," most of it aimed at the business traveller, who represents 38 percent of the market. The research has led not only to changes overall, but to marketing hotel rooms specifically to appeal to women business travellers, who take 22 percent of overnight business trips in Canada. Having first determined what these women would like to see in their hotel rooms, many hotels are now offering such extra touches as restricted elevator access with a special key, makeup mirrors with better room lighting, hair-driers, bathrobes, and even Q-Tips and soap for sensitive skin, all for the same price as a regular business-class room. Hilton Canada alone had spent about $1 million in the eighteen months prior to the *Globe* article on focus groups and personal and telephone interviews, trying to determine how best to adapt to changing customer needs and tailor not only the services offered, but the advertising and marketing, to their guests.

In addition to the sheer volume increase in market research, there has also been a marked increase in the use of technology to measure public opinion. The May 1988 World Association for Public Opinion Research (wapor) convention in Toronto, for example, featured lectures on the impact of *computer-assisted telephone interviewing* (cati); *computer-aided personal interviewing*, which means using portable, lap-sized computers rather than pen and paper to record in-home interview responses; *random-digit automated dialling* and automated recordings, which involves automated dialling of random numbers, presentation of a prerecorded set of questions, and the respondents reply by dialling or pushing telephone numbers corresponding to particular responses; and a *portable polling and telephone promotion* system, which uses a "synthesized voice" that sounds so human people try to have conversations with it. (That system was used effectively in 1986 when the Republicans employed ten of these gadgets and a Ronald Reagan voice to call 780,000 people and get their vote out for the Florida governor's race.)

In addition, there is the whole field of *computerized audience-opinion systems*, dominated by the California-based Quick Tally system and the Toronto-based Program Evaluation Analysis Computer (peac). Both feature hand-held electronic handsets much like your tv remote-control device, with respondents continually pressing buttons to record their second-by-second reaction to whatever it is they're watching.

At the wapor convention, Quick Tally demonstrated its usefulness to three hundred pollsters. A complete system can be carried in two medium-sized cases, and it can collect data from five to five hundred individual handsets. The systems also have instant analysis of collected data, including frequencies, percentages, and cross-tabs with broadcast-quality graphics easily displayed on any television set or monitor.

peac Media Research Inc., which has a Chicago subsidiary called Viewfacts Inc., first introduced its system commercially in 1979. TVOntario had developed a similar product in pursuit of a method to measure the reaction of children to programming for the Children's Television Workshop ("Sesame Street"). The network devised a remote, wireless hand-held unit with a series of happy-faced buttons indicating a range of positive and negative measures of emotional response to programs.

In the 1984 U.S. presidential campaign, the Republicans used the peac system to good advantage in the televised debate. In fact, Walter

Mondale's advisers aired a commercial on national networks in the closing weeks of that campaign, which featured the single most-unpopular minute of the hour-long debate. The Democrats didn't know that at the time, of course, but the Republicans did. After that debate, as Reagan flew home to California, he was accompanied by his pollster Richard Wirthlin and by James King, executive vice-president of PEAC. They showed Reagan a video replay of the debate, featuring a moving graph showing continuous viewer response to each moment of the debate. It happened that Mondale's advisers picked up on a segment where he was attacking Reagan's Central America policy failures, believing it made their man look both knowledgeable about foreign affairs and decisive, two of his perceived weaknesses. But the preselected focus group who had measured the debate by continually pressing five buttons (scaled from very positive to very negative) on their handsets had chosen that particular segment as the most negative in the debate for Mondale.

CBC has a PEAC system it uses to evaluate its programs, and King tried to convince them to use it in the 1988 campaign to monitor the leadership debates, but they wouldn't.

King says the system has advantages over the traditional focus group because it avoids bias caused by a particularly loud and aggressive member of the group, who might influence the others, or shortcomings in group directors. "This system is quick and it's anonymous. And we can custom-recruit the people we want. Typically, we run four or five sessions of twenty to twenty-five people. If we're looking, say, for undecided voters, we'd find them. If it's something we're doing for an airline, we'd get a mix of frequent and infrequent flyers, that sort of thing."

King says they have not used the system in Canada for a political party. "We've certainly shown it to politicians and they are fascinated with it ... but there's been resistance from the traditional party pollsters." It is being used in the United States and Europe, and King says it's probably a case of some day a Canadian political organization will "discover" the technology abroad and bring it back to Canada, even though it was developed here initially.

One Canadian who makes extensive use of the system, however, is Concordia University professor of education John Baggaley. In addition to using it commercially, Baggaley has monitored political debates federally and provincially for ten years. "It's unfortunate and unnecessary the traditional pollsters regard it as threatening, which they obviously do," he says. "It's a powerful way that they would have to sharpen their own senses or their own methods. This system doesn't replace traditional methods, it complements them, and gives you a deeper ability to go and sift the sand, to search for reasons why people respond in a certain way."

Baggaley says people can't always articulate precise responses to something after they've watched it, particularly a long political debate, and the second-by-second responses, all recorded on a graph, which can be shown on the TV screen, tell researchers precisely how the focus group was responding at any one time. The trick is to look for major ups and downs in the graph, when the whole group responds negatively or positively to a particular statement or action.

He says research through the years has shown that Brian Mulroney gets negative ratings, for example, when he takes his glasses off while he's speaking. "It's a bit of visual rhetoric and it inevitably gets a negative rating. People are beguiled by the flow of images, the way they talk, the way they move, and they may not have taken in the substance of what they said. This system is perfect for measuring those moods."

For the 1988 campaign English-language debate, Baggaley had a group of twenty people, preselected so they would be evenly divided among supporters for the three parties and undecided voters, watching the debate in their own homes, continually pressing their handsets to register their second-by-second reactions. Baggaley said Turner instantly did well responding to the opening question on patronage. None of them did well during the second hour, on women's issues — "they were just fumbling around trying to avoid the issues" — but Turner scored heavily in the now-famous exchange with Mulroney over free trade.

However, Baggaley's study, unlike the public-opinion polls, showed that Broadbent, not Mulroney, was second. "I would swear by that," he says. "On the data basis it was plain that Mulroney had not won any points. He had even lost a few voters. He lost two of the three who had voted Tory last time. Both Turner and Broadbent picked up people. . . . Broadbent did poorly when he was talking about NATO, but he did well, even against Turner, when talking about social issues. . . . If Broadbent's people could have had this data, I'm sure they would have responded better to his performance than they did.

"Politicians are getting short-changed by their advisers and by their pollsters who refuse to look at this new technology. Why do they refuse? Because they have a stranglehold on the design of the campaign, especially those pollsters who play that role," says Baggaley.

Which brings us, finally, back to Mulroney. In the political arena, nobody spends more money on polling than he does. But apparently, if we can take him at his word, he thinks he's not getting value for his money. In the spring of 1988, when both he and his party were faring poorly in all the polls, including his own private ones, Mulroney said, "Polls are a dime a dozen. Everyone's got one coming out of his ears and quite frankly I don't pay much attention to them."

Just before he said that, of course, he removed his glasses.

7

Allan Gregg: The Icon

Technology talks. So does money. And Tory pollster Allan Gregg has both in abundance.

Much like the manager of the victorious World Series team who automatically enjoys a reputation for baseball genius, regardless of what sort of players he has to put on the field, Gregg, the oracle, is rarely mentioned without a string of laudatory adjectives attached. He is called a genius, brilliant, and a whiz kid (although, at thirty-seven, he's getting past the "kid" stage, and he's remarkably sensitive about his age). He is, by his own account, ahead of his time too, although he did confess in one interview that he was twenty-five years ahead of everybody else when he began, and is now only ten years ahead. Still, not bad for a guy who has only been a pollster for a decade.

When the Liberals were winning elections, Martin Goldfarb was all those things. In the 1960s and early 1970s, when Bob Teeter was helping Conservatives to win elections in Ontario, Nova Scotia, and Alberta, he was a genius too. Beyond compare.

Now it's Gregg's turn. And he has some personal experience with the genius-one-day-bum-the-next syndrome. He's enjoying the genius phase now, but for a time in 1980 and for several months during 1983 and 1984, he was a bum. "If you believe your good press clippings you should also believe your bad press clippings," he told Robert Fulford in a 1985 *Saturday Night* magazine piece. "If you want to believe it when they say you're a genius, you'd better believe it when they say you're a bum."

Gregg was a bum in Brian Mulroney's eyes after the Tory leadership convention in 1983. Gregg, a Clark loyalist, was part of a CBC television panel during that convention. When news of Mulroney's fourth-ballot victory hit the booth, he turned to Barbara Frum and said, "That's it for me. I'm finished." And until the spring of 1984, he was finished, at least as far as Mulroney and the federal Conservative party were concerned. They turned to Gallup instead.

A few weeks after winning the Tory leadership in June 1983, Mulroney had a meeting with a group of Big Blue Machine operatives in Toronto. They, of course, were trying to convince Mulroney to keep Gregg on as pollster. He'd worked for them in Ontario under Bill Davis, and polled for several other Tory premiers, so he was not without his political boosters. But Mulroney would have none of it. Not then. When Gregg's friends praised the pollster, Mulroney said, "Yeah, you really don't know what he said about me." With that, he put a cassette into a VCR and played the tape that an aide had put together for him, a collection of all the critical comments made on TV about Mulroney during the convention. One of the startled witnesses at the meeting later described the tactic as "Nixonian." But whatever it was, Gregg would have to wait while his pals kept pecking away at Mulroney's resolve. It didn't help, of course, when Gregg co-authored the book *Contenders*, an account of the 1983 convention that paints an unflattering portrait of Mulroney.

Gregg enjoys being what journalist John Sawatsky called the "punk pollster." He boasts of hiring street kids with Mohawk haircuts and pierced ears. But his life-style doesn't exactly fit the image. He has a Jaguar in the garage, for example, and a place in Nassau.

The media always loved him. After all, he has long hair and an earring, he loves rock-and-roll music, and he gives good quotes. One of his closest personal friends, a regular poker and golf partner, is CBC star Peter Mansbridge. Gregg is a colourful character in a world dominated by pin-striped automatons, an apparent free spirit, seemingly independent, not only in the way he dresses, but in the way he plays the game.

Gregg didn't set out to be a pollster. Growing up in Edmonton, he dreamed of becoming either a teacher or, preferably, a rock star. Gregg's father sold men's clothing at Eaton's and his mother was active in the political campaigns of local Tory Douglas Roche. Gregg graduated from high school at age sixteen and worked his way through the University of Alberta, promoting rock concerts (he once brought in Led Zeppelin), and running local playgrounds. An honours student, he wrote his M.A. thesis on the voting record of Parliament during Lester Pearson's minority government in the 1960s. In 1974, he went to Carleton University to pursue a Ph.D. in political science, a pursuit he later abandoned. A year later he landed a job as research assistant with the Tories. By then, he had married his teenage sweetheart and had a son, Christian. Two years later, after Joe Clark had won the leadership, Gregg had become a key strategist and the party's in-house pollster.

In the summer of 1978, Gregg went on a ten-day exchange program sponsored by the U.S. State Department, where he met several prominent American pollsters. Among them was Richard Wirthlin, with whom Gregg would soon go into the polling business. Gregg had been writing the questionnaires for the Tory polls, printing them at party headquarters, then sending them along with a sample design to a private polling company, Canadian Facts of Toronto, for the telephoning. Party volunteers would then code the results and Gregg would take them to Ottawa Keypunch for processing, then, using his graduate-student account at Carleton, he would take them to the university computer. The whole process took nearly a month, hardly useful for day-to-day politics, particularly election campaigns. Having met the American pollsters, and been entranced by their sophisticated tracking methodology, Gregg convinced the Tories they should hire a professional polling company. He interviewed many, but couldn't find any in Canada to his liking, so they went back to the United States and hired Teeter again.

In his book *The Insiders*, John Sawatsky explains how that worked: "Teeter's people conducted their interviews from a phone bank in Toronto off a questionnaire drafted by Gregg, and then fed the responses into a computer at Wayne State University outside Detroit. The data rolled off a terminal in Gregg's office in Ottawa where he interpreted the results. While Teeter gathered the data and tabulated them, Gregg manipulated the figures and worked out what they meant."

In the meantime, the Ontario Tories had become disenchanted with Teeter — who had written their man Bill Davis off in 1976 as a political liability — and Tom Scott of Sherwood Communications entered a 50–50 joint venture with Wirthlin, who had the technology, to run a new Canadian company called Decima Research Ltd., with Gregg owning 20 percent of the company.

Two weeks after Clark won the May 1979 election and was sworn into office, Gregg moved to Toronto and Decima began its run as the official Tory polling company in July 1979. Unfortunately for Gregg, Clark's government fell less than a year later, time enough for only four polling contracts to be sent his way (two from the government, two from the party). One of these contracts called for a critique of Clark's campaign for the party's strategists. Gregg's brutal conclusion was that "Clark's image problems at the end of the campaign, by and large, were the same as at the beginning. He suffered primarily from being perceived as unqualified to assume the senior office of government, as uninformed and lacking in strength. In fact, it may not be an exaggeration to suggest that a national leader has rarely, if ever, assumed office with lower expectations concerning his ability to govern."

Even with Clark out, however, Decima quickly grew by taking on a combination of business contracts and partisan provincial contracts — most provincial governments were Tory. Gregg's reputation as a guru grew with the business. His big catch in those early years was the Canadian Petroleum Association, for which Decima conducted a single poll in the summer of 1980, and which evolved into a $350,000-a-year contract.

Earlier that year, Gregg convinced David MacNaughton of the giant polling and consulting firm Public Affairs International (PAI) to join him 50–50 in starting up the *Decima Quarterly*, a detailed compilation of polling data to be sold to business clients for $20,000 a year. They signed up only two corporate clients (Labatt's and Allstate) and three government departments (at half-price) and lost $170,000 the first year. But eventually, several government departments subscribed, corporate clients were lining up, and the quarterly became the milch-cow it remains today, with well over fifty regular clients. Now the price is $24,000, which includes a presentation, either from Gregg or from another company official.

During the winter of 1980–1, things were not going that well for Decima. Wirthlin, who had been Ronald Reagan's California pollster, suddenly became the pollster for the U.S. president and had no time for Decima. Scott was also getting edgy about losing so much money in the venture, so Gregg approached Rod Bryden of Kinburn

Capital (a venture-capital firm that had financed a 1979 PAI takeover) and Decima subsequently became a division of PAI, which itself was a wholly owned subsidiary of Kinburn Capital.

The arrangement did not please Gregg's Tory clients. After all, PAI was controlled by Liberals, and suddenly the Tories were concerned about the security of their data. Things grew so tense that the party executive privately organized a special treasury committee to examine the issue, and an unsigned memo was circulated through party ranks, detailing the parent firm's Liberal background. Gregg did not handle the situation with aplomb. He basically dismissed the critics as right-wing, anti-Clark Tories who were out to embarrass Clark rather than to protect party data. There was something to that, of course, but even Clark became alarmed, particularly after the executive committee of the national party approved a motion calling on the Tories to stop doing business with Decima.

Gregg weathered that storm, only to find himself in more serious trouble when Kinburn's stock collapsed. So Gregg, David MacNaughton, and Michael Robinson scraped together $1.25 million to buy Bryden's interest in the company. MacNaughton borrowed $450,000 for 60 percent of the common shares; Gregg and Robinson each borrowed $150,000 for 20 percent of the shares; PAI and Decima employees contributed $350,000 in non-voting shares, and the final $150,000 was raised through company debt. The three men then formed a holding company, Public Affairs Resources Group (PARG), in the fall of 1983, with PAI and Decima as its two subsidiaries.

By August 31, 1988, the end of its fiscal year, PARG's revenues were $25 million, up 22 percent from $20.5 million in fiscal 1987 and up 58 percent from $15.8 million in 1986. While the political side of the business represents only about 20 percent of revenues, the publicity that results from the political work probably brings in much of the corporate business.

In his 1985 interview with Fulford, Gregg said Decima had bought a public-affairs research company in Washington and opened a London office. The firm has also conducted polls in Israel (where its 1987 election predictions were way off) and Australia. "I'd like to see Decima Research as an international company within three years," he told Fulford, "operating initially in the English-speaking world." He almost made it. In February 1989, Investment Canada announced that it had approved the sale of PARG to the WPP Group PLC, a London-based marketing company. News of the complicated deal was leaked in November 1988, when it was learned that PAI and Decima would be sold for about $12 million to Hill & Knowlton Inc., an American public-relations company owned by giant advertising agency JWT Group Inc. which itself was taken over by WPP in a $566-million deal in July 1987. All of which means that Decima is no longer wholly Canadian, but has become a small corporate cog in a giant international wheel.

Gregg, of course, has always boasted of being his own man, a claim that is at least partly responsible for his unconventional dress habits, although lately he's been seen more often in a business suit than in his traditional cords and suspenders.

In a January 1988 interview with Warren Caragata of Canadian Press at Decima's spacious Yonge Street headquarters, Gregg said, "There's nothing I've ever done that I feel compromised on, or for that matter something I think my mother would think is bad."

He must have forgotten his embarrassing command performance late in the 1980 election campaign when a Gallup poll showed Clark's Tories twenty-one points behind Trudeau and the Liberals. The Tories issued a press release making their private poll public, just four days before the election, showing the party twelve points back, not twenty-one, as Gallup showed. Gregg was hosting dinner in his home that night with Peter Mansbridge, Nancy Jamieson, and Lowell Murray, then Clark's senior aide, Bill Neville, telephoned from the campaign plane to say the media wanted to see Gregg at the Hotel Toronto to explain his figures. "I was reluctant but I went," Gregg said in a 1982 interview with Rosemary Speirs in the *Globe*. "I looked terrible — dressed in old clothes — and I'd cracked a beer, figuring it was just a backgrounder. Suddenly the cameras and the microphones were in front of me and reporters were asking 'Will you win?'

"I'd been thrown to the dogs. I was there to tell them not to give up on us. I had to tread very carefully between gilding the lily and telling a lie," he said. In truth, Gregg came out looking more like a press agent attempting to fudge his own data. "The costume of a detached social scientist fell away and he appeared no more than a party hack," wrote Fulford. In fact, his numbers were much closer to the mark than Gallup's were, come election night, but Clark still lost and the whole episode didn't do Gregg's reputation any favours.

Still, Gregg has managed to maintain an impressive stable of political clients, among them Nova Scotia's John Buchanan, the country's longest-serving premier. Buchanan is without peer in his slavish adherence to Gregg's survey numbers. In August 1981, Buchanan was discovered by local journalists holding a secret confab with Gregg and his cabinet colleagues. They were studying a poll he claimed was on federal-provincial relations. In fact, the Decima poll numbers — left behind by a minister and found by journalists — showed Buchanan's Tories with 45 percent of decided voters, compared to 35 for the Liberals and 20 for the NDP. Buchanan flatly denied Gregg's presence in Halifax had anything to do with election planning. A week later he called an election.

It is because of Buchanan's lengthy love affair with the flamboyant Toronto pollster that many of the four hundred guests at a closed-door blue-chip prayer breakfast in April 1989 — including Mulroney, Turner, and Broadbent — were taken aback when Buchanan, the guest speaker, said he gets his political advice "at church every Sunday on the front steps," rather than relying on the advice some politicians get "from those high-priced pollsters from Toronto." Imagine saying that at a prayer breakfast.

Other pollsters, without exception, acknowledge Gregg's tremendous methodological skills, although most point out they could get the same amount of data if they had as much money to work with as he does.

In the Speirs interview, Gregg boasted, "We can target not just the possible swing ridings, but the swing polls within those ridings, and key voters within those polls. We can identify on a block-by-block basis their historical voting behaviour, their demographic profile, their inferred preference — and reach them, not by the old mass-media techniques, but by telephone and direct mail." Gregg said he identified twenty-five volatile ridings in the 1981 Ontario election, and of those, six were Tory when the campaign started and nineteen were Tory when it ended.

But that was 1981. In 1985, Gregg told newly elected premier Frank Miller he had the support of 56 percent of the electorate, a finding that encouraged Miller to call a quick election not long after succeeding Bill Davis. Miller finished second to Liberal David Peterson in the popular vote, although he did win the most seats. Before the end of the summer, a Liberal–NDP compact made Peterson premier and Miller was gone. Gregg had also advised Miller that the issue of funding for Roman Catholic high schools wouldn't hurt him in the election. It did. In fact, Gregg played a key role in the surprising decision by Davis, shortly before he retired, to extend funding all the way through the Catholic high schools. (Until then, funding went only to Grade 10 for the Catholic schools.)

The issue had been a tough one since Confederation. In his first campaign in 1971, Davis won a huge majority by opposing separate-school funding, while the Liberals favoured it. Eventually, Davis made a secret pact with G. Emmett Cardinal Carter to extend funding before he left politics. Part of his rationale was based on arguments advanced vigorously by Gregg that, with Ontario becoming less WASP-ish, the Tories, who had ruled the province since 1943, had to extend their traditional core vote. Gregg argued that the bulk of immigration during the 1960s and 1970s was Roman Catholic, much of it from cultures where Conservative was a four-letter word. Davis took the advice and so sealed the fate of the long-running Tory regime in Canada's largest province.

Gregg may never have done anything his mother "would think is bad," but it's unlikely either he or his mother would be proud of the use made of his block-by-block data in the 1986 Manitoba election. Tory organizers used Gregg's numbers in their campaign against NDP House leader Andrue Anstett in the sprawling riding of Springfield, which runs from the eastern boundary of Winnipeg all the way to the Ontario border. Anstett had been the man given the unenviable task of shepherding the NDP government's wildly unpopular language bill, designed to entrench French-language services in that province, through the legislature. Mulroney had received considerable praise for going out to Manitoba in 1983 to fight for the French-language services, but now the provincial opposition Tories staged a bitter, protracted fight against the legislation. Because he had toured the province, holding hearings and speaking on behalf of the divisive language bill, Anstett became a particular electoral target for the Tories, and Gregg's detailed polling revealed significant pockets of anti-French hostility in Anstett's own riding. "They [the Tories] ran ads in the local papers suggesting that I was trying to make the province bilingual, and require people to speak French," said Anstett later. 'None of this was being said elsewhere in the province.

"They knew exactly where to target," he said. "They'd done some very sophisticated polling in that area. I didn't know it until after the election.... Where I did worse was where the Tories used this specific targeting stuff ... and it was different literature designed to appeal specifically to people who were most inclined to get riled up about the French language issue." Anstett said they used the same technique against him on the abortion issue. "They did that very subtly as well. They were hitting Catholic and Mennonite households with letters. . . . They didn't do it on a massive basis, just several thousand Catholic and Mennonite households."

Anstett, himself a former pollster, said, "They need demographic profiles to do that . . . some pretty sophisticated polling to be able to identify things that specifically.

"Let's accept the fact that polling is a tool that is known and proven in terms of substantial utility to political campaigns. It's not going to go away," he said. "The kinds of things that were done in Springfield will probably continue to be done. I don't think it's right. . . . Polling should be used to enable parties to package, much as we do soap on Madison Avenue. . . . that's the game we're in unfortunately . . . to package what they stand for, their policies, their philosophy, in a way that allows the voter to best understand it. . . .

"The way it tends to be used, unfortunately, by all parties, is to say, 'What is it they want?' Now we'll give it to them.

"It's very different from what was done in Springfield, however, which was specific targeting directly intending to influence on an emotional basis. If you use polling for that purpose, then I think you're undermining some very fundamental things about democracy and about rational voting," he said.

Anstett lost by fifty-five votes. His Tory opponent, Gilles Roch, denied using different literature targeted on the French issue to different parts of the riding, yet there were newspaper articles at the time quoting some of the anti-bilingualism stuff from his pamphlets.

While everyone who works with Gregg at Decima respects his ability with numbers, there's been no shortage of resentment over the years about his high media profile. "There are a lot of professionals at Decima," says one former employee, "which Gregg, by the way, would be the first to acknowledge. But apart from some references to Ian [McKinnon, Decima president] how often do you hear about anybody else? For the most part, when people think of Decima, they think of Gregg, and that is a double-edged sword. His profile brings in business, but they want Gregg personally because he's Decima to them. Good as Allan is, he can't serve all the clients."

Indeed, Brian Mulroney also thought Gregg was getting too much publicity. One of the terms in his resurrection as Tory pollster in 1984 was that he wouldn't be seen so much, talking on behalf of the party.

"The company has tried to depersonalize Decima as well, although with limited success," said the former senior employee. "You still see Allan's face all over the place."

Gregg still sometimes embarrasses Mulroney. In his annual mood-of-the-nation poll for *Maclean's* magazine in 1986 he found 59 percent of 1,500 respondents said Canada needed a new prime minister. However, they were indifferent to all three federal party leaders. In an October 16, 1986, speech to a blue-chip Conference Board of Canada business conference, Gregg said Canadians were suffering a bad case of "economic illiteracy," which made it difficult for the government fundamentally to repair the economy. Gregg said before the 1984 election, Canadians wanted an "initiator" to solve their problems. Afterwards they wanted a "facilitator" to help the private sector solve their problems. "Now they want a policeman to set the rules and punish those who break them." Gregg said government and business had to "make the benefits of free trade more tangible and real to the average Canadian.... Canadians aren't very smart. But they're eminently reasonable," he said.

In early 1987, Gregg was publicly predicting that both Brian Mulroney and Gary Hart could make a political come-back. On CTV's "Question Period," with the Tories trailing the Liberals by fifteen points in the latest Gallup, Gregg said, correctly, the Tories needed a string of identifiable successes. "It's a performance problem."

The Decima verification centre looks like a hospital nursing station, on a raised platform, with supervisors at the centre who can tap into any line unnoticed at any time. When conducting telephone surveys the Decima interviewers identify themselves as representatives of Summerhill Research. About 25 percent of the callers ask the respondents if they would mind a supervisor calling them back to verify the interview, but not all those respondents are called.

One university student who worked there said, "It's the kind of job you do for a couple of months and then leave. They had a black book and if you called in sick and you didn't have a doctor's note, they'd put you in the black book. If you had three marks, they'd kick you out."

If you work four hours, you can take an unpaid fifteen-minute break. If you work five hours, you're paid for a fifteen-minute break. Work eight hours, and you get a half-hour break. You can work a minimum of two four-hour shifts a week, but one had to be a Friday or Sunday. "They had trouble getting people to work those days. . . . About 50 percent of the people I called [on Sunday mornings] would get very angry."

One former Decima official says, "If you want to see where pop culture is at today . . . go to Decima." Chances are the street kids hired to make the calls didn't drop by the office on the way home from church. "The punkers wouldn't be getting stoned on the job," said the student who worked there. "They'd come stoned. I had a supervisor ask me if I wanted to do drugs, in the lunch-room. I said no. He said, 'You mean you've been coming here every day sober?' I said yes. He said, 'You've got to be kidding. Everybody comes here stoned.'" The student said they used "acid, pot, hash, not really any heavy stuff. Nothing to get out of control."

None of the polling firms offers terrific conditions for their workers, of course, but most of the others tend to hire middle-aged and older people, usually housewives or retired people wanting to earn a few extra dollars. Gregg's operation has a preponderance of younger workers, which perhaps explains why his company, unlike the others, uses such high-school methods as demerit points in a black book. In this respect, the polling industry rivals banks for returning fat profits to the executives while paying the interviewers, or tellers, minimum wages.

In the 1988 campaign, Gregg made much of leadership being an issue with Canadians. But back in 1982, when the Tories were trailing the Liberals because of Clark's lousy leadership, Gregg argued the opposite. "It's not a question of leadership. It's a question of issues and the party, not the person perceived by people as most capable of solving their problems. Leadership is irrelevant now," he said. "It's the issues that really cut today" — except of course if your leader is more popular than their leader, as Mulroney was compared to Turner.

Oh well, things change. And one of Gregg's constant themes in his partisan and non-partisan speechifying is that people and parties must change too. That's what prompted him to push separate-school funding in Ontario, and that's what identifies him as being on the left side of the Conservative spectrum, a pink Tory. In May 1984, for example, Gregg pointed to U.S. Democratic presidential candidate Gary Hart, the self-styled "new ideas" man, as a leader who would "take off like a rocket in Canada." That, of course, was before Hart's "new ideas" ran afoul of some age-old personal practices.

Gregg showed his capacity to change according to circumstances again a few months later, when he explained the 1984 Mulroney election sweep by saying that it was old ideas, not new ones, that Canadians wanted. Gregg told the *Globe*'s Patrick Martin that people longed for a return to the past. "They wanted to put an end to the way things have been for the past 10 to 15 years."

For all his blathering about methodological and philosophical purity, Gregg, like all other pollsters, has an amazing ability to come up frequently with results that mesh perfectly with the pre-survey desires of his corporate client. In March 1987, during the rancorous debate over drug-patent legislation, the Pharmaceutical Manufacturers Association of Canada announced with considerable fanfare that a Decima poll of 1,200 Canadians showed that "after hearing the main arguments for and against [the bill] . . . 65 percent felt [it] was a good thing and 31 percent thought it was a bad thing." A look at the questions explains why. For example, 82 percent said they would support the bill if the government made sure "that drug price increases would not be higher than the rate of inflation." Fine, but there was no such mechanism in the bill. In fact, the government was arguing — falsely, it turned out — that the bill would not increase drug prices at all.

Respondents were given a rotating series of pro and con arguments on this bill before being asked their views. The questions were loaded. One of the arguments offered "against" the bill was: "Just because other countries offer greater protection to brand-name companies doesn't mean Canada is being unfair and needs to change its laws." The clear implication was that the legislation was unfair to the drug companies, but so what?

In February 1989, the Canadian Nuclear Association hired Decima for a survey of 1,200 Canadians over age eighteen and discovered that 61 percent favour nuclear energy as a source for generating electricity. But Adele Hurley of the Canadian Coalition on Acid Rain accused Decima of asking loaded questions. When a question was prefaced, for example, with: "Scientific data and opinion indicate that coal causes acid rain and contributes to the greenhouse effect, while nuclear power does not," 68 percent chose nuclear energy; 19 percent, coal. "You don't have to be a rocket scientist to figure out why a biased question like that was allowed," said Hurley. "Let's face it, Decima is the Conservative party's pollster, and I think it's a well-known fact that the Conservatives support nuclear energy from a big-business, economic standpoint."

One complaint voiced by Conservatives who are not plugged into the power elite of the party is that while party money pays for the expensive collection of polling data, ordinary party candidates have no access to the numbers. If an individual Tory candidate wants numbers for his riding from Decima, the poll costs him $5,000. Many candidates either don't take constituency polls of their own or, if they do, opt for local pollsters. London East MP Jim Jepson, who lost by 102 votes, spent less than half the cost of the Decima results to hire York Research, the same pollster who was "bang on" in 1984 when Jepson won by 8,000 votes.

"In a way it's sad [that] we are so poll-oriented," says Jepson. "I'm the kind of person who says, 'Here's where I stand. Take me or leave me.' I don't think polls should be . . . released during a campaign. They do a disservice to the public. You won't get candour from politicians because they want to be seen to be on the popular side of the issues. They're useful tools, but they're also a cruel instrument by which politicians can manipulate the electorate, and various special-interest groups can structure polls to get a particular result and then claim the public supports them. It's not going to change though."

Nearly all of the media reportage after the 1988 election campaign portrayed Gregg as the shiny white knight who came rushing to the rescue of the tarnished Tories after Turner caught them unprepared with his impassioned plea for Canadian nationalism. Gregg, of course, makes no effort to deflect the praise. Indeed, he happily contributed to it in a series of post-campaign interviews.

The campaign does raise a few questions, however. If Gregg's in-depth psychographics are as good as he claims, why were the Tories unprepared? Tory strategists, based largely on Decima polls, had not counted on Turner's tough attack on free trade. Why not? Surely Turner had signalled his intentions with his Senate gambit back in July?

The Tories began deliberately with what veteran policy adviser Bill Neville described in a November 28 *Financial Post* article as a "low-key, positive campaign. . . . The thing to do is not make waves. . . . I don't know what else you're supposed to do when you're well ahead." The Tories, like the NDP, flatly underestimated the gut impact of free trade on Canadians. And, as was the case for the NDP, this mistaken assumption came directly from their polling numbers. While NDP pollster Vic Fingerhut took considerable flak for his judgments, Gregg emerged as the man who saved the day.

The common belief is that, after the Liberal rise and Tory fall resulting from the TV debates, Tory campaign strategists huddled in the Langevin Block across from Parliament Hill to plan their counter-attack. In the November 28 *Financial Post* article, "How the Tories Turned the Tide," Gregg was quoted as saying, "What we had to do is bomb the bridge. And that is precisely what we proceeded to do." In short, they got tough on Turner, launching a direct, nasty assault on his personal integrity and leadership qualities, and before long, voters who'd been impressed by Turner's debate performance began having the same old doubts about his abilities that had kept him at the bottom of the leadership sweepstakes for nearly five years. Gregg, the story goes, had the numbers to show the Tories that, despite his debate ambush, Canadians were still dreadfully uneasy about Turner.

This interpretation of events has been widely published and broadcast and no doubt has already taken a place in Canadian political history as yet another example of Gregg's brilliance. But is it true? Well, the Tories certainly did meet after the debate, but then campaign-strategy teams do tend to meet regularly during campaigns. And they were worried about the turn-around in Liberal fortunes, although on this point Gregg and others have been quoted as saying that they never doubted for a moment that Mulroney would win. Gregg told a group of fifty campaign workers the day after the controversial Gallup "rogue poll" that the numbers were "absolutely, unequivocally, take-it-to-the-bank, 100 percent wrong."

Gregg has subsequently told people that, based on his numbers, he and other party officials completely rewrote the television advertisements to key on Turner's credibility or, to be more precise, lack of it.

But just how much of this is self-serving mythology, and how much is real? Did the Tories really need a poll to know that Canadians were uncertain about John Turner? Surely not. But the more important question is, did the Tories really change their game plan based on Gregg's sophisticated tracking samples after the debate? Common wisdom says yes. But Tory senator Finlay MacDonald, a respected veteran of dozens of Tory campaigns, says no. MacDonald, who has a well-earned reputation for bluntness, has not held formal campaign posts in recent years, but he is one of those well-placed back-room boys whose access to and knowledge of the system gives him an independence not enjoyed by others, and places him in the position of being sought out periodically for campaign advice and, in return, enjoying the privileged view of the campaign insider.

"I think Turner just ran out of steam," he said. "The negative aspect of his particular campaign was finally exposed. I really don't know if it was anything we did.

"I may be doing a hell of a disservice to the people who were actually there making the decisions, and I was not, as to whether there was a time after the debates and they said o.k., here's what we do, we take off the gloves . . . and, ergo, that was the momentous day the decision was made that caused the thing to turn around.

"Well, you have to sort of prove it to me. I know damn well that the advertising was based on polling that took place before the writ was issued. It was the result of intelligence being received by Gregg and Tom Scott that caused the advertising, for all practical purposes, to be locked in. During the campaign it's extraordinarily difficult to change it.

"The advice Peter Lougheed gave me in 1972 [MacDonald was campaign chairman then] was, get the game plan and stick with it. That was always Lowell Murray's approach. The game plan. Don't be thrown off by anything. . . .

"I remember being told before the campaign began that the first part of the campaign was going to be positive and that the gloves would come off later on, but that was the game plan," said MacDonald. "I remember clearly being given that understanding. We followed the game plan and it worked.

"I just felt in the last two weeks, John Turner's passion was spent. We never had any doubt what the outcome was going to be."

Whatever the precise truth of the campaign strategy, there is no doubt that Gregg, at least while the Tories maintain power, will hold the position of Canada's top pollster, in much the way Goldfarb did when the Liberals held power. But Goldfarb, while widely quoted, was never personally venerated by the media and his own partisans the way Gregg is, largely because Goldfarb, like his patron-saint

Trudeau, was not readily accessible to the media, while Gregg, the long-haired bon viveur, not only looks more colourful but is always ready to pass on a quick quote or tidbit of scientific wisdom to his legion of media friends.

Goldfarb for a time held the lofty position of Canada's premier pollster, as we shall see in the next chapter, but he never achieved quite the influence over the prime minister, mainly because his boss, Trudeau, did not completely trust polls — and often did what he wanted despite the numbers — while Gregg's boss, Mulroney, generally lives and dies by the latest data, a characteristic that makes Gregg, apart from Mulroney himself, as powerful and influential in the political process as any other living Canadian.

8

Government by Goldfarb

Five days before the last federal election, Baton Broadcasting planned to run the final campaign Martin Goldfarb poll on its weekly public-affairs program, "Sounding Board," on six television stations, Toronto's giant CFTO, Ottawa's CJOH, and CTV affiliates in Regina, Saskatoon, Prince Albert, and Yorkton.

The poll didn't run. Goldfarb, the veteran Liberal-party pollster who has been criticized often for doing both partisan and media polling at the same time, had John Turner's Liberals still two points ahead of Brian Mulroney's Tories. By that stage in the roller-coaster 1988 campaign, every other public pollster had the Tories five to eight points ahead, and cruising.

Baton boss Doug Bassett, scion of a prominent Toronto Tory family, says the poll was out of date, "so we decided not to go with it." On the question of a possible conflict between Goldfarb's private partisan role and his public role, Bassett said there was no conflict. "Everybody knows Goldfarb is a Liberal pollster. It's like 'Canada A.M.' having Caplan, Segal, and Kirby on their political panel. Everybody knows they're partisan. I believe Goldfarb thinks his name is the most important thing he has, just as I do and I'm sure you do. He's not whoring for the Liberal party and giving misleading information."

Earlier in the campaign, on "Sounding Board," Tory partisan Hugh Segal had in fact raised the issue on air, saying he had "some problems" with Goldfarb acting as pollster for both Baton Broadcasting and the Liberals at once.

Tom Clark, Baton's political editor and host of the show, says Segal mentioned it before they went on air. "I told him in no uncertain terms he should raise it. I agreed it was an issue. I think there's a very legitimate concern about that . . . an ethical question."

Clark says it was his decision to cancel the poll's planned broadcast. "I checked with friends at Environics and Gallup, and my contacts within the Tory party and of course with Marzolini . . . and they all thought Goldfarb's numbers were off. Even Marty agreed that the poll was out of date. We had the feeling at that point the campaign had taken a significant shift. I got the raw data almost a week after he went into the field and it didn't make any sense.

"We were the only organization using a partisan pollster," says Clark. "He had a good reputation. I never suspected for a moment Marty was cooking the books. I saw the raw data . . . but I had nothing to do with the selection of Goldfarb. That was done by Bassett. I had to live with it as best I could, but I felt the only ethical thing I could do if it was raised as an issue was to air it on our show."

Clark says, it's "the appearance that doesn't stack up. I think it's an error which can't be repeated. It's a naive error, but an error none the less."

For his part, Goldfarb dismisses the criticism out of hand. "They're making an assumption that your private polling would influence what you publish in the media. In that particular circumstance I had the approval of the party. Segal didn't say anything when my poll was very much in favour of the Tories, but when the numbers switched and the Tories were behind the Liberals after the debate, suddenly Segal decided this was a big issue. As long as the Tories were ahead it didn't bother him.

"I could stretch that argument and ask about Segal, who is obviously a partisan player, whose company was responsible for the advertising in selling free trade, then obviously the public didn't get a fair shake on the meaning of free trade. . . . I don't agree with that. I can't work for General Motors and Ford. Yes, I was giving Liberals strategic advice to help run the election, but I didn't tell anybody what our strategy was publicly. All we did was publish numbers," he says.

Not quite. He also did interviews on air about those numbers, and Clark says that's where he personally had a problem with Goldfarb's partisanship: "I don't think it was legitimate criticism to say to

Goldfarb he could cook his numbers. . . . If there was any skewing Marty was trying to do, however, it was in trying to direct the issues.

"We would have him in to interview him about his poll. What he tried to do was bring up issues he'd say soon would be the big issue in the campaign, clearly Liberal-party issues . . . it was his selection of comments after we had the poll on [TV] that was sometimes troubling."

On the November 2 show, for example, Goldfarb talked about the "extremely volatile" electorate, said it "looks like the Liberals have a shot at forming a government," but added that the numbers were "fragile." However, Goldfarb went on to talk about free trade and the leaders' personalities being important issues, and said the national sales tax was the "sleeper" that the Liberals could turn into a "big issue, just as they've done with free trade." That, of course, was precisely what the Liberals were hoping to do. Certainly Goldfarb was. He told the author in a post-campaign interview, "We begged him [Turner] and pushed him to get off free trade. We felt from our polling that the value-added tax was the best issue to go to. We tried, we really did. But you're dealing with an individual and he just wouldn't change. He'd staked his fate on [the free-trade issue] and wouldn't alter the course."

Goldfarb may feel that he, personally, is unaffected by his sometimes seemingly contradictory roles, but he does not always view other pollsters so generously. In a May 1984 interview with Linda Diebel, then of the Montreal *Gazette*, Quebec politician Richard French was quoted as saying, "The polling industry is just not reliable, not honest. They trade data all the time and the ethics of the whole industry are highly questionable." French said he was particularly concerned about the commonly accepted practice of pollsters and consultants working for companies, federal and provincial governments, political parties, and candidates — all at the same time. "They might as well be walking the streets," he said.

French offered MP Donald Johnston's bid for the leadership of the Liberal party as an example of how the roles blur. Johnston's campaign strategist was volunteer David MacNaughton of PAI, generally regarded as a Liberal firm. But Tory pollster Allan Gregg is Mac-Naughton's business partner (along with Michael Robinson), and Decima and PAI co-sponsor Gregg's *Decima Quarterly*. Rick

Anderson, president of PAI data, was Johnston's full-time campaign manager.

Asked about this mixing of functions at the time, Goldfarb rolled his eyes and said, "I'm frankly surprised that David is working for Don because he sells the report and it's difficult to keep things separate."

Indeed, it is, which is why it's ironic that Goldfarb would see the difficulty with other pollsters working for two masters at the same time, but not recognize the problem of having "to keep things separate" in his own case.

Goldfarb also displayed a cold-blooded detachment about the morality of his partisan masters using his numbers to pander to the voter's basest instincts to win an election. In Diebel's *Gazette* article, he says his company probed "public fears and dreams" for the Liberals during the 1974 campaign when Tory leader Bob Stanfield wanted to bring in wage-and-price controls to stop the double-digit inflation of the time. Goldfarb said he discovered the voters feared wage more than they did price controls and he helped devise a strategy to attack the wage-restraint bogey man.

Asked how he felt when Trudeau imposed controls himself in October 1975, Goldfarb said, "That's a whole different issue. It is completely independent of the fact that we won an election on our strategy." Or, one could add, efficacy is far more significant in political life than ethics.

Goldfarb argues that the polling industry itself needs higher standards. "There should at least be a minimum standard so that we don't allow anybody to stick a shingle out and say, 'I'm a pollster,' when he may not have the academic credentials and technological know-how to get the job done.

"In the same way we license doctors after they've mastered a certain body of knowledge, perhaps we should license public pollsters. If a company wants to hire me as a pollster and it's not published, that's up to them. But there has to be some criteria," he says.

There are, in fact, standards in the industry. Two organizations, the Professional Market Research Society (PMRS) and the Canadian Association of Market Research Organizations (CAMRO), promote non-binding guidelines. Until 1987, Goldfarb was a member of CAMRO, but he resigned in a huff because they were investigating complaints made against him. These complaints stemmed from wildly conflicting poll results released during the Ontario Conservative leadership race in November 1985.

The Ontario Tories, after an unbroken forty-three-year reign, had finally lost power to the Liberals, led by David Peterson. When Frank Miller had won the leadership earlier that year, former cabinet ministers Larry Grossman and Dennis Timbrell were his main opponents. Now, Miller had quit, and the two men were going head-to-head. (Alan Pope, also in the race, was clearly trailing.) Goldfarb, Gallup, and Environics, all published media polls taken in late October or the first week in November. Both Gallup, for the *Toronto Star*, and Environics, in the company's quarterly, *Focus Ontario*, concluded the Liberals would continue to lead public opinion easily — between 46 and 54 percent support — regardless of which of the three Tory leadership contenders won. Goldfarb, however, polling for Toronto's CFTO-TV, discovered some startling support for Grossman, saying that under his leadership the Tories would be well ahead of the Liberals, with 44.8 percent support, compared to 35.2. This result was nearly nine points higher than Gallup showed and twelve points higher than Environics. Goldfarb had the Timbrell-led Tories at 38.5 (Gallup, 34; Environics, 30) and Pope at 31.5 (27 under Gallup and 23 for Environics). Goldfarb had both Timbrell and Pope trailing the Liberals in support.

A few days before the vote, the Grossman campaign handed delegates a flyer headlined, "Only Grossman Can Win!" The flyer cited the Goldfarb poll of six hundred eligible Ontario voters as showing their man "clearly identified as the only Tory leadership contender who can beat the Liberals led by David Peterson."

As it turned out, Grossman beat Timbrell on the final ballot by just nineteen votes, making it extremely likely that the Goldfarb poll made the difference. After all, the Ontario Tories had become accustomed to power. If just ten Timbrell delegates were persuaded by the poll that a vote for Grossman would get them back in, that was enough to determine the winner.

The Liberals had been hoping that Grossman would win. Timbrell, more of a Davis clone, was seen as a much tougher opponent. In her book, *Out of the Blue*, veteran newspaper columnist Rosemary Speirs wrote: "The [Goldfarb] poll may have helped Grossman at the convention. No doubt it also caused Liberal backroom boys to raise a glass to Goldfarb. They knew the Liberal pollster had found different results when he polled privately for the Ontario party a couple of months earlier. For the Liberals, Goldfarb had tested Timbrell and Grossman as possible election contenders against Peterson, and he had then found that Timbrell was the greater threat.... Timbrell looked more dangerous as a potential premier."

An Environics poll, two months after Grossman won the leadership, showed Liberal support among decided voters at 46 percent, with Grossman's Tories at 31, and the NDP at 21. In the September 10, 1987, provincial election, Grossman finished third, with 25 percent of the vote, compared to Peterson's 48 percent and NDP leader Bob Rae's 26 percent. During that election, Goldfarb was Peterson's pollster.

As a result of complaints about the discrepancies among the three 1985 leadership polls, CAMRO launched an investigation in 1986, but Goldfarb, the man who calls for polling licences and academic credentials, resigned from the organization and no conclusions were reached. "They [CAMRO] were too selective," says Goldfarb. "There was some polling that [Michael] Adams did which said the [Ontario] Liberals were in a free-fall after the debate with Grossman. It turned out to be a bunch of bunk ... but they didn't investigate that. We thought they were very selective in who they investigated."

Goldfarb did not start out as a man of wealth, controversy, and influence. His parents immigrated to Canada in 1927, and Martin, now fifty-one, and his two brothers lived in a cramped walk-up over his parents' tiny grocery store on Dundas Street West in Toronto. He graduated from the University of Toronto with a bachelor's degree in anthropology and a master's in sociology. He once described himself as "pretty much an average student" until he met Joan Freedman in his second year. "Joan gave me a raison d'être, a purpose," he said. "She had a calm, intellectual approach that opened up a whole world to me." Less than a year later they were married.

Goldfarb taught high school in North York and got a research job on the side with MacLaren Advertising. He conducted his first survey for the firm on adolescent behaviour. After five years, he quit teaching. His company began as a cottage industry in his own front room then graduated in 1968 to a small office near Bathurst Street and Lawrence Avenue "in two dumpy rooms, with only me and my mother-in-law, Ida Freedman, to do my typing and be my secretary."

Politically, he had done some work for former Liberal MP and cabinet minister Paul Hellyer, but the bulk of his business then (as it still is, in dollar terms) was corporate work. In his first few years he expanded about 20 percent annually, gradually renovating his offices and hiring more staff. He inspired several well-known commercial campaigns, among them, "We Care About the Shape You're In," for Wonderbra, "It's Ours," for Petro-Canada, and "Ford Has a Better Idea," for the Ford Motor Co.

He met Liberal strategist Keith Davey through his work with Hellyer. After the 1972 election, when Trudeau brought Davey back in to run the Liberal election machine, Davey brought his friend Goldfarb with him as party pollster, a position he has held ever since. Goldfarb quickly became a charter member of the so-called Coutts-'n'-Davey Gang, a group of about eight power-brokers who exercised almost complete control over the Liberal party and hence, the government, for most of the 1970s and the early 1980s. Indeed, of the whole gang, Goldfarb is now the only remaining member still considered a major party insider. The others have either gone on to other things or been shunted aside.

Goldfarb does not like to talk about being rich. But he is. His luxurious offices in a high-rise tower in North York house a staff of more than fifty. There are two suites for Goldfarb alone, including a spectacular sitting-room with moss-green velvet-covered walls, magnificent hardwood floors, several Persian rugs, Inuit carvings, a painting by Canadian Indian artist Norval Morrisseau, and assorted lithographs by Surrealists Miro and Calder.

He has a mansion in the Bridle Path area, a Porsche and Rolls-Royce, and a cottage in Muskoka. "I don't like to draw attention to the fact that I make a lot of money," he said in a 1983 interview. "It's not the most important thing in my life, and it makes me sensitive."

Perhaps. But over the years, other people have delighted in calling attention to Goldfarb's money. The late Tory MP Tom Cossitt, Trudeau's nemesis in the House of Commons at one time, tabled a question in April 1977, asking how much Goldfarb had collected from the public purse. In December 1980, he was told the company had been paid more than $1.3 million in federal-government contracts over the decade.

Goldfarb is noted among other pollsters as the one most willing to interpret results of his surveys, often venturing far beyond conclusions that his numbers actually support. He has acknowledged in past interviews, "I know some people question the degree to which I interpret. All I can say is that to say what people think is only the beginning. Anyone can come up with statistics, good statistics. It's another thing to say why."

To discover the "why," Goldfarb uses a technique called "psychographics," a psychological term to describe a graph indicating the relative strength of individual personality traits, a kind of psychological biography that attempts to tell not only what people believe, but why they believe it, based on certain overriding characteristics. Goldfarb breaks his individual profiles into six specific segments: "day-to-day watchers" constitute 25 percent of the population, and are defined as people who are unsure of themselves and tend to follow trends; "old-fashioned puritans" (18 percent) stick to their principles; "disinterested [sic] self-indulgents" (14 percent) don't care about much besides themselves; "joiner activists" (16 percent) love to get involved but never as the first one in; "responsible survivors" (12 percent) understand the system and know how to use it; and "aggressive achievers" (15 percent) are the real leaders in society.

Goldfarb argues that knowing what group people are in helps to determine the likelihood of behavioural change. He concedes that some "sociological imagination" is needed. "We don't just analyse data, we interpret it based on our understanding of society."

In 1977, Goldfarb got into a terrible row with the media, politicians, and pollsters in Quebec for his rather rosy interpretations of the decline of separatist feelings in the months after Lévesque's electoral victory.

It was at this time that Lévesque coined the phrase "Government by Goldfarb." Goldfarb was accused of allowing his federalist and Liberal sympathies to cloud his results, and Lévesque at one point dismissed the massive project as a "political operation." (During his time in opposition, Tory leader Joe Clark often picked up on the "Government by Goldfarb" theme to indicate the Liberals paid more attention to polls than to doing what they thought was right. But then the Tories were no different, and the wonder is that "Decision by Decima" hasn't become the slogan of current critics of the Conservative government.)

Not all the criticism of Goldfarb was warranted. Given the temper of the times, a charter member of Toronto's anglophone power elite wasn't likely to be well received, regardless of what he said. The attack on his work was so widespread, however, that Goldfarb felt compelled to respond to it in a December 1977 article in the Montreal

Gazette, in which he denied any bias and claimed the results of his studies and other studies were not at odds. Actually, they were.

The controversy began September 27, 1977, when the *Gazette* headline, based on the Goldfarb findings, read: "Separatism Support Drops." The same day, the front-page headline on the French-language *Le Devoir,* highlighting the findings of a CROP poll, said: "Quebec Is Ready To Give The PQ A Mandate To Negotiate." At the time, of course, Goldfarb was also doing polls for the federal Liberals, who, naturally, were devising strategies to combat Quebec separatism. Goldfarb had done three polls worth $120,000 for the federal Finance department and the Anti-Inflation Board, plus a $90,000 poll for the secretary of state on what Canadians thought about federal bilingualism programs.

The Goldfarb and CROP polls differed on almost every major question. According to Goldfarb, for example, 56 percent of French-speaking Quebeckers opposed Bill 101. CROP found 59 percent supported it. Goldfarb found 25 percent favoured "separation," but CROP's numbers showed 38 percent in favour of "sovereignty-association" and 50 percent in favour of giving the provincial government a mandate to negotiate "sovereignty-association" with Ottawa. CROP's Quebec sample was 2.5 times larger than Goldfarb's. More to the point, asking people questions about "sovereignty-association," which is what the PQ government was actively promoting, and outright "separation," which was (and remains) such a loaded word in Quebec, was not the same thing.

Goldfarb also found the Quebec Liberals were the most popular party, while CROP said 51 percent of decided voters supported the PQ. Goldfarb found 30 percent of Quebeckers supported the status quo. CROP's figure was 4 percent. And so it went. McGill pollster and sociologist Maurice Pinard accused Goldfarb of having a federal bias in his questions and of "taking advantage of the ignorance of their clients [Southam–*Star*] in order to make money." He attacked the Goldfarb poll for its "show-business–like character, its excessive dramatization and its absurd hypothesis." He said, on some questions Goldfarb received only 132 responses for the entire province, giving a margin of error of 9 percent.

Some of Goldfarb's questions were extreme. For example, respondents were asked if they thought it was likely Canada would have to fight a civil war over Quebec separation; if there was a war, would it be French versus French, or French versus English; would it be a guerrilla war or a formal war with armies. In addition, he asked whether, in the event that Quebec became an independent country, its government would be: communistic, revolutionary (like Cuba or Argentina), democratic, fascist/dictatorial, or other." The poll generated huge headlines across the country by predicting that one million people would leave Quebec if the province separated. In a survey in which separation was equated with a shooting war followed by a fascist or revolutionary government, the surprising thing is more people didn't say they'd leave when the shooting began.

The poll, designed by Goldfarb, was considered so important by Southam that the company assigned a committee of senior editors and six experienced journalists to write and edit the published stories. For all that, however, the news stories ignored the fact that breaking out the Quebec numbers in the poll just about doubled the statistical margin of error, a constant problem in media reportage of polls. The CROP poll, however, took its complete sample from Quebec, and therefore was not subject to the arithmetical vagaries of regional breakdowns.

Worse, Goldfarb wrote that the poll showed a desire for "Less federal power and more regional and provincial power." It didn't. Quite the contary, in fact. Asked if the federal government should have more, less, or the same amount of power, 18 percent nation-wide said more; 34 percent, less; and 47 percent, the status quo. Asked if the provincial governments should have more, less, or the same power, the results were: more power, 40; less, 42; and the same amount, 42.

In short, despite Goldfarb's personal interpretation that Canadians wanted less federal and more provincial power, his numbers showed the opposite, that 65 percent did not favour a weaker federal government, while 59 percent didn't want stronger provincial governments, a majority in both cases.

Finally, Goldfarb was quoted uncritically in a Southam article as saying, "The strong feelings that are expressed in many parts of the country with respect to the role of the provinces in the national unity debate maybe suggest a new order of debate that should be considered. . . . That is, one of the options that should be considered is that the federal government should not participate at all, except to chair the meeting. The role of the federal government would then be to administer or manage the kind of government the provinces or regions evolve. . . ."

Journalist George Radwanski, writing on that point in the *Financial Times*, said, "Nothing in the questions and answers in the survey documents a desire that the federal government abdicate all its responsibility for guiding the nation's future, and Goldfarb's suggestion is no part of the pollster's or even the sociologist's art. But to the casual reader without access to the full report, its inclusion in the survey series may endow it with an aura of scientific respectability."

Three years after claiming to have found that Canadians wanted a weaker federal government, Goldfarb was quoted in Ron Graham's book *One-Eyed Kings*, advising Trudeau to push ahead with constitutional reform because: "The country didn't want confrontation, but it was prepared to support federal authority. It felt that, in the crunch, it needed Big Daddy." Goldfarb was also quoted, describing the Liberal 1980 energy package, which included the disastrous National Energy Program, as "a clear signal that we knew where we were going, that we knew what was best for Canada, that we will speak for the little guy." In some respects, he was right. It sure told Canadians, especially westerners, where the Liberals were going, and when the "little guy" next got a chance to speak, he tossed them out on their ear.

In *The Rainmaker*, Keith Davey wrote, "Right after the 1980 election, we had begun work on a battery of sophisticated analytic techniques. Specifically, Marty Goldfarb developed two computer-driven models: an issue leverage model and an issue interaction mapping model. It would become possible for us to maximize our various policy positions as well as to develop separate strategies for different segments of the voting marketplace. Every Liberal candidate in Canada could be made aware of major issues riding by riding, along with advice on what to say and how to say it. Direct-mail response could be organized literally on a house-to-house basis. However, this operation was under the auspices of the PMO, which meant that changes in personnel — most notably Tom Axworthy — left no one on board who knew how to use the equipment.

"Goldfarb made both John Turner and Bill Lee aware of the scope of these models, but they both chose to ignore them. Bill Lee snidely told Marty, 'You're worried about old Liberals. I want to reach new ones.' This most effective technology was simply shelved."

So, too, were Davey, Axworthy, et al. But not Goldfarb. Despite his lukewarm support for pollsters, Turner realized that a decade of

data could not be easily replaced, although for a time, when Angus
Reid turned up doing leadership polls for Turner, it looked as if
Goldfarb's position was in jeopardy. Goldfarb would probably have
been displaced if Reid had learned to keep his mouth shut.

In September 1985, key Liberal strategist Senator Michael Kirby,
an associate in Goldfarb's firm, told the Liberal caucus about a
Goldfarb poll that supposedly was instrumental in creating "the new
John Turner." Obviously, not many Canadians noticed the new and
improved model, but there were some surface changes, most notably
a more aggressive style in the House of Commons — not long after
the poll Turner called Mulroney a "shameless hypocrite" over his
position on patronage.

In March 1986, Goldfarb told about 450 people at a *Vancouver
Sun*-sponsored lecture at UBC: "If anything, politicians have become
more fixated upon affecting public opinion than on doing what they
think is right. Frequently politicians may readily admit that they
think they know what should be done to alleviate a problem, but the
fear of making a mistake, a crippling error, deters them from taking
such action." It seemed an odd lament from a man who is as responsible as anyone in the country for the situation. Obviously, Goldfarb
had been reading, and believing, his own press clippings, since he
went on to say that pollsters have eclipsed the traditional policy-
making role of Parliament, caucus, and the bureaucracy. "We now
have government by pollster."

At the end of 1987, both Goldfarb and Gregg conducted national
polls on free trade, Goldfarb for the anti–free trade *Toronto Star*, and
Gregg for the pro–free trade External Affairs department. Typically,
both pollsters got the answers most pleasing to their particular
clients. Goldfarb found 44 percent supporting the deal and 42 percent
opposed, essentially a draw given the margin of error, enabling the
Star to trumpet the news that support for the deal was slipping.
Gregg, however, whose poll was taken two weeks earlier, discovered
51 percent of Canadians supported the deal (and, by extension, truth,
justice, the Canadian way, and Mulroney), with those opposed at 42
percent, the same opposition number Goldfarb would find.

Goldfarb said, "Historically, this issue has always stimulated
highly contradictory emotions among Canadians. This time, it's apparent that Canadians clearly understand that we made a bad deal,
that we are giving up a lot of our sovereignty and political control.

However, free trade has always held out the hope of some wealth to Canadians, and sovereignty is always less important when you are poor."

In case you've forgotten, that was Goldfarb the detached media pollster speaking, not Goldfarb the partisan Liberal strategist.

On January 22, 1988, while taping a show with Tory MP Patrick Boyer on CTV's "Question Period," host Pamela Wallin introduced her guest to the television audience by saying that Goldfarb had been invited "to discuss the role of polling in Canadian politics, although you don't do that much polling for the Conservatives, mostly for the Liberals."

"We only poll for the Liberals," Goldfarb interjected.

Not true. Among others, Goldfarb has done considerable polling work over the years for the Ontario Tories. Liberal MPP Pat Reid once accused Bill Davis of, ironically, "Government by Goldfarb." Goldfarb has also done work for the B.C. Socreds.

When polling for political parties, Goldfarb interviewers identify themselves as representatives of the Canadian Polling Institute. During the 1987 Ontario election, won easily by David Peterson, Goldfarb's firm was conducting a two-hundred-calls-a-night rolling poll using his sophisticated new technology, Computer-Assisted Telephone Interviewing (CATI), the same technology used by Environics. Each interviewer has a headphone and a computer terminal, dials a number from a randomly selected list, keys the answers, and the data is fed into a master computer.

When Goldfarb's poll in the *Toronto Star* showed Peterson's Liberals well ahead of Larry Grossman and the once-mighty Tories, it was consistent with other polls. Still, the old question of appearances came up, and Grossman dismissed the numbers as the work of the Liberal-party pollster in the Liberal-party house organ. It wasn't necessarily fair comment, but Goldfarb's dual role allowed the Tories at least to attempt to soften the blow of their third-place standing by playing to a common public perception.

Goldfarb did not win universal acclaim among federal Liberals in October, five weeks before the election, when he and Tom Axworthy published a book, *Marching to a Different Drummer*, widely seen as critical of Turner's leadership. "The book wasn't an attack on Turner," says Goldfarb. "The media picked that up and continued to play it, and for the most part they never read the book. There were various scenarios in there, showing how the Liberals could be first, second, or third; the NDP could be first, second, or third; or the Tories could be first, second, or third. So the media picked up the one line where we said the Liberals could be third and selectively chose not to include the opposite, that the Tories could be third and the NDP could be third. So they implied we were anti-Turner in the book.

"It's unfortunate that the book gave Turner the press it did. He didn't deserve it. It wasn't in the book," says Goldfarb. "It was an academic book, not meant to be a large seller. And it wasn't. Guys called me for weeks, hammering me about the book."

That may be because much of it was, in fact, anti-Turner. Neither Goldfarb nor Axworthy was ever really a Turner-led Liberal in the way that he had been a committed Trudeau-led Liberal. Their book showed it. For example, they wrote that the party "is not identified in the voter's mind with any distinctive policy. It was once the party of minority rights and strong national government. That image has been blurred."

That may be how they saw it, but it was hardly a testament to Turner's leadership. Nor was their view of Turner's support for the Meech Lake Accord. "John Turner's endorsement of the pact repudiated his party's intrinsic heritage," they wrote. "With one stroke, the Liberal party's traditional positioning as the advocate of strong activist national government was traded in for a temporary peace [with Quebec]." Now, why would anyone interpret that as criticizing Turner, eh?

Indeed, Goldfarb himself told journalists at the time that Turner had recently vowed to significantly amend the constitutional accord. "He's come a long way. And that's what the book argues as well. This isn't meant to criticize Turner or any one Liberal. It's about two parties," he said.

Axworthy went one step farther, claiming the book's conclusions weren't necessarily those of the authors, but were from surveys of delegates to the 1984 and 1986 Liberal conventions. "It's a survey of what the Liberal delegates believed," Axworthy said. "They had serious doubts that their positions were the same as Turner's position."

Ironically, the authors wrote what might have been Turner's epitaph (although they naturally had directed it at Joe Clark): "a leader who cannot even unite his own party gives little reassurance that he will be able to govern the nation."

And the fact that Turner would put up with a published attack on his leadership by his own pollster in mid-campaign makes the point more eloquently than anything else that could have been said about Turner.

While Goldfarb continues to prosper with his private clients, he has also maintained his grip on the Liberal polling apparatus, although that does not have the same prestige when the party is out of office as it does when they are in office. While Goldfarb may have lost some of his clout then, he certainly hasn't lost any of the Trudeau-esque arrogance that he and many of the former prime minister's senior aides seemed to have inherited from their spiritual and political leader. Early in the spring of 1989, Goldfarb was approached by TVOntario as part of a series on pollsters. He, at first, consented to take part, thinking he would be the key figure in the series, but upon learning later he was slated to be but one of several pollsters, Goldfarb refused to have anything to do with it.

Goldfarb is an intensely studious man, more a polling artist, if you will, than a technician, a man given to taking his numbers and using them to paint societal attitudes with broad brush-strokes. His most enduring, and uninspiring, characteristic is that despite his constant pleas for more professionalism and higher academic credentials in the business, Goldfarb continues to play the often-conflicting roles of pundit, pollster, and political partisan, all at the same time as if these roles are mutually exclusive, and his various personae are totally unrelated to one another. The evidence simply doesn't support this conclusion and, given the problems of the 1988 campaign, his future as a pundit doesn't seem all that bright. But then punditry doesn't pay as well as the other two roles anyway.

9

Galluping Ghosts

George Gallup would not have been pleased. Back in the 1970s, newspapers carried such headlines as, "When Gallup Polls Speak, Everyone Listens — And Believes." But if Gallup's ghost had visited Canada during the 1988 federal campaign, he would have been shocked to learn that, while people were still listening to the Gallup poll, most of them weren't believers anymore.

Clearly the most venerable of the polling organizations, Gallup was suffering as never before. And at least part of the reason was that, unlike the 1970s, when it was really the only polling firm engaged in the public dissemination of opinion, the 1980s had spawned a host of firms whose work could be compared to Gallup's. And the comparisons weren't flattering, particularly during the 1984 and 1988 campaigns when Gallup results fluctuated wildly from week to week, prompting many of the true believers to publicly question the organization's findings.

Gallup, formally the Canadian Institute of Public Opinion, is one of forty-three affiliates world-wide. The Canadian operation is owned by a group of Toronto-based investors and survey researcher, Owen Charlebois, who used to operate his own firm in Ottawa, is CIPO president. Current vice-president Lorne Bozinoff, who acts as the company's chief spokesman, says Gallup "was a poor businessman. He could have made a fortune, but he didn't set up a system of royalties."

While the real heart of the organization remains at Princeton, N.J., where it began, each affiliate pays a modest fee, depending on the size of the organization, to support a bare-bones, non-profit office in

London, England, called the Gallup International Secretariat, which organizes an annual meeting of all the affiliates, publishes a newsletter, and acts as a conduit through which the affiliates often share work and technical expertise. Each country is allowed just one company that can use the Gallup name, a choice recommended by the Secretariat and approved at the annual meeting of the affiliates.

When the CIPO began operations in Canada in 1941, Wilfred Sanders, a *Financial Post* journalist, became the first Canadian co-director. Originally, the Canadian studies were based on about 2,000 interviews with Canadians twenty-one years of age and over, living in about two hundred electoral districts in the country. Interviewers polled ten respondents in each district. Early tabulations of the results were subcontracted to IBM in Toronto, and the company issued about three releases each week, two Canadian and one from either a U.S. or a British Gallup survey.

At the end of the Second World War, the CIPO sample was halved, to 1,000 interviews. In 1958, it was cut to 750, but was raised to 1,000 again in 1974, when the Gallup omnibus service, which allows paying clients to tag on to the regular monthly survey, was beginning to pay financial dividends.

Because Gallup was the first major polling organization, the best-known, and for many years the only organization conducting public polls — as opposed to corporate market-research polls — Gallup's reputation always exceeded their performance. Despite the fact that late-campaign polls are the easiest to do, since most people are aware there is an election on and actually have a view to express, Gallup and the other firms are usually judged on the basis of those polls. The unreliability of polls between elections and earlier in campaigns is inevitably forgotten, and Gallup, like the other firms, tends to boast only of their final tallies. For the most part, they haven't been bad in this one simple category. They missed the winning Liberal margin by seven points in 1957, and the Tories' by five. For the next several elections Gallup was within a point or two, but in 1980 they overestimated the winning Liberals by four points and missed the Tories by four. Two days before that vote Gallup reported a gap of twenty points between Liberals and Tories, about eight points more than the actual result, prompting Joe Clark to wonder aloud if the results were tainted by Gallup's main customer, the *Toronto Star*, which supported the Liberals, and convincing out-going Treasury Board president Sinclair Stevens Gallup should be "seriously investigated" and polls should be banned during campaigns.

In May 1984, Gallup was again publicly criticized when their poll showed the Liberals up fourteen points, six points ahead of the Tories among decided voters, an unlikely shift of twenty-eight points in less than a month. Tory pollster Allan Gregg called the Gallup poll "dead wrong," and NDP national secretary Gerald Caplan said, "Gallup methodology is so screwed up that the results are beyond the realm of anything possibly happening in this country today."

Gallup recovered somewhat in calling the 1984 results accurately and wasn't that far off the mark in their final 1988 poll. But what will be remembered from that campaign is Gallup's dramatic, most say absurd, post-debate poll showing the Liberals holding a commanding twelve-point lead over the Tories two weeks before election day, a time when every other pollster had the Tories rapidly recovering from the immediate effects of John Turner's strong debate performance.

Gallup asks a single question in their monthly survey: "If a federal election were held today, which party's candidate do you think you would favor?" It is just one question among 150 to 200 in the Gallup omnibus. Many pollsters believe the one-question sampling can exaggerate real political opinion. Most others ask two or three questions to reduce the number of off-the-cuff responses and undecideds. Gallup argues, questionably, the higher proportion of "undecideds" they get is a reflection of the number of people who don't vote.

Gallup also uses the cluster technique in all of the major urban census areas, a method that leaves out vast, albeit sparsely populated, regions of the country, which tends to skew the results somewhat, creating a bias in favour of urban voters and against rural voters who, in many regions, tend to be Conservative supporters. If, for example, a sample design required eight respondents from northwestern Ontario, other pollsters, operating by telephone, would likely get a couple of respondents from Kenora, one from Rainy River, one from Dryden, and maybe three or four from Thunder Bay, but Gallup, using the cluster technique, would be inclined to get them all from Thunder Bay to save the cost of sending in-home interviewers around, even though the political attitudes in Thunder Bay vary greatly from those in Rainy River.

Because of Gallup's traditional pre-eminence in the polling field, however, politicians know that, even if they worry about the accuracy of the results, the public more readily accepts a Gallup poll than it does any other. That reality prompted then Justice minister Jean Chrétien, in December 1980, to release the results of three polls, worth $160,000, done for the government on the question of constitutional patriation. Chrétien had refused to release the polls until Gallup came out with a poll of their own showing Canadians opposed to unilateral patriation with an amending formula by an overwhelming margin of almost two to one. Chrétien's polls, however, showed the opposite, and the whole thing even prompted Pierre Trudeau, who rarely felt compelled to explain anything, to call a formal news conference to pooh-pooh the Gallup results.

In March 1981, Joe Clark said he was pleased that the Gallup showed his popular support up three points, to 37, but added, "We probably pay too much attention to this poll. It's shallow. Gallup is a notoriously weak polling organization."

Despite the criticisms, various lobby groups understand the weight a Gallup carries with the public. In 1982, for example, the pro-choice Canadian Abortion Rights Action League tacked a question onto a Gallup omnibus and were able to announce that 72 percent of Canadians supported the pro-choice position, and they had a Gallup to prove it. In fact, what they had was the response to a terribly biased question, which didn't prove anything. Respondents were polled on: "A decision on whether or not to perform an abortion should rest with the consenting patient and should be performed by a licensed physician in conformance with good medical practice."

Winnipeg pollster Greg Mason calls that "a classic case of the distorted question. Whether people favour abortion or not, there are few who would disagree that it or any other operation should be performed by a 'licensed physican in conformance with good medical practice.' Not many favour a quack doing abortions . . . or appendectomies, if they need to be done, for that matter. As a consequence, a significant majority appeared to favour abortion." Even Gallup realized they'd been had on that one and, in March 1984, turned down another request from CARAL to include an abortion question on their omnibus poll.

Gallup's credibility came under attack again in September 1986, with the leaking of the results of a recent Gallup commissioned by an unidentified person showing Jean Chrétien was favoured more than two-to-one over John Turner among those who said they had voted Liberal in the last election. (Turner, incidentally, was the constant "most popular leader" for years in this sort of Gallup popularity sweepstakes, until he actually got the job, after which he was replaced by Chrétien in the same out-of-office category.)

There were strong suspicions at the time that a Chrétien Liberal had commissioned the poll — which showed that Chrétien as leader would be fifteen points ahead of the Tories, while Turner was just five points ahead — prompting Peter Schmidt, head of the Gallup poll in Canada, to threaten to "blow out of the water" the person who commissioned the Chrétien questions. "This chap will not be in the same limelight in the future," Schmidt said. "We will not allow anyone to damage Gallup's reputation for integrity." In fact, Gallup did not reveal their customer's name.

This, of course, did not stop Gallup from asking what the *Winnipeg Free Press* called "tendentious questions in search of predictable answers" on behalf of pressure groups. The newspaper was responding to an advertisement in the *Globe and Mail* in September 1987, from a group called the Immigration Association of Canada, which announced it had hired Gallup to conduct a poll designed to elicit hostile comments about immigrants.

"Sure enough," read a *Free Press* editorial, "it asks the right questions and gets the desired answers. Question one purports to set out two views of immigration. One 'holds that Canada's immigration policy should be designed in the interests of the majority of Canadians,' the other that it should be designed 'to provide safe haven for the disadvantaged people of the world' and should not be concerned with 'employment qualifications of the entrants or the changing ethnic and cultural composition of the country.' Guess which option most of the respondents chose?

"The slanted questions in this poll, as in so many others, make it worthless as a measure of public opinion. The main question it raises is how the organizations which lend themselves to such tactics can make any claim to credibility," the editorial commented.

Which brings us, finally, to the 1988 election campaign and Gallup's role in it. Gallup vice-president Lorne Bozinoff, thirty-five, with a Ph.D. in marketing from the University of Toronto, had been with Gallup for two years and was experiencing his first federal election campaign. Despite his inexperience in the field, however, Bozinoff considers himself an expert in Canadian politics. "If you understand politics, you'll see marketing and politics are very similar," he says. "Not in a derogatory way, not the hard sell we associate with marketing . . . but politics is looking at people's needs and how to meet those needs, selling ideas, selling leaders is sort of like selling a product."

So, too, is selling polls. To keep up with the competition then,

Bozinoff decided Gallup would poll weekly for the first time, which meant resorting to telephone polls, not just the in-home interviews, which have been the mainstay of the Gallup technique. He angrily dismisses arguments that weekly campaign polling means skimping on the normal checks and balances as a "first-year-undergraduate type of criticism. . . . Now I don't want to sound arrogant, but I think after fifty years in business we can get a little beyond this. Gallup does not cut corners, no matter what the poll. . . . Those criticisms are just ignorance. It just shows a lack of understanding and it obviously bothers me when I hear these criticisms. . . . It's insulting." But some people with far more experience in polling than Bozinoff has have made these observations — referring not just to Gallup, but to all the firms conducting weekly campaign public polling. Their objection is simply that the quick turn-around required does not allow pollsters to do the proper call-backs. So there is corner-cutting to meet the weekly deadlines.

Bozinoff cut a deal with the several subscribing newspapers to provide weekly polls. In addition, his deal with the *Toronto Star* was to provide some special polls, one on Metro Toronto, for example, and another published the day after the English-language debate, asking Canadians if the Liberals would be better off with Chrétien instead of Turner as their leader. It showed the Liberals ahead 49 to 30, with Chrétien, potentially a 212-seat majority. "The overall conclusion from this data is that, with a popular leader, the Liberal party could easily regain its position as Canada's dominant party," said Bozinoff in the *Star* story. Even Liberal opponents, such as New Democrat Gerald Caplan, found the poll, coming in mid-campaign when there was no chance of a leadership change — despite a CBC story about a supposed coup — "irresponsible."

Bozinoff's methodology was seriously biased against Turner. Respondents were also asked how the other parties would fare with different leaders (the Tories would go up a point; the NDP, down six), but those results weren't reported in the *Star*. Most likely they weren't reported because Bozinoff did not offer respondents any specific options for Tory or NDP leader as he did for the Liberals. Asked about this at the time, Bozinoff said, "With the other two parties we didn't use specific names because we couldn't think of an alternative."

Asked if he thought this was a fair question in the midst of a campaign, Bozinoff said, "Well, it was sparked by last week's talk about a two-party system." But was it fair? He didn't say. In a post-campaign interview, however, Bozinoff boasted, "We were the only pollster that never had the Liberals disappearing in the whole length of the campaign."

Ottawa Citizen columnist Marjorie Nichols, a tireless critic of the polls, noted that one of Bozinoff's mid-campaign seat projections gave the Tories 65 percent of the House of Commons seats with just 40 percent of the popular vote. When Nichols called the pollster for an explanation — no government in Canadian history has ever won a majority with 40 percent of the popular vote — Bozinoff told her his computer extrapolations were "conservative" compared to those done by Mulroney's pollsters. "It came as a surprise to me that Gallup's man would be exchanging information with the PM's men," said Nichols, "but then I confess to ignorance about the code of conduct for the polling business."

Gallup, and every other polling organization, professes to maintain complete security until the results of their polls are published. In truth, the security is not complete. Veteran Liberal campaigner Keith Davey says, "In all the years I worked on campaigns we always knew, in advance, what the numbers were." And Conservative campaign strategist John Tory said they knew because the pollster tipped them off the day before. That's how Mulroney was able to respond with such assurance to the November 7 so-called rogue Gallup poll.

The question of security is normally not that significant, but in this campaign, with the high stakes over free trade, at least as perceived by Canada's business community, it became a major point of concern.

Brokerage houses called polling firms with offers of up to $60,000 for advance information. All the pollsters deny giving or selling this information, but all admit they were asked for it. "I was told some guy made $25 million on the market," says Bozinoff. "To make that kind of money, you've got to move a lot of money around. Gallup did have a major impact on the dollar. It dropped 1.5 cents. That's a big amount if you follow these things. Millions were at stake here. One brokerage firm did ask us conceptually how they could become a subscriber the way the newspapers do. I told them I didn't think it was ethical."

Bozinoff says that, with a twenty-four-hour market, all somebody had to do was go down to the *Star* at midnight and get the first editions, "then run over to his office and make a few deals with Japan, or whatever."

Insight's Michael Marzolini says, "People were phoning us too. The *New York Times* even blamed the initial decline in the dollar on our Sunday-night poll.... We had calls from Americans, Morgan Trust for one, and a call from a vice-president of Merrill-Lynch asking about a rumour he'd heard that I had a poll showing the Liberals in first place."

Michael Adams of Environics says his firm was called, "but we were not receptive to this sort of thing." Adams was criticized by some of his competitors, however, for doing parallel campaign polling for a large investment house. "We were hired, and I'm trying to be circumspect about this, by a company interested in public opinion to do survey work during the election for their own use," says Adams. "That's not the same thing as selling advance information."

Angus Reid says, "I heard from brokerage houses that never returned my calls in the past. Pollsters could have made a lot of money. There were lots of big offers, but it would have been completely illegal, immoral, and irresponsible."

That depends who you talk to. Ira Katzin, director of research at the Toronto brokerage firm Merit Investment Corp., says, "I would certainly consider it insider trading. If I knew beforehand what the next release of the pollster was going to be, it would certainly be a great thing to know. You'd have to buy index options, which means you buy an option on the stock exchange index ... but a fortune could be made if the numbers had a major impact on the market as they did in this campaign with free trade."

But Stanley Beck, chairman of the Ontario Securities Commission, disagrees, "I'd take all that with a grain of salt. I don't think the polls really did a hell of a lot to the market. That's hard to know. It's interesting, but you'll hear a lot of chatter. That it's possible to buy the Toronto 35 index options, but you're gambling on the entire market to go up. You might get a blip in interest rates the same day, or the Ayatollah may do something. It's a crap shoot.... I don't think the market did move all that much."

In fact, the day after the Gallup, the TSE dropped 75.09 points, making it the second-biggest drop of 1988 to that point. In addition, the dollar closed Monday at 80.94 cents U.S., down more than 0.5 cents from Friday's close and more than 2 cents below its level a little more than a week earlier when the Liberals first shot into the lead in election polls. After publication of the first post-debate polls measuring the Liberal surge, the dollar dropped almost 1.5 cents, its worst single-day performance ever. Sherry Atkinson, chief economist at giant stockbroker Burns Fry Ltd., was quoted as saying, "If the . . . trade deal is ripped up, I think the dollar will go below 80 cents. And the stock-market drop we've seen would be only the beginning."

Bozinoff insists that the mix-and-match approach they practised in the campaign, using both telephone and in-home interviews, is a statistically valid technique. "I'm not going to tell you all our secrets, but the phone sample is matched to our personal-interviewing sample. . . . The personal-interview sample is the best sample you can get anywhere. . . . It doesn't rely on a phone number. The house is there or it's not. Furthermore, people are a lot more likely to open the door when you knock than they are to pick up a telephone when it's ringing. My feeling is they're much less likely to refuse to be interviewed if you're there in person. That's why we do it in person if we can. Sometimes we can't." When doing weekly campaign polls, for example.

Bozinoff says Gallup has a complete collection of city maps for the whole country on microfiche from Statistics Canada. "We just randomly draw a set of those maps and we mark on them with a little X where the interviewer is supposed to start.

Say we're sending him to Gander, Newfoundland. We have a map, not of all Gander, just a few blocks. We mark which block they are to do with a little X showing where to start. We don't want them to pick the house. They might say this is a nice big house, I'll start here, or I don't want to go to this run-down house. . . . We just randomly pick the X. We don't know what these blocks look like. We're in Toronto. We always put the X in a certain corner just because it's easier, but in essence it's random because we don't know what's there . . . and we put an arrow and say, walk in this direction. . . .

"There's an art and there's a science to this business," says Bozinoff. "The science at Gallup we've perfected. We're as close as we feel we can ever get in terms of being accurate."

Bozinoff describes the company's media polling as "5 percent of our business, but 95 percent of our [public] awareness. . . . We wouldn't be Gallup if we didn't do that . . . and because it's Gallup it attracts more attention."

They certainly attracted attention in 1988. No doubt about that. Too much for their own good.

10

"Gloomy Gus" Reid

Nova Scotia Liberal leader Vince MacLean was remarkably sanguine as he sat in his campaign bus, entering the picturesque fishing hamlet of Eastern Passage nestled along the rocky shore at the mouth of Halifax harbour, just outside of Dartmouth.

He had reason to hope. With five days left until election day, things were looking good. The crowds had been large, the polls showed it was a tight contest, the media had been positive. It looked as if the ten-year regime of Tory premier John Buchanan was counting down.

And then the phone rang.

It was MacLean's press aide Jim Vibert calling the bus from party headquarters directly across the harbour in Halifax. Lightning had struck. An Angus Reid poll showed the Tories eleven points ahead, 45 to 34 in decided votes, with the NDP at 20 percent. Worse, the Tories had momentum. They'd gained four points from an earlier Reid poll, while the Liberals had slipped three.

"That poll cost us the election," says MacLean flatly. "It cost us several seats. . . . Ever since John Turner fired him [Reid] as the pollster for Turner's team, we [Liberals] have been getting bad results, and I think people should know about it."

Losers, of course, always hate the polls. MacLean is hardly the first politician to blame a pollster for his defeat. But he may be the first politician who has a point.

For when the votes were counted, the Liberals lost a squeaker, just three points behind. Buchanan had gone into the election with 40 of the 52 seats. MacLean had 6. When the dust cleared on September 6, 1988, the Tories had fallen 12 seats, to 28; the Liberals gained 15, to 21;

and with two New Democrats and one independent, Buchanan's once-massive majority was hanging by a thread.

"When you're that close, all you've got to do is take two seats from the government, it's a tie," says MacLean, then rattles off the names of several ridings he says the Liberals could have won had it not been for Reid. Indeed, MacLean's party lost nine seats by fewer than five hundred votes, three by fewer than three hundred.

"What happened once the poll came out is the media became, well — 'Is it right?' you know, that was the only question. It dogged me the next four days. . . . This wasn't like any other bad poll that I had gotten beforehand," he says. "It was different in that there was no time to react, no time for people to settle down, and no time to correct it."

The poll shattered the morale of Liberal workers, and MacLean spent the final forty-eight hours non-stop, delivering forty-four speeches, each one in a different location. But it wasn't quite enough, not in a province where it's critical to be on the government side.

"A few thousand votes spread around would have tipped the scales," says MacLean. "And it's very important in a place like Guysborough, which relies on the government to get its road paved, or Yarmouth or Bridgewater. These are seats that are influenced directly by politics and political patronage."

In late August, Tory candidate Joe Burke, with Buchanan sitting quietly by, nodding his head in approval, told his nomination meeting in Sydney that the riding's Independent MLA Paul MacEwan couldn't get any money for projects because he wasn't a Conservative. "I'm saying that the people of Cape Breton–Nova, if they want improvements, we must get with the government to get those improvements."

A few weeks after the election, when the voters of Cape Breton West had booted out Tory incumbent Donald MacLeod and elected Liberal Russell MacKinnon, a local contractor was ordered by the government to stop work on a new school. "The guy was clearing the site and preparing the foundation," said MacLean. "We raised such a stink about it that three weeks later they had to call them back and get them started working again. But it shows you what happens here if you don't vote with the government."

MacLean's campaign manager, Ron MacDonald, now Liberal MP for Dartmouth, says that, going into the campaign, their party polls showed "that the one thing which might kill us was the perception people had we couldn't win. We had to get them to start thinking of us as winners. . . . And by the end we felt comfortable we'd win at least a minority. The worst poll we did in the last week we were within three points of the government, a Goldfarb poll. We had momentum, and we went into the last week feeling nothing could happen to change it. But Angus Reid was the disaster we didn't think should happen."

"When the headline in the *Daily News* read 'Tories Surge Ahead,' it was the darkest morning of my life," says MacDonald. I knew it was wrong, but how could we convince people this late in the campaign it was a bum poll? His methods are bad. His polls don't accurately reflect, and never have, where the Liberal party is at. He consistently polled the Liberals lower than other pollsters. I don't believe for an instant he's a friend of the Liberal party. That poll cost us the government.

"In a close, volatile election, a pollster can have a tremendous impact. He can play God. I think in that election he [Reid] saw the opportunity to play God and he issued the numbers," says MacDonald. "Why didn't he issue them on Monday, and another firm could do a poll to check them? He did it on Thursday when we had absolutely no chance to refute. I think it was unprofessional and irresponsible. . . . He interfered with the democratic process."

Even Reid himself was concerned enough by his August 26–30 telephone survey of 601 Nova Scotians to go back for another 300 before releasing it. Ron MacDonald says: "We called Reid to say we were concerned about his numbers, that our campaign was going well and it was a tight election and this could affect our chances. He said he was recrunching his numbers. He said he was surprised at the major change in voter intentions. . . . We knew it wasn't good for us."

Reid himself was unapologetic. In 1984 he was publicly predicting he'd soon replace Goldfarb as the federal Liberal pollster. But it didn't happen, and Reid admits he was bitter, but he denies accusations from MacLean and other Liberals that he's skewing his numbers to make the party look bad. In fact, never short on gall, Reid claims his poll actually helped MacLean because anti-government voters left the NDP and voted for the Liberals. How Reid would know this is uncertain, since he didn't do a post-campaign study on the votes, but it doesn't stop him from saying it. It's part of the reason Reid has become not only one of the best-known pollsters in Canada, but certainly, in the polling fraternity — and the Liberal party — the least admired.

"MacLean has argued their polls showed something different," says Reid. "I checked with some of my friends and found out they did no polls."

Not so, says MacLean, declaring that the party had province-wide polls from Goldfarb and Omnifacts, a Halifax firm, and constituency polls from another regional pollster, Criterion.

"I'm not one of those who believe the measure of public opinion is a neutral force," says Reid. "I think it causes things to happen. In that sense, I would probably agree with Vince MacLean. Whether it caused things to happen in his particular campaign or not, who knows? And so what if it does? I think the overall public-opinion process is far more important than the fate of one Nova Scotia politician."

Reid doesn't seem to care what people think of him. He does care, however, what they think of his work.

"There are an awful lot of arrows being shot at me and I'm not one to take the arrows lying down. I fought back," he says. "And I suppose that makes me appear anti-Liberal. Well, so be it. The fact of the matter is my great-grandfather was a Liberal MLA in Saskatchewan for twenty years.... I come from an Irish Catholic family in Saskatchewan. My mother is probably more Liberal than Catholic. I've got Liberal blood flowing in my veins, whether I like it or not, and this short-term skirmish with John Turner and his peope is absolute bullshit."

University of Toronto political-science professor Nelson Wiseman, a university classmate of Reid's, says, "He was a Conservative then. He was very active in the PC party." And moments after talking about his Liberal bloodlines, Reid was boasting that senior Tories had recently made overtures to him to replace Allan Gregg as the party pollster. "I basically said I'm not interested.... But this is a wing of the Conservative party which has some strong feelings. It really didn't have to do with the quality of Gregg's work. It was the fact that Decima is part of the Big Blue Machine power structure that other forces within the party would like to knock off.... That's one of the things that hurt the Liberals, was allowing Goldfarb to be so dominant for so long that it basically ended up allowing this dry rot to set into the Liberal party," he says.

Reid has some harsh words for Gregg too. "Polling is becoming demystified now that there are more pollsters out there, unlike the old days when there were just Goldfarb and Gregg, and you kind of had to book six months in advance to even get in to see them. I'm surprised they didn't have a little altar there. Now that there are the rest of us guys out there as journeymen, trying to do our job, these guys aren't seen as the icons they were.

"Gregg would argue that we're neanderthals, a C-minus player involved in a very simplistic surveying who doesn't really deserve comment. Allan did an interview with a Winnipeg publication which did a feature on me, and Gregg is quoted as saying, 'My mother told me if you can't say anything nice about somebody, don't say anything at all.'

"These people at Decima use every opportunity to smirk away about this guy out in Winnipeg. It's part of the myth-building process. . . . In commercial terms, he's really running scared."

In September 1987, Reid threatened to sue the equally outspoken Hamilton Liberal MP Sheila Copps who accused him in an interview on CBC-TV's "The Journal" of working for the NDP and having been fired by Turner for blabbing to the media. Reid dismissed the accusation as "trash," but had Winnipeg lawyer Donald A. Primeau fire off a letter to Copps, threatening "to commence defamation proceedings" unless she provided "a complete and unqualified retraction . . . together with a sincere apology to Dr. Reid" within ten days.

At the time, Reid had the NDP at 44 and the Liberals at 29. Gallup, however, had it: NDP, 37; Liberals, 36. Both pollsters had the Tories in the low 20s.

As for Copps, she said in an interview, "I absolutely don't deny any of my accusations."

"Regardless of how I feel," says Reid, "the question is, is that in some way affecting the nature of the public-opinion polling that I'm doing? . . . That's the implication. But I think that accusation, which speaks to the very heart of professional trust in our business, is where, you know, that's what the Copps accusation was all about, and I seriously considered going to court over that."

To demonstrate his impartial survey technique, Reid pulled out a document called 'For the Record,' which contains comparisons of party-preference polls with both Gallup and Environics between January 1986 and September 1988. The sample contains results of thirty-three Gallup, twenty-four Reid, and twelve Environics polls. The Reid polls show the Liberals either the lowest of the three parties or tied for low twenty-one out of twenty-four times. Gallup has the Liberals lowest once; Environics, twice. The Reid polls have the NDP lowest six times and tied for last twice. They have the Liberals at the top twice, but the NDP in first place thirteen times and tied for first three times. Reid has the Tories at the top fifteen times and at the bottom or tied for last five times. In short, Reid consistently finds the Liberals lower and the NDP higher than the other pollsters.

At least part of the reason for this result stems from Reid's controversial methodology. He asks respondents which of the three leaders they prefer before asking which of the three parties they would support. Given Turner's consistent unpopularity, argue Reid's critics in the polling industry, making the respondents think about Turner first contaminates their party preference. Reid, of course, disagrees.

"We developed that technique in the 1984 general election, working for John Turner, and of course in doing 20,000 interviews you play around with a lot of different approaches. It turned out that's the very best one. . . . Keith Davey will tell you in 1984 our numbers were spot on the money, spot, spot, spot on the money, in terms of what happened not only nationally but also regionally. We use that technique because we think it works . . . regionally," Reid says. "I believe it does a disservice to the system to think we can talk about parties in the same generic terms we used to talk about them back in the age of print. A party is its leader, philosophically, theoretically, sociologically. . . . Leadership is a party's central dynamic. . . . Why did the Liberals soar in the middle of the [1988] campaign? It had nothing to do with a change in Liberal policy. It had to do with the fact that John Turner looked good in the debates."

Michael Adams of Environics has been one of the toughest critics of Reid's methodology, and to demonstrate how intense these disagreements are, when CTV's Mike Duffy did a show on political polling, both men agreed to be interviewed, separately. They wouldn't come on the show together.

Winnipeg pollster Greg Mason says, "This business is like any other business. One has stars that raise huge egos and so they tend to take shots at each other.

"Reid will typically put his questions at the end of a survey under the argument that what you do is you present people with policy choices, so you're talking about health care, tenants, the whole range of issues, so they get in their mind how they feel about things in general, and then ask how they're going to vote.

"That's quite different from what Environics does," says Mason. "They put the political question right up front and then talk about policy. There's a lot of debate, but the consensus is you should put your political question right up front. The stuff that comes before really tends to influence how people would vote. And the stuff up front really reflects a kind of summary judgment without having thought through a very complex process.

"Either way, it doesn't make a lot of difference as long as you're consistent in all your polls," he says.

In a recent interview, Reid said, "[It's] healthy we have some differences. . . . If we were all a bunch of goddamn lemmings, everyone doing things the same way, that would skew the results. Good polling, like good science, involves repeated measures and involves measures from different perspectives."

He said asking the voter preference questions right off the top doesn't make any sense. "You've got to think of the context of the interview. You're at home eating dinner and the phone rings and there's an interviewer on the line who says, 'Hi, who do you plan to vote for?' . . . You probably weren't sitting there over dinner having this little political discussion with your family. You probably were a lot smarter than that, watching TV or farting, or whatever. So you can't begin that way. You have to develop some rapport. No one begins with the question of voting intentions. . . . You end up with too many undecideds. That's why Greg Mason had 40 or 45 percent undecided in one of his Manitoba polls. . . . People say, 'Just fuck off, I haven't even thought of this stuff.'"

In the 1952 U.S. presidential elections, Gallup demonstrated that questions about party preference and leadership preference garner different results. Republican Dwight Eisenhower was immensely more popular than his Democratic opponent, Adlai Stevenson, and when respondents were asked to choose between the two men, Eisenhower had a substantial 47 to 40 lead. But when respondents were asked to choose between the two parties, it was almost a dead heat — Republicans, 45; Democrats, 44. Liberals argued that Turner suffered this same syndrome, only in reverse, since the party did better when respondents were asked to choose the party names, and worse, because of Turner's personal unpopularity, when Reid put the leaders' names up front. In the United States, of course, the popular vote counts much more directly than it does in Canada, as voters choose which of the two major candidates will become president. Here, popular votes count only indirectly, since the vote tally in each individual constituency determines winners and losers. Since many parties have won an election in the Canadian system but lost the popular vote, the argument against Reid's method of putting the leader's name up front is that it inflates the importance of the leader beyond what it really is.

It wasn't that long ago when Reid desperately wanted to become the Liberal party's official pollster, replacing Goldfarb, and for a time it appeared as if he would get his wish. Reid first met Turner one early summer day in 1983 at the cottage of his brother-in-law, former Liberal cabinet minister John Reid, near Kenora in northwestern Ontario, less than a mile from Turner's wilderness retreat. It was a time when Trudeau was still in power but was expected to retire soon, and the two Reids and Turner chatted about the possibility of Turner making a political come-back. That resulted in a meeting in Turner's downtown law office the next month, and Reid was subsequently hired by Turner to do some preliminary polling for him to determine his potential delegate appeal. In the spring of 1984, leading up to and during the actual leadership convention, Reid continued to poll for Turner. When Turner won, Reid expected to get the job as party pollster."

"After Turner won the leadership there was a period of about two weeks in which Turner had to make a lot of decisions," says Reid. "One of them was who was going to do the polling. . . . He couldn't make the decision, so he ended up going with both of us [Reid and Goldfarb].

"From the beginning of what turned out to be our rather short relationship, John Turner and myself didn't see eye to eye. I felt extremely bitter after the leadership convention. Here I'd been standing by this guy Turner, like it or not, and all of a sudden I had the weight of the party, or to be more accurate, the weight of the Toronto mob, weighing down on me. So I headed into the 1984 campaign, not as the Liberal pollster, but as a guy who was hired to do the daily tracking."

In June 1984, Reid told the Montreal *Gazette* he had been tabbed to replace Goldfarb as Liberal pollster. Reid, mocking about "Government by Goldfarb," said, apparently in earnest, "I plan a very low profile. John Turner is not a man to set policy through polls." In an interview with the *Globe*, Reid repeated his claim that the Liberals were worried about Goldfarb's image of running the government by polls. "My own style is to conduct high-quality research that can be fed into the grist mill. . . . I'm an expert in reading the Canadian public, not an expert in proposing creative solutions." He said it is a "conflict of interest" for pollsters to recommend policy. The pollster who also advises a client "isn't detached enough to accurately, objectively, read the public."

Right after the 1984 campaign ended in disaster for the Liberals, Reid conducted a $75,000 election autopsy — "which I wasn't paid for until 1987" — then wrote a campaign synopsis, "which I did gratis, really, as part of the purging process for myself. At the end, I was very satisfied with my polling. I felt the Liberal party and John Turner in particular had been unable to make a break with the past. . . . The experience left a bad taste in my mouth about how polling interacts with internal party politics."

Reid says his "contractual obligations" were completed after that poll. In late November he held his final meeting with Turner in his Commons office. "It was a bizarre meeting. I was sitting there, talking about the post-election poll, and how all of our tracking had shown that Turner had blown it in terms of perceptions of Canadians that he had a feel for the average person and that he could make decisions on public issues.

"He had started really high in public perception on these and had gone steadily downhill," says Reid. "And while that one-hour meeting was going on, the phone kept ringing and Turner would lean back and get on the phone and be berating some person on the other end of the line. He was trying to rent a ski chalet for his family. I was frankly personally offended at the way this man would treat obviously some receptionist or booking person on the other end of the line.

"I was simply dumbstruck, in awe of the contrast of what I was saying to him and his own personal behaviour at the time."

Just after the new year, the Liberals gathered in Montebello for their own post-mortem and Reid was invited by Axworthy to attend. "I didn't get a nickel for doing that. I told them they had to wipe the slate clean, had to begin setting new policy now, not to slide back into the traditional opposition mode. And they had to begin a process of revitalization of their policies."

Unfortunately, he came out and told reporters much the same thing, an action that did not endear him to the party elite. Around the same time, Reid delivered a speech in Ottawa in which he also criticized the party, the Senate, and the leader.

"Well, I was told, but I wasn't there, that Turner hit the roof and shouted for anyone to hear who was there that the goddam Reid is fired. Well, when does one quit and when is one fired?

"I had frankly lost total respect for this individual, and since I'd already made the decision to walk over and become a public pollster, to be true to one's self I couldn't stand up after the '84 campaign and say all sorts of wonderful things about John Turner. That would be dishonest and immoral."

David Walker, Reid's former partner, says, "Traditionally, of course, market research is considered confidential. Angus does not always recognize that fact. He sometimes talks too much."

Walker, now a Liberal MP, says Reid was "really hurt" when he wasn't made official party pollster. Walker blames Davey. "Davey came in and he was up to his old tricks. He and Goldfarb go a long way back, so he put the blocks to Angus. It was really frustrating for Angus to come so close yet fail. Davey is one of the old school that you do what you have to do to win."

Reid said the problem had to do with the centralization of power within the party, "the development of this very tight clique. That's why the selection of a pollster is so absolutely important. He who controls the polling, to some extent controls the party. You control that because polling in the last fifteen years has acted like the principal point of legitimacy for policy actions.

"That's part of the reason why it became such a heavy issue in 1984 between Goldfarb and I. The real issue was not this battle of the pollsters . . . but who was going to be controlling a party. It was on that subject that John Turner could really never make a decision. It wasn't so much that Keith Davey or Tom Axworthy or whoever liked Marty more than Angus Reid. Marty was their guy. If Marty was there, they'd be there."

It turned out that Marty was there and Reid wasn't. So he went back to Winnipeg to attempt to expand his five-year-old firm. It didn't take long for his resentment to show. On January 5, 1985, Reid told Canadian Press that the NDP could surge ahead of the Liberals by six to twelve points as the second choice of Canadians over the next several months. "It's too soon to tell whether or not we're going to see a sustained third-place position for the Liberal party," he said. "But clearly it does raise questions not only about Turner but also about the whole structure of the Liberal party right now in Canada." He predicted "the next eight to ten months are going to be critical" for the struggle between the Liberals and the NDP for second place.

At the end of 1985, Reid announced he was going to become a "national pollster" to compete against Gallup. "I think there have been a number of people in the industry, in the media and people in government [who] have felt for some years that probably the time has come to have more than one national polling service," said Reid. He promised six surveys in 1986 and a faster turn-around than Gallup through a special electronic hook-up with his company offices in Halifax, Montreal, Toronto, Winnipeg, Regina, Calgary, Edmonton, and Vancouver.

In September 1986, Reid was predicting a Liberal minority after the next federal election. "If I was a betting man, and if the numbers we see today hold true, you're probably looking at a Liberal minority government," he said. Eight months later, Turner's "minority" government had disappeared and Reid was the first to put the NDP in top spot (a first for the NDP as well). By July, after other pollsters also had the NDP leading, Reid was predicting the party would win at least a hundred seats in the next election. "We're not dealing with a one-day wonder," he said. "And we're not dealing with a blip. We're dealing with a party that will gain up to one hundred seats in the next election, and maybe more."

Reid said NDP support was "hardening . . . [and] leading to increased momentum, rather than any sort of screeching to a halt." He said voters' experiments with the NDP were akin to "glue sticking or cement drying," adding the only way NDP support could collapse would be if Mulroney or Turner "were to step aside, giving their parties a fresh face." Both leaders declined his invitation. By September 1987, a Canadian Press computer analysis of Reid's numbers showed how silly the whole exercise can get. It resulted in a minority NDP government, with 134 seats; the Liberals, 93; and the troubled Tories, 55, only 5 in Quebec, compared to 22 for the Liberals and 48 for the NDP, a party that has yet to win its first seat in Quebec, let alone sweep the country's second-largest province.

While Reid seems to spend considerable energy battling with the other national pollsters he also gets into the odd dust-up with those on his home turf. In March 1988, Reid was quoted in a *Winnipeg Free Press* story — identified both by name and as an unnamed "city pollster" — accusing the then NDP provincial government of playing favourites with survey contracts, the sort of thing the federal Liberals did for Reid when they were in power and he was first starting out.

The story accused the government specifically of giving at least 65 percent of its $500,000 in survey work, untendered, to Viewpoints

Research Ltd., a new firm set up by a former cabinet employee and two other New Democrats. David Gotthilf, a former $35,000-a-year employee with the provincial executive council, is secretary-treasurer of the firm, while Ron Pradinuk, owner of Pradinuk Advertising, which billed the province $1.7 million for advertising work during the previous six years, is vice-president. Ginny Devine, wife of current Manitoba NDP leader Gary Doer, is also with the firm.

Reid, quoted as an "industry source" in the news story, argued that Viewpoints was involved in a conflict-of-interest situation because the company did market-impact studies on government advertisements prepared by Pradinuk Advertising. Later in the story, Reid, quoted by name, said it was time to investigate the relationship between the NDP government, Viewpoints Research, and Pradinuk Advertising. "It's outright patronage," complained Reid. "Here's a new company set up by a former staff of the premier getting the lion's share of the business when my ten-year-old company can't even bid on government work because they won't tell us." Reid said his firm billed the province $15,000 in 1987 out of its national billings of $6.5 million.

Asked about the story in a 1989 interview in his Winnipeg office, the former U.S. consulate building there, Reid said, "I'm not going to comment on that." Then he went on for fifteen minutes, explaining how it wasn't personal about Gotthilf or his staff — "I've never even met the guy . . . but I just felt that as a national pollster with headquarters here and with twenty-five or thirty staff, that some of the patterns were unfair. One of them was on the board of the Manitoba Telephone System and they were doing research for them." Reid himself did some work for the NDP government while serving as a director for eighteen months of A.E. McKenzie Co. Ltd., a provincial crown corporation. "I got so tired of what I saw, I quit," he says. "At one point, I considered moving out of Manitoba as a result of the lack of tendering. We went for a year without seeing a single offer to tender on, so I wrote the premier and quit.

"But I share the concerns in that *Free Press* story about having an ad agency that owns part of a market-research firm that in part is doing the evaluation of advertising that firm is doing," he said. "You don't have to be stupid [sic] to realize that that is a conflict of interest. But I had no axe to grind."

Dave Gotthilf disagrees. He blames Reid for the story. "It's factually incorrect. Those figures, I wish they were true. In the year they were talking about, we actually lost money, and in fact, we weren't the major supplier of government research, Criterion Research was." (Criterion, now the second-largest survey firm in Winnipeg, was founded by former Reid employees who left after a bitter dispute with him.)

"We did some government work," said Gotthilf, "and I used to be a government employee. But beyond that, there's not much truth to it. The problem Angus had with government . . . is that he talks too much to the press. When you're dealing with sensitive material, governments are inclined to not want to give information to people who have a tendency to blurt it out holus-bolus without any kind of restrictions. He's put himself in a difficult spot. His agenda was to get back at the government for what he perceived to be unfair allocation of contracts."

Gotthilf concedes the government handed out some "untendered contracts in particularly sensitive areas, but they were allocated to two or three suppliers fairly equitably. . . . But we bid against Angus on some contracts. He was bidding higher than everybody else and he didn't win. It's sour grapes."

Ginny Devine says that now, with the Tories in power, their firm has not been asked to bid on a single contract. Either Decima, or the local firm, Western Opinion Research, which has Tory ties, is doing most of the government work now, she says. "Maybe some of it is tendered, but it hasn't been offered to us."

Reid's style, of course, has not always endeared him to his polling colleagues or, for that matter, to some of his clients, but he's long been a darling of the media. He's outspoken, brash, and most of all, accessible. Two former senior *Maclean's* magazine writers said Reid used to give them "all sorts of good information. . . . He was so anxious to get the contract with *Maclean's* [which ultimately went to Decima] he used to feed us stuff from other polls he was doing. It was great for us."

Unlike other pollsters, in fact, Reid allows journalists from Southam to actually participate in helping form survey questions, a practice condemned by other pollsters. In an April 1988 feature on Reid, "the new bad boy" of the industry, in the Montreal *Gazette*, Goldfarb objected to Reid's dubious practice of allowing Southam journalists to have a hand in drafting the questionnaire. "A poll like that isn't a poll," he said.

Reid says he is simply applying a little more art to polling, where

Goldfarb is too rigidly scientific. "We try to set a context with our questionnaire. We try to simulate what is going on in the voter's mind in an actual campaign. They think about issues, then they judge leaders, and then they vote."

Sometimes, however, this practice can undermine the credibility of Reid polls. In August 1987, Southam journalist Ken MacQueen reported the findings of a Reid–Southam poll that purported to show that Canadians were no longer frightened by the old socialist bogeyman. Respondents were asked a series of questions on NDP policy, and the results were reflected in such headlines as, "NDP Not So Scary, Poll Finds." Perhaps not, but you couldn't really tell it by this poll. What's more, MacQueen, who covered the NDP for Southam and wrote the poll story, also helped Reid write the questions. MacQueen is a fine journalist, but he is not a pollster.

"Guys like Marty [Goldfarb] claim it's terrible we'd ever allow a journalist to have anything to do with the phrasing of a question," says Reid. "I don't think it's terrible. We try to get our input from as many sources as we can."

The problem in this survey was that questions phrased specific NDP policies as vague generalities. Before answering a series of questions on policies, respondents were asked: "According to a lot of opinion polls, the federal New Democrats now have more public support than they have ever had before and people are paying more attention to the party's policies. Regardless of which federal party you yourself favor right now, I'd like to get your opinion about some NDP policies."

The preamble itself creates an unmistakable bias in favour of the NDP by telling people, who may or may not have known, that the party has "more public support than . . . ever before."

Worse, when the interviewers get to the actual policy questions, most of them are not exclusively NDP policies at all. Of the eight policy questions, only two were really specific NDP policies — pulling out of NATO and the nationalization of banks — and the party got its lowest rating on those two, 33 percent and 28 percent support, respectively. All the other questions garnered support from a low of 51 percent to a high of 80 percent (that's for "changing the tax system so high-income people pay more tax and low-income people pay less tax," a proposition all three major parties support).

On day-care, respondents were not asked how they felt about the actual NDP policy of free, universal, government-run day-care. Instead, they were asked if they supported or opposed, "Creating a

national daycare policy that would provide affordable daycare services for all families that require it." Not surprisingly, 72 percent
thought this was a swell idea. But NDP policy has no requirements at
all. It's universal. Period.

In March 1989, Reid sold 60 percent interest in his polling firm to
Southam Inc. No price was announced, but it was for around $4.5
million. Reid says the deal will allow him more muscle in the U.S.
market. "There's an opportunity with free trade to work increasingly
on a continental basis — it was there before free trade and I think it's
going to accelerate after free trade." Reid, however, continues to head
his four companies: the public-opinion polling division, Angus Reid
Associates Inc., with headquarters in Winnipeg; Toronto-based
Hutchinson-Reid Ltd., which does research and consulting on consumer products; Agristudies Canwest, which supplies marketing and
policy research to the food and agriculture industries; and Access
Survey Research, an umbrella polling division with centres in
Canada and the United States. Reid had billings of $6.1 million in the
fiscal year ended August 31, 1988, and projected about $7.5 million
for 1989. Only about 5 percent of it comes from his public political
polling, for which he is best known.

   Now that Southam actually has a major stake in the Reid poll, we
can expect to see even more direct involvement by the media chain in
Reid polls, the questionable practice of meshing the journalist's and
the pollster's functions as if they were the same and required the same
skills.

When all is said and done, however, the main issue with Reid comes
back to his relationship with the federal Liberals. When he worked
for them during the 1984 campaign, he became known as "Gloomy
Gus," because his scenarios were always worse than Goldfarb's. It
turned out that Reid was right.

   But Reid-watchers note what they claim is a pattern of Reid polls
coming out just when things look good for Liberals. There was, of
course, the Nova Scotia poll. But, in April 1988, the day the Liberals
were gathering for a convention in Windsor, Ontario, newspaper
headlines read, "Liberals Last," the result of a Reid poll showing the
party had fallen to third place.

   Winnipeg North Centre Liberal MP David Walker, Reid's former
partner, who actually sold the first Reid polls to three Southam

newspapers in Ontario during the 1985 provincial election, says, "Angus is brilliant at selling services to clients. The best there is. The media loves him, too, because he's willing to take people on. He's great at smelling out a story. And he's always willing to be quoted.

"But Angus and Turner were never friends. They never warmed up to each other." Asked if Reid was biased against Turner and the Liberals, Walker says, "Against John Turner, definitely. There's something personal there. Against the Liberals, well I'm not so sure. Angus jumps back and forth and this upsets partisans who see themselves as part of a team. He'll become friendly with the Tories when they're in. In the West, he makes friends with the NDP. . . . He talks too much."

Reid now says he believes in "the separation of church and state." He says public pollsters shouldn't be doing party work. Yet, in 1984, he was publicly lusting after the Liberal job and, after the last election, was flirting with going after Tory pollster Allan Gregg's partisan job. Also, during the 1988 campaign the NDP hired Reid's subsidiary, Access Survey Research, to do the actual field-work for the party, the same service it has performed for the Ontario NDP in the past. Reid says he doesn't see the numbers. Access simply collects them and sends them along to party pollster Vic Fingerhut for his analysis.

Walker says he and Reid had a constant disagreement over the relative strengths of the NDP and the Liberals. "During the 1985 Ontario election we had many arguments. Angus saw it as the rise of the NDP. I saw it as the rise of the Liberals. It turned out, it was the Liberals. We also disagreed on the significance of the NDP rise between elections. I didn't agree with Angus about the basic restructuring of the three-party system.

"But, you know, Angus built a national organization from a regional centre against tremendous odds. Goldfarb and Kirby were always very hostile toward him."

Walker says he decided he'd leave the firm after an argument the two men had immediately following the November 1986 Liberal leadership review, where Turner won the support of 76.3 percent of party delegates. (Reid's pre-vote survey set Turner's support at 65 percent, although he added it could go as low as 60 or as high as 81, pretty well covering all contingencies.)

"Angus wanted to go right out into the field and do a survey on Turner's leadership," says Walker. "The guy had just been given a resounding vote of confidence by his own party, and going out into the field then, with the firm's history, would look bad. I remember we were arguing about this in Reid's office and he said to me, 'What's the worst possible thing that could happen?' I said, 'I don't know, what?' And Angus said, 'The worst possible thing that could happen is that John Turner could become prime minister, that's what.' It was then I realized that Angus and I had a different agenda."

Reid acknowledges the remark, but says all he meant was if Turner became prime minister the company wouldn't get any federal business. Anyway, says Reid, the problem he and Walker had was that "David Walker is a good guy, but he's partisan.

"It's not anti-Turner. I don't go out and tell our interviewers in Montreal or wherever to find some shit to lay on about John Turner. If there's anything that is personal it was all the messages I got from the Liberals and others that John Turner hated my guts. . . . Speaking privately with David Walker at the time . . . I felt that, for whatever reason, the statement that came loud and clear from everyone is that, if Turner gets elected, then he's going to get you.

"Turner can be a vindictive man. That's not me having it in for Turner, it's that he had it in for me," he says. "Fortunately, not all Liberals out there feel that way."

11

Michael Adams: The Mother Teresa of Polling

Michael Adams, like his colleagues in the public polling industry, will never be accused of humility.

Nor of being short of things to say. He tends to talk in stream of consciousness. A telephone call just to set up an interview sparked: "I tend to be the conscience of the profession ... the pollsters' Mother Teresa."

Adams, a thin, frizzy-haired, affable, studious-looking man, is president of Environics Research Group Ltd. of Toronto, a firm established in 1970 and now well known for its regular surveys in the *Globe and Mail* and *Le Devoir*.

"I came up with the term 'strategic voting' in 1984 and was amazed that, during the [1988] election, the focus groups the CBC and CTV had, ordinary voters, were using the term to describe the kind of voting they were doing.

"People voted for the Tories despite Mulroney and despite free trade. If the Liberals hadn't been such a pathetic collection of nincompoops, well. I read in *Maclean's* where Goldfarb was talking about if the media had focused on the Liberals' forty-point plan it would have been better. Doesn't he know that's the politics of the past, the vote-buying approach of the past? Voters are more sophisticated now.

"This campaign was remarkable. It defied the rules. The party that went in ahead is supposed to come out ahead. Of course, that didn't happen in 1984. This time the Tories went in ahead and came out ahead, but there was an incredible turn-around in mid-campaign. No journalist, pollster, or politician really understands yet what went on in this campaign. I think I'll write about it. I'm half journalist these days," he says.

There's no doubt it's the half he likes. He tried for years to break into the media before latching on to the prestigious *Globe* in 1983. In the late 1970s and early 1980s, he and his vice-president Donna Dasko wrote in the *Financial Post* and *Toronto Sun* for what he then called National Polling Trends Ltd. Two days before the May 22, 1979, election, Adams published a poll he had done for the *Toronto Sun* on the twenty-three federal ridings in Metro Toronto. Adams predicted the Liberals would win fifteen seats; the Tories, six; and the NDP, two. In fact, Clark's Tories won twelve, two more than the Liberals, and double what Adams said they would win. The NDP won just one Toronto seat.

A week earlier, he had written in the *Financial Post*, "The real problem is translating popular vote into seats. No one has yet developed a fool-proof formula, because each general election is really made up of a number of mini-elections, in each of the ridings [this time 282], in which the party with the most votes wins the seat. Our single-member-district/plurality-vote system sometimes creates strange anomalies between popular vote across the country and who wins the most seats and forms the government." He should have thought of that himself before translating his popular-vote numbers into seats.

In any event, Adams now goes to some length to explain that he does not do polling for political parties, apparently believing that public media polling is somehow a less unsavoury activity. He admits, however, that "there was a time in the 1970s when we could have been hired by a party to be a party pollster and I would have said, great, because there were no media opportunities there. The *Globe and Mail* didn't believe in publishing polls then."

Adams, in fact, has polled for politicians. He worked for Alberta businessman Peter Pocklington, for example, when Pocklington sought the federal Tory leadership in 1983. And he polled for Larry Grossman, when Grossman was Ontario treasurer, in 1984. Indeed, that secret polling for Grossman became somewhat of a political issue around Queen's Park, since the purpose was to feel out what sort of support Grossman would have in a bid for the Tory leadership. It only became public when Frank Miller mentioned it at his news conference announcing his candidacy and Grossman flatly denied he had anything to do with it.

Donna Dasko, however, admitted that Environics had been "doing polling for a candidate or potential candidate." She said it involved a survey of riding presidents and executives. "I don't think I can really say anything else. We don't comment on who we're doing polls for."

Nor did Adams act like a guy who sees working with political parties as a blot on his professional purity when, in the spring of 1986, he approached the Liberal party to sell them some questions on his omnibus survey. His actions became public only after Liberal MP Jean Lapierre accused Adams of trying to entice John Turner's office into buying a poll that was critical of Turner's leadership.

Adams had just released a poll that showed Jean Chrétien was favoured over Turner as Liberal leader by a two-to-one margin, 41 to 20. Lapierre said Adams not only offered Turner's office the poll before it was published, but "they billed us for it." Adams denied he tried to fool anybody, but he did admit approaching Turner's office, asking them to buy questions on an omnibus poll. "We thought they were interested. They weren't, so we ripped up the invoice and that was the end of it."

He said the spring poll was independent of the poll he had offered the Liberals, although the results were similar, because it was done "independently for the *Globe and Mail*." Adams said he and then *Globe* managing editor Geoffrey Stevens "even worked on the questions together," another odd admission for a self-professed purist.

Adams sees himself rather grandly: "I guess in a sense we're the gurus of polling.... I don't know that I want to call myself a guru, but let's say people who are trying to interpret social trends, political trends."

He had no such qualms in a May 1987 article for *Policy Options*, saying, "Today's pollsters have become the modern gurus of our society. They have replaced Shakespeare's clowns and witches as Cassandras of truth and prediction."

The guru side of Adams, as opposed to the raw-researcher side, was demonstrated during the last election campaign when he told Canadian Press three weeks before election day that Mulroney should defuse the trade issue by promising voters a referendum. It was just after the Liberals had enjoyed their post-debate resurgence. Adams said the Tories couldn't "run the next three weeks on free trade or they are in serious trouble." He drew a parallel with René Lévesque, who won a majority government in 1976 after promising a referendum on independence. Lévesque lost the referendum vote, but came back to win another majority. The Tories dismissed the suggestion out of hand, but still managed to stumble home with another majority.

Adams says the work his firm publishes is just a small fraction of their market research. The firm has more than 150 private- and public-sector clients and a total of 9 ongoing syndicated research studies. "And then we have fifty or a hundred other clients giving us 20,000 bucks a year to tell all the in-depth stuff on what is going on with public-affairs issues. The two best quarterly reports on public-affairs issues are *Decima Quarterly* and *Focus Canada* [his own]," he says, modestly. Angus Reid, Insight's Michael Marzolini, and now even Gallup, also have quarterlies, which, while not as well known, are a fraction of the cost. This has become an extremely lucrative field for pollsters. For the most part, somebody has already paid them to collect the data anyway, so they just recycle it, tarted up a bit, and the cheques come flowing in.

Environics also sells questions on its omnibus surveys. "People can put a few questions on for something like $5,000 to $7,000 rather than $50,000 to $75,000 for a national survey."

Adams himself holds an Honours B.A. in political studies from Queen's University (1969) and an M.A. in sociology from the University of Toronto (1970). He's also a past president of the Canadian Association of Marketing Research Organizations and sees himself as a champion of promoting higher standards in the Canadian research industry.

Adams has also had a long and mutually profitable association with Yvan Corbeil, the man who built his Montreal-based CROP firm into a major polling concern. Around 1982, Adams says, he decided he had to become a national pollster, and he met Corbeil at a conference at Princeton, N.J.

"We took a walk in the woods. He helped me out a lot in 1982 and 1983. The two firms published several joint polls," says Adams. "I'd do the English and he'd do the French. In 1985, he sold me the CROP report that he'd started in 1976 and I turned it into my own *Focus Canada*."

Since then, Corbeil has withdrawn from the business, suffering the effects of the debilitating Lou Gehrig's disease, and has sold the company to his colleague Alain Giguere. CROP is still an independent company, with 51 percent ownership in Quebec, but late in 1988 Adams bought 49 percent of the firm and became partners with CROP on an international study of social change involving work in twenty countries. The study, begun in France in the mid-1970s, now has many of the largest corporations in the world subscribing to it. Asked about the business deal with CROP, the normally talkative Adams said, "I'll have to be somewhat circumspect about it. Let's just say our relationship is one of sovereignty-association."

Adams boasts he's so squeaky clean he even announced a computer error in an October 1985 poll. A month earlier he, Dasko, and Jordan Levitin had written a piece in the *Globe* entitled, "Canadians Have Faith in Their Pollsters." And, wouldn't you know, 80 percent said they felt polls "are at least somewhat representative of public opinion," whatever "somewhat representative" means. In any event, some of that faith must have been shaken a tad when Environics's October poll showed the Liberals at 47 percent in Ontario, the Tories at 33, and the NDP at 22. In fact, it should have been 36 for the Tories and only 35 for the Liberals, but a mistake occurred when a computer operator put some data from rural Quebec in with Toronto numbers. It didn't affect the national numbers at all. Adams promised to tighten up his checking process — from two checks to three, with a statistician on hand — but said, "I'm not really very embarrassed. The overall numbers were correct."

In an interview in his downtown Toronto offices, Adams said, "You do not see a lot of pollsters retracting when they make a technical error. Environics did once.... It was about our third or fourth national poll."

As in other businesses, however, sometimes the high road becomes a little rockier if there's a major contract at stake.

In March 1985, for example, Environics was one of several companies to bid on a three-year contract, at $80,000 a year, with the Ontario Ministry of Energy, an energy-tracking study on the long-term behavioural patterns of Ontario residents on energy and energy conservation. Environics had designed the original questionnaire, and Adams was eager to get the main contract as well.

Michael Van Dusen, who was director of communications for the ministry at the time, was one of four members on a panel hearing all the presentations. Because the contract involved market research, the ministry had invited Lucia Kosninsky, a methodologist with the research department at Foster Advertising, to be a panel member.

CAMRO, the organization Adams is active in to improve industry standards, does in fact have some guidelines, as does the Professional Marketing Research Society, called "rules of conduct and good practice." One of those rules is that telephone interviews should be under thirty minutes because experience has shown that respondents get impatient after that time and either begin to slough off the questions or simply hang up, thus making the time spent with them a total waste. That is why, incidentally, some firms tell their interviewers to lie to respondents at the beginning, claiming the interview will be shorter than it is.

As it is, pollsters are sometimes lucky to get one in ten people to answer their questions, although they all claim a much higher success rate.

In any event, says Van Dusen, Kosninsky had tested the questionnaire prepared by Environics for the study and found it took about an hour, much too long for a successful telephone sample. All the other bidding firms had pre-tested the questionnaire and estimated it would take between forty-five and sixty-five minutes. They had all asked if it could be cut back or switched to in-home interviews, which can be longer. Not Adams, however. He told the panel it would take between twenty-five and thirty minutes.

He also argued that people were really interested in energy right then and would have no problem staying on the phone to discuss it. The ministry people knew better. In 1981, energy was really hot, but not in 1985. Yet Adams told the panel he'd done a pre-test and nobody had refused the interview. They didn't believe him.

"The fact of the matter is that Decima made a much better presentation," says Van Dusen. "That's why they got the job. But Michael accused us of giving it to them because of partisan connections. It wasn't true.

"I recall the incident. It wasn't a huge flashpoint. Lucia just kept asking him questions on the topic. I don't think he'd expected such a technical approach. And the more she asked, the more apparent it became he wasn't going to get the job."

Rhonda Hendel, another panel member, who worked at the ministry, says she was "shocked" when Adams's inconsistencies were pointed out to him and "he just shrugged, as if it was no big deal. He was basically trying to lie to us, and he didn't seem to care very much."

Van Dusen had known Adams for some time. "I used to have lunch with him frequently. But when he didn't get the contract, he phoned me several times, even after I'd left the ministry and gone to work for

Abitibi-Price, to voice his concerns. The vehemence of his follow-up phone calls was incredible. He was accusing us of bias because Decima got the contract. . . . It certainly wasn't very professional."

Yet Adams probably spends more time than any other pollster does talking about standards and professionalism.

In *Policy Options* in July 1987, Adams wrote, "Within the Canadian marketing and opinion research industry where the professional standards already exist, there must be greater emphasis on the enforcement of those standards, if the industry is to maintain its credibility with the media and the public."

One thing you would expect from a pollster is an acute sense of the importance of statistics. No doubt Adams has that, along with all his colleagues, at least nineteen out of twenty times anyway. Still, it's odd that in three speeches just a few months apart, a man who earns his living with statistics would cite significantly different numbers for the value of the market-research industry in Canada. On June 1, 1988, speaking to the Canadian Managing Editors Conference on "the accuracy and impact of public opinion polls in Canada," Adams said, "Today market and opinion research is a large and sophisticated industry in North America, with over $2 billion in annual sales in the U.S. and over $200 million in Canada alone."

In September, he offered the same paragraph to the Public Affairs Association of Canada, except he added $1 billion on the U.S. total and $100 million on the Canadian figure.

In November, he sawed it off, telling officials from the Department of Regional Industrial Expansion in Renfrew, Ontario, the "large and sophisticated industry" has sales of over $3 billion in the United States and $250 million in Canada.

The spread between $2 billion and $3 billion and $200 million and $300 million is well outside any pollster's margin of error.

Something else Adams shares with his fellow pollsters is his penchant for attacking his competitors' methodology. Asked about Goldfarb working for both the Liberals and the media, he said, "That's not right, you know it's not right. In fact Marty did a couple of things in the last election . . . and I shouldn't be the critic of this. I used to be critical of other pollsters, now I'm saying I'm not going to be critical because I feel that it sounds as if I'm doing it for competitive reasons rather than that I have some professional interest.

"But when I look at Gallup's performance in this campaign, and I have intellectual disagreements with Angus, and with Martin Goldfarb I disagreed . . . [with his] coming out as a party pollster, doing media and writing a book criticizing his leader in the middle of a campaign. . . . It's quite a commentary, somebody would do that and not get fired on the spot. That's a commentary on the power of that person, that his tenure is probably more secure than the leader's . . . and then polling for a television station, whose charter I suspect when it comes to the CRTC, you would think the objectivity in journalism, which should apply to television as it does in print, would preclude that."

Which brings us to some of Environics's own work during the 1988 campaign. Environics is unique among media pollsters in that Adams and Dasko get not only to do the survey, but also to write the story about the results. Despite their long experience in the survey business, however, and constant criticism of the way journalists frequently mishandle data, Environics was guilty of some of the same data distortions they have criticized other media outlets for in the past, to the point where the *Globe* decided after the campaign they wouldn't use as many Environics polls and a *Globe* reporter, not Adams and Dasko, would write the story.

In a May 1988 speech entitled "Media Polling in Canada," Adams said, "Journalists in Canada must do a better job in evaluating what poll data they will present — just as they check the credibility of other news sources — and they should be educating the public on how to use and interpret polling data." He added that "we should see more critical investigative journalism on polls." Absolutely.

Yet during the campaign, Adams routinely broke down his national sample into regional and provincial groupings, wildly distorting the margins of error in the process, but not always telling that to his *Globe* readers. And since he wrote it himself, he can't blame it on journalists. He did try, however.

"What we did, Environics actually did something new. We actually broke down all the provinces except Atlantic Canada, where they were too few, we broke them down because the journalists at the [*Winnipeg*] *Free Press* or the [*Saskatoon*] *Star-Phoenix*, you know, papers all across the West, would call Environics and say, 'What are the numbers for Saskatchewan?' And we'd say, 'We put you guys in with Manitoba,' and they'd say, 'Aaagh!!!' They'd go nuts. Or, 'We put you in with Alberta,' and they'd go even crazier. So we said, o.k. in this election . . . we will break it down in the West so the four provinces report separately. . . . We know the samples are small, we'll give you the margin of error, the sample size, and then if those papers want to report the Environics numbers, as to what they say in Saskatchewan, they can also say this is a very wide margin of error."

They can, but few newspapers bothered reporting anything but the overall numbers and, as Adams knows, radio and television simply don't take time in their newscasts to get bogged down with margins of error.

Granted, the *Globe* does a better job than most newspapers in telling its readers how a poll is conducted, but in its March 29, 1988, poll, it reported, "The margins of error are slightly wider . . . for the regional and demographic data."

Slightly wider? In fact, error margins grow astronomically, not only when the national numbers are repercentaged with the undecideds factored in, but with any regional, provincial, or major metropolitan-area breakdowns, such as Toronto and Montreal, which were reported in Environics polls, often without the margin of error.

On November 1, for example, the *Globe*–Environics poll put the Manitoba Liberals ahead of the Tories by 41 to 30, but Adams's story did not say the Manitoba sample was 64 people out of the national sample of 1,538, and the margin of error for Manitoba was plus or minus 12.2 percentage points. "You've got a sample that small in a province this size and that's ridiculous," said Manitoba Tory campaign chairman Terry Stratton. "We're totally upset because it's not our reading."

Stratton said that, with the margin of error included in the Environics poll, his party could have had between 36 and 60 percent support at the start of the campaign and between 18 and 48 percent in late October. Incredibly, Adams also said that another significant number was the opposition to free trade in Manitoba, 51 percent, which was higher only in one other province, Saskatchewan (at 54 percent). "When you get a number like that, you know it's significant, however many people were sampled." No, you don't. Adams knows full well that 51 percent could have been as low as 38.8 percent, given the 12.2 percent error margin.

After the heavy criticism, however, Adams did include a chart on the inside page in the final pre-election *Globe*–Environics poll published November 10, just eleven days before the election. But Manitoba Tories still weren't impressed to see their party listed at 33, a full thirteen points back of the Liberals, on a total of 61 Manitoba respondents, and a margin of error of plus or minus 12.5. But the 46-to-33 Liberal lead was widely reported, with little reference to the error margin, particularly on radio news reports, even though statistically the two parties could have been tied, or the Tories could have been ahead, and Adams could still claim his numbers were within the statistical tolerances. Saskatchewan, with 53 respondents, was plus or minus 13.5 percent. Even Ontario, with the largest sample (460) had a 4.6 margin either way. So what's the point?

Manitoba pollster Greg Mason called Environics's provincial breakdowns "absolutely bizarre. These national pollsters are just . . . [irresponsible] . . . in this business of foisting off regional analysis when the sample is below 200. Everybody knows that, yet they keep repeating it. . . . The pollster just should not release that information. It's kind of like releasing a handgun to a minor and being caught. There are certain groups you just don't want to pass bullets out to and I don't know why pollsters continue to do it.

"I think the pollster has to take the fall for that," said Mason. "It leads people into believing that you can make that kind of comparison, so if you present a chart and Manitoba is sitting there with sixty-odd people and then you turn around and say, well, they shouldn't publish that information, that's just negligent on the part of the pollster. . . . They know in fact that competitive journalism will reproduce those numbers."

Mother Teresa would have simply said no.

12

Michael Marzolini's Pizza Polls

Michael Marzolini likes to say that polls are like pizzas. "They have to be served hot."

And hot is how the thirty-one-year-old president of Insight Canada Research has been feeling ever since he upstaged his better-known polling rivals and called the 1988 federal election campaign dead on for "CTV News."

Marzolini, a self-taught computer whiz, prides himself in speed, getting the numbers to his clients before they have a chance to cool off. "We had the first poll after the debate. Our methodology — I'm into streamlining and getting things done as quickly as possible. We had 611 interviews done in a three-hour period, and also tabulated. I did the analysis in the following ten minutes. The logistics were incredible. We had three telephone banks spread around the city [Toronto] . . . the information was flowing into the computer as it was coming off the phone . . . it was being coded and zapped through. We had three different data entries. We had thirty-five or forty people on the phones and another ten or fifteen support staff," he says.

Critics will say that Marzolini is too fast. There certainly is little time for call-backs, which means heavy substitutions and a less "scientific" sample. Taking him at his word, for example, if forty people did 611 interviews in three hours, that means each person had to average a little more than five interviews per hour, a remarkable turn-around rate.

Marzolini acknowledges his reponse rates are low. "We have to be very careful of that. . . . We generally make one pass. You've got a telephone number, you contact that telephone number, and if they're not home, do you call them back? Not usually, if you're doing a one-night poll.

"Generally what you try to do is pick up 60 percent of the people ... but in a political survey you're lucky to get 30 percent or 20 percent. That is not quite the same calibre we would do for a corporate client or advertising client."

Even so, CTV got a lot more than it paid for. "They took a bit of a risk. We had no track-record as far as the public was concerned ... but we did daily tracking, which had never been done before for a media poll. We started with 100 interviews a day, and that's what we billed them for. But we never did 100 a day. We did more. They were expecting a very easy election, a milk run from start to finish for the Tories ... we were soon doing 150 a day, then up to 200, and sometimes 300, 400, or 500.... We tracked the campaign from Day One."

When Marzolini started work, he lied about his age, saying he was twenty-one. He was fourteen. Putting on a $49 Woolco suit, the Don Mills native marched into a computer company called Multiple Access Canada Systems Group and stayed there ten years, working mainly a 4:00-p.m.-to-midnight shift while he completed high school at Don Mills Collegiate and graduated in 1980 in political economy from the University of Toronto. The quintessential self-made man, when Marzolini applied for the job he says, "I'd never seen a computer at that point, but I had a book and read up on it. I taught myself the language and I read a book on public-opinion research. I always thought I knew behaviour better than most. I always liked the idea of politics. I liked to look at the mechanics, the strategy. I never wanted to be a politician, but I could always see Goldfarb being the kind of guy who knows things. I was the North York Trivial Pursuit champion."

Marzolini's polling pursuits took him to a Kent State campaign managing seminar in the early 1980s, where he met some major American political consultants and got to watch the Republicans in the 1984 presidential election conduct their nightly tracking and rolling samples. He also experimented with the PEAC system and, basically operating a business out of a suitcase, signed up more than forty Liberal MPs for customized campaign work, operating a firm called Kenwin Research Associates. At the time, Welland MP Gilbert

Parent, Turner's caucus chairman and one of Marzolini's early clients, said, "Mike is the new Allan Gregg. He's a computer genius." He may be, but it didn't do Parent any good. In the 1984 election, he lost the seat he'd held for ten years to Tory Allan Pietz by 4,000 votes.

Marzolini was also helping York North Liberal Aldo Tollis, who had applied his sophisticated techniques to identify and sign up 4,000 new party members and win the nomination to fight the sitting Tory, radical right-winger John Gamble. Marzolini did a computer search on Gamble's complete parliamentary record. The strategy was to send personalized (computer-printed) memos to specific target groups. For example, Marzolini discovered that, when a motion was introduced in the Commons asking for unanimous consent for a sympathy letter after John Lennon's murder, Gamble was the only MP to dissent. That information was then sent to the eighteen- to twenty-five-year-old voters in the riding. "As far as we're concerned," said Tollis, in an interview shortly before the campaign began, "Gamble is dead in the water." As it turned out, he was. But he lost to Independent Tony Roman. Tollis finished a distant third.

Not all of his MPs lost, however. "We managed to get over half of them elected," he says, with the assurance that pollsters have it was their data and not a host of other factors that determined the outcome."

Marzolini began doing delegate tracking for John Turner leading up to the 1984 leadership convention, ending up completing 2,500 psychographic interviews with delegates. "We even projected the second ballot within 1 percent."

After the 1984 federal election, Marzolini was hired by the Ontario Liberals to do tracking in the 1985 provincial campaign, which ultimately saw the end of the long-running Tory regime. The media polls at the time (Reid, Gallup, Environics) were showing a comfortable win for Frank Miller's Tories, "but we showed a shift with about two weeks remaining in the campaign that wasn't seen by the other pollsters, and [David] Peterson became much more confident near the end," he says.

"It was a case of segmenting the poll results as much as possible to try to find out how to get, say, 10 percent more among Mediterranean Catholics, 5 percent from Indian Oceanics, to really squeeze as much out of the vote as possible. In the last week or so these things started to be believed. Decima was picking pretty much the same numbers, but none of the media polls were. The *Toronto Sun* had a particularly bad one on election eve, showing 51 percent PC, 28 for the Liberals, whereas we had it 38 to 36 Liberals." The vote was 38 to 37 for the Liberals.

Marzolini then set up his current company, Insight Canada. His first client was the Toronto Stock Exchange.

"We take it into communications strategy, almost the public-relations area, in making use of the numbers. It's just not enough to go out and do a poll and say, 'Well, 42 percent of the people think you're a jerk.' What you have to be doing is to find out that while 42 percent of the people think that now, you can get that down to 28 percent if you do certain things. . . . We put together everything from computer graphics, strategy maps, poll-by-poll analysis, social demographics . . . pretty much a campaign blueprint. This is what you do: you follow it from page 1 to 45, you go to these places I tell you to go to, you say these things."

Traditionally, political polling has been pretty well confined to federal and provincial candidates. Not any more. Marzolini conducted surveys for a host of municipal candidates in and around Toronto. A 1986 *Toronto Star* story reported that thirteen of the forty members of Metro Toronto Council had commissioned a poll of their constituents during or before an election campaign. Several unsuccessful candidates used polling as well. Former Liberal MP Norm Kelly, who mounted a strong campaign but failed to unseat veteran Scarborough mayor Gus Harris, spent $10,000 on polling during his 1985 challenge, saying they "reinforced what my own nose told me. They [politicians] don't like flying blind at the federal and provincial level but, strangely, many politicians are prepared to do this at the municipal level."

Toronto councillor Derwyn Shea was quoted as saying he once spent $7,000 of his own money to survey issues of concern to senior citizens in his west-end ward. He said he was shocked at the price, but, "I don't regret a penny spent. . . . It's one of many ways to keep your fingers on the pulse of your constituents." Not all local politicians agreed. Scarborough alderman Brian Ashton said, "Politicians are making deals with the devil for the sake of a few percentage points."

Marzolini doesn't see himself as the devil, but he did concede that, "some opinion polls have been used by politicians like a drunk would use a lamppost — more for support than illumination." Given the cost, and the fact most local politicians don't have access to party coffers — or tax write-offs — polling is likely to continue in most major cities but not to the extent it's used federally and provincially.

In the 1987 Ontario election, for example, Marzolini alone signed up twenty-eight Liberal candidates, only one an incumbent, and all of them were elected in David Peterson's Liberal landslide.

At the 1986 Liberal convention, where Turner's leadership was endorsed by 76.3 percent of the delegates, Marzolini did extensive delegate tracking. "I can't show you the 65 recommendations we made for John Turner in 1986. We tracked him going from 55 percent to 76. I feel our recommendations kept him in the job. Whether that was a good thing or not, we didn't really care. We just did the work."

By this time, Marzolini's corporate-client base was expanding, but not quickly enough. He was still unknown. "We'd always tried to be quiet. That's the way I was taught in the States. . . . I found out we were able to keep quiet, but at the same time, nobody knew who the hell we were. . . . That made it tougher to develop business. We thought it would be good first to remove ourselves from being perceived as partisan. Campaigns pay very little money. It's more like a hobby and it was unrealistic to expect we would become the Liberal pollster."

Marzolini's toughest moment during the 1988 federal election campaign came with his October 30 numbers, the first post-debate poll, showing the Liberals bursting into the lead for the first time, 39 to 35. The next day, Gallup reported the Tories were still ahead, 38 to 32. "After the CTV show I remember Lloyd Robertson came over and said 'How do you feel, putting the Liberals back on track?' I said, 'I feel like Oppenheimer. I only made the bomb, you had to decide to drop it.'"

Still, it was gut-wrenching day after the Gallup. "We had sixty calls from the media. They were all abusive . . . very nasty. They were all calling to ask about our qualifications. Had we done this sort of thing before? What right had we to do it? The New York Times even blamed the drop in the dollar on our poll. Environics called us that morning, wanting to know what other numbers we had for the parties out west, so we gave them the stuff. I remember thinking, why are they calling? It's unusual to call another polling firm to check numbers. . . . They said they were coming out the next day and I felt, if they had numbers like Gallup, we might as well start looking for work elsewhere because it would be impossible to have any credibility. Then at 10:20 on the national news, they had the Environics numbers, which were damn near identical to ours.... We were back in business, although nobody ever called up and said, 'Hey, I guess you guys were right.'" Within a couple of days, both a Goldfarb and a Reid poll also published similar numbers. Then came the infamous Gallup that had the Liberals way ahead, "by which time the Liberals had started to fall back down again."

Marzolini's favourite campaign question was asking respondents to give a one-word description of each party leader. Mulroney came out as "dishonest," Turner as "weak," and Broadbent as "sincere . . . but we did a computer search and found 'asshole' twenty-three times for Turner, forty-two times for Mulroney, and only five times for Broadbent." That wasn't used on family television, of course.

Marzolini credits Tory strategy for combining the issues of free trade and Meech Lake in Quebec, and says the major blunder for Turner was "his positioning himself on the outside of the mainstream, giving the impression business is bad, unions are bad, everybody's bad.... Then there was that remark by Kirby, comparing business with the Ku Klux Klan. I think that did more to deep-six the Liberal campaign than any other thing in the election. We could see those numbers start to turn the next day. People were saying they thought Turner was a business guy, and now he's against it. He's obviously not trustworthy, not focused, he's disorganized, he's desperate. He's attacking anything that gets in his way. I've never met Michael Kirby actually, but I'm told I don't get along with him."

Of all the competing pollsters, Marzolini's least favourite is Gallup. "I have no respect at all for their methodology.... They mix their methodology."

Marzolini's main complaint is that Gallup does both at-home interviews clustered in urban areas and telephone interviews in different areas of the province and treats them as if the results are comparable. He says not only the different interviewing techniques but the different methods used to determine which areas to call upon mean that the numbers will be suspect.

"Just to go to the urban centres and interview people and say that that's a national poll does not work, and it caused everybody a lot of anguish during the election campaign. All the political campaigns were sort of disoriented by it. While you can find a polling firm that is erratic, and you can say it is erratic, it's not so easy when you have the Gallup name. Gallup is like Kleenex. A Gallup poll is a Gallup poll.

It's always going to be listened to, no matter how many people raise their eyebrows." Marzolini also dismissed Gallup's claim of a rapid movement between their final poll and election day as "absolute nonsense. We looked at every single day's results and broke them down. There was no difference between any day [during the last week].... I got very resentful having to explain Gallup all the time. They take Gallup as being *the* word. I'd always wondered why Allan Gregg was so down on Gallup. He said the day after the election, 'Those guys don't know their ass from their elbow.'

"Their rogue poll had a 17 percent swing upwards in Quebec. Bozinoff said it was because Jean Chrétien was campaigning for local candidates. There's no way Jesus Christ himself campaigning is going to bring up one party 17 percent in one province."

Marzolini says he respects Decima and Environics. As for Reid's method of asking the leadership question before party preference, he said, "I worry about that because, when you're making a decision to vote, it's based on more than leadership." Indeed, in Marzolini's final tracking poll, with a fat sample of 2,720 eligible voters, just 17 percent of declared Tory supporters said they were voting that way because they liked the leader. (For declared Liberal voters, it was 16 percent; for the NDP, 18 percent.) For Tories, 33 percent said their vote was pro–free trade, while 38 percent of declared Liberals listed anti–free trade as the main reason for their vote.

On Goldfarb's dual role as party and media pollster, Marzolini said, "There's no way you could ever change a poll ... but I realize the perception could be a problem itself.... I was very sensitive to that during the election campaign. We don't consider ourselves partisan ... but our political work had been for the Liberals.... CTV probably had some concerns about that as well, but it was a deliberate move on my part to distance ourselves from any party. I had a personal friend who was a Liberal candidate and I wouldn't go to his fund-raisers. I bought a ticket, but that's it.... Non-partisan is the best way to be and that's certainly the way I want to keep the company."

Marzolini says the television exposure was helpful. The company does an annual survey of executives for the Board of Trade journal. Before the election, "when we called all those chief executives, nobody had any idea who we were. This year, of the three hundred executives, about twenty-five of them said, 'Oh, you guys were the

CTV pollsters. You did the election stuff.' So it made it easier to do that poll. It also means when business is developing and a company is looking for public-perception work, they'll at least consider us."

So many clients have been considering the firm as a result of his election success that in July he moved from his cramped King Street East offices to some spacious digs on ultra-trendy Yorkville Avenue, complete with an 800-square-foot sundeck. He also purchased a sophisticated CATI (Computer-Aided Telephone Interviewing) system, an advanced model of those used by both Environics and Goldfarb, with ten lines to start and room to expand to twenty-four.

Which brings us to a sore point with Marzolini, the tendency of the media to identify him as a "small-time pollster. . . . It's been written up three times that way now. . . . We have a system where all our telephone numbers are on compact discs. They come right off the enumeration areas, no clusters involved. It's probably the purest sample of any of the research companies. . . . I think our record in the election speaks for itself.

"We'll have the same technology Wirthlin is using in the States," he adds. "We'll have the fastest system north of the forty-ninth parallel."

Pizza anyone? Guaranteed hot.

13

Here Comes the Judge

On May 19, 1978, fourteen-month-old Albert Iutzi was found dead on a sofa in his filthy home in Thamesford, a sleepy farming community of about 2,000 people just east of London, Ontario.

The boy weighed less than fifteen pounds. He died of a massive skull fracture. There was evidence of older fractures to his skull, arms, ribs, and a wrist, and previous bruising to his head and face. He had been beaten over a two-week period before his death.

His parents, Royden, fifty-five, and Vera Elizabeth, thirty-four, were both charged with second-degree murder. Two years later, the mother was convicted of manslaughter, sentenced to two years less a day in reformatory, and ordered to notify officials immediately if she ever became pregnant again. Her husband was acquitted.

The case, as you'd expect, caused a sensation. It led to a special probe of regional social agencies ordered by Keith Norton, then Ontario's minister of Community and Social Services.

The *London Free Press* and local radio and television stations ran lengthy accounts of the case. Both parents had worked at odd jobs between stays on welfare. They had no car and were regularly seen hitchhiking along Oxford County roads. The father was a small, wiry man who drank heavily and argued incessantly. The mother, a large woman with unruly blonde hair, had a history of psychiatric problems. Married at sixteen, she had a Grade 8 education and an IQ of 75. Four pregnancies ended in stillbirth or miscarriage. She had been diagnosed as psycho-schizophrenic in 1964 at the Goderich Psychiatric Hospital and entered St. Thomas Psychiatric Hospital in 1966 at age twenty. She was back there again five years later, after being judged incapable of looking after herself. After the birth of a daughter in 1974, she was admitted with post-partum psychosis, impaired memory and judgment, and had developed a father-daughter relationship with her husband. She was given electro-shock therapy. The daughter was taken away from her by the Oxford County child-welfare agency in 1974 and made a ward of the crown after authorities presented evidence in Woodstock family court of abuse and neglect. The daughter was eventually adopted by another family.

Vera Elizabeth was back in psychiatric care in 1976, and again in 1977, shortly after Albert was born. She had been on medication, but medical evidence at the trial showed she understood little of the events leading up to her son's brutal death.

Both parents pleaded not guilty and immediately reported they had been subjected to a series of threats. Local passions ran so high that two law students working for the defence team were threatened with physical violence. These reports convinced lawyers that there was considerable prejudice against their clients, so they asked Neil Vidmar, then a psychologist at the University of Western Ontario, to conduct a public-opinion survey in the hope of persuading the court that local opinion made it impossible to get a fair trial and that, therefore, the defendants should be granted a change of venue.

Vidmar had done this sort of survey work in court cases before, and has done them many times since. The defence did not get its change of venue, but the survey information was convincing enough that the judge allowed defence lawyers to grill prospective jurors with a series of questions based on what the research had uncovered, hoping to weed out jurors who had a predisposition against the Iutzis. A pre-trial questioning period, called the *voir dire*, is routine in the United States. The use of experts in the jury-selection process has been around a long time, but "scientific" jury-selection methods, which often include surveys, basically began in the 1972 conspiracy trial of Catholic priests Philip and Daniel Berrigan and five other anti–Vietnam War protesters. It has now become commonplace in U.S. courts, but, in Canada, the process of "challenge for cause" is still the exception, not the rule.

In the Iutzi case, Vidmar conducted in-depth telephone interviews with 197 randomly selected households in Oxford County. He discovered that, because of heavy media coverage and word-of-mouth, 60 percent of respondents were familiar with the case. Pushed for more details, 39 percent mentioned such words as "child abuse, battering, neglect, or mistreatment," even though Vidmar had carefully avoided using those terms in his questionnaire. Asked if they could serve as impartial jurors, 50 percent said they couldn't. Many respondents talked about the mother's psychiatric history, previous involvement with the Children's Aid, allegations about the couple's drinking habits, and even wild stories about killing the child for insurance money and putting him in a washing-machine.

Vidmar also asked if respondents believed that, if "both the father and mother are equally guilty, that the mother is probably more guilty than the father, or that the father is probably more guilty than the mother," and a substantial majority, particularly among women respondents, said the mother was responsible for the welfare of her child, even if the father killed the boy — a concept of maternal responsibility called "strict negligence," which fortunately is contrary to law.

Based on the survey results then, a total of seventy-five potential jurors (veniremen) were subjected to a list of fifteen questions, which had each been approved by the judge, during a process that lasted one and one-half days before the jury of six men and six women was chosen.

Vidmar, currently on the law faculty at Duke University in Durham, North Carolina, has conducted pre-trial survey research in several high-profile cases, including the "Squamish Five" case involving the Litton bombings, the Helmut Buxbaum murder case, and the Sidney Jaffe bounty-hunter case. Polls were also used in the Supreme Court case of abortionist Dr. Henry Morgentaler.

"Poll evidence has been used in a number of cases," he says, "much of which has been unsuccessful. While it has become reasonably routine in the U.S., it is still not used all that often in Canada. You have to have special circumstances and legal aid has to be convinced that the poll should be undertaken, since, of course, the survey costs money."

Surveys are most commonly used in the courts in trade-mark and obscenity cases and combines matters dealing with monopolies and misleading advertising. In a 1982 case, for example, a Federal Court of Canada judge made considerable use of a public-opinion survey in overturning a government decision to deny Pizza Pizza Ltd. exclusive rights to its name. The poll showed that the chain was better known than other pizza parlours, convincing the judge to override the federal argument that it was against the public interest to grant the "Pizza Pizza" trade-mark because it served food other than pizzas.

A bibliography in the 1988 *Canadian Journal of Marketing Research* lists thirty-nine Canadian cases of this nature where public-opinion polls were used. An article in that issue by Toronto lawyers Mary Jane Stitt and Nicky Hug on the legal status of legal research concludes that the courts will not allow surveys to be used to prove that statements made by the respondents are true. That would be classed as hearsay, not admissable. "If, however, the surveys are submitted to show that certain statements were made, then the surveys will be admissible. Proof that the statements were made can take various forms such as the testimony of the interviewers or affidavits sworn by the interviewers or interviewees." In any event, the survey must comply to strict rules of methodology.

"Public opinion surveys are also often admitted in obscenity cases to establish community standards existing with respect to obscenity," they wrote. "The judicial approach to survey material in such cases is to admit it where the survey has been properly conducted. Expert opinion evidence will only be admitted, however, where the witness is an expert in market research and in the field of obscenity."

In November 1985, then Revenue minister Elmer MacKay came under fire in the Commons for having spent $50,000 on a poll to confirm that nine out of ten people asked believed Crest is a brand of toothpaste. Procter & Gamble Co., which makes Crest, had challenged a federal cosmetics tax by claiming that Crest is a health product aimed at reducing cavities and therefore not subject to the tax. The issue was worth more than $12 million in federal tax revenue, and MacKay said, "When you have to present evidence before a court and when there are high stakes, as the saying goes, one doesn't want to go there inadequately prepared." But Liberal MP Don Boudria mocked the minister for spending that kind of money to prove the obvious, telling the Commons that, "for all of us who thought all this time that Crest toothpaste was foot powder or shaving cream, we need not worry anymore."

Still, in a 1988 paper on the use of surveys in trade-mark litigation, Daniel R. Bereskin of the Toronto firm Rogers, Bereskin & Parr, wrote, "There is usually no problem in persuading a court to admit a survey as evidence. The problem today is to persuade the court to give the survey some weight. Surveys are expensive and the client who has to bear the cost will want to know whether the survey will be given sufficient weight to justify the cost. From the client's point of view, not only is it uncertain whether the survey will produce favourable results, but it is also not guaranteed, even if the results are favourable, that the judge will pay any attention to them."

One well-publicized case where the use of a Gallup opinion poll did not impress a judge — to some extent because of the poor methodology — is the ongoing case of Northern Ontario community college teacher Merv Lavigne. Backed by the right-wing National Citizens' Coalition, Lavigne is fighting the use of forced union dues for political (read: NDP) purposes. In 1985, he challenged the widespread practice under the Charter of Rights and Freedoms. In July 1986, the Supreme Court of Ontario ruled that the use of compulsory union dues "for purposes other than collective bargaining . . . cannot be justified in a free and democratic society." But in January 1989, the Ontario Court of Appeal overturned that judgment, and a month later Lavigne sought leave to appeal his case to the Supreme Court of Canada.

The Gallup questions, paid for by the NCC — $700 for a straightforward question, $1,085 if it requires more detail and analysis — were three of about fifty questions on a regular Gallup omnibus, an in-home survey of 1,044 Canadian adults taken September 5 to 7, 1985.

The poll asked the following questions:

Many Canadian workers are required by law to pay dues to unions.

a. Should or should not a union be allowed to use some of the dues of such a worker to support a political party the worker may not personally support?

b. Should or should not a union be allowed to use some of the dues of such a worker to support a political cause the worker may not personally support?

Do you think unions should or should not engage in political activities?

The survey found 86.8 percent of those asked felt unions should not use union dues to support a party that the worker may not personally support. Only 7.7 percent felt it was all right. On the question of using dues to support a "political cause" that the worker may not

support, again there was overwhelming support for Lavigne's position, 84.3 to 9.1 percent. On whether unions should engage in
political activity, 71.2 percent said "no," while 20.5 percent said
"yes."

While the introduction of the survey by Lavigne's lawyers had no
measurable impact on the Ontario Supreme Court itself, it did provide a useful glimpse, by witnesses under oath, into what often passes
for scientific methodology in the polling business.

Not a single reputable pollster will argue against the fact that the
question itself, both its wording and its placement in the questionnaire, is of key importance in the ultimate outcome of the survey.
Pollsters acknowledge, without exception, that questions can easily
be designed to elicit a particular answer, and the key to getting good
survey results is to ask good questions. Yet, for all this talk, most of
these same pollsters do what Gallup did in this instance: they include
questions on their money-making omnibus surveys that fall far short
of proper standards, questions that may have been written partially,
or totally, by clients whose only qualification is that they paid for the
question to be asked.

In this respect, the Lavigne case is an object lesson in the difference
between what polling firms say and what they do. Clara Hatton, a
Gallup vice-president who first joined the firm in 1947 and has spent
most of her career there, admitted under cross-examination from
lawyers representing the unions who are fighting the Lavigne case
that the questions in this particular survey were written by the NCC,
not by Gallup.

Hatton testified that she was unaware at the time that the NCC was
involved in the Lavigne litigation, and consequently had more than
an academic interest in the subject, when they commissioned Gallup
to ask three questions for them. Hatton also agreed that, "Yes, question wording could . . . will affect the answer to some degree or
another." Asked how the NCC engaged Gallup she said, ". . . they
phoned up and said they had questions they wanted to ask from a
national sample and sent us copies of these questions." Hatton
testified she did not know who wrote the questions for the NCC or
whether that person had any experience in polling or in formulating
polling questions.

She also admitted that the poll does not indicate whether the
respondents had given any thought to these matters prior to being
asked. (Polling critics will argue that polls, by suggesting issues, also

prompt answers that are not representative of what a person really thinks.) Hatton's response was, "They [respondents] are asked a question as to opinions, and they have to think of it while they are being asked the question." She did say they are given "as much time as they need" to reply to the questions, although her testimony also showed that the typical fifty-question survey takes thirty minutes, an average of thirty-six seconds for each question to be asked and answered, not an awful lot of time to formulate thoughtful replies.

Hatton insisted that the NCC questions were "not biased" and were pre-tested by the company. Again, that sounds more impressive than it is. In the standard pre-test, ten people are simply asked the questions. They aren't even asked if the questions are biased; only if they volunteer that they find them biased will pollsters rewrite them. The ten test respondents are usually chosen at random, five men and five women, but according to Hatton's testimony, if this isn't possible "we would pre-test with a small group in the office or over the telephone."

In a sworn affidavit in this case, University of Waterloo political-science professor John Wilson argued that omnibus surveys by definition are "unsatisfactory instruments for eliciting reliable portraits of popular opinion on important issues of public policy and debate. The respondent's attention is distracted by the general lack of focus of the study."

The problem is that one minute you're being asked your preference in toothpaste, the next whether Wayne Gretzky should have been traded to the Los Angeles Kings, then a question or two related to political issues. Essentially, the omnibus survey is a series of usually unrelated questions that come at you out of the blue. They have no particular value except that somebody, for whatever reason, paid to have the questions asked.

Wilson, both in his affidavit and under cross-examination in court, testified that these particular Gallup–NCC questions were "biased and might have encouraged a particular kind of response. To say that many Canadian workers are required by law to pay dues to unions may in some cases be true, but it does not indicate that, in many other cases, the payment of dues to trade unions is a matter voluntarily negotiated between an employee and a trade union." Wilson said many companies give money to political parties as well, without consulting their customers, employees, or shareholders, and a fairer question would have been to ask respondents their opinion on such contributions by public and private companies, unions, and various interest groups, rather than singling out unions and setting up a "negative response set which would lead the respondent to be less likely to approve of trade unions making political contributions when asked."

Wilson said "measuring public opinion at any time is a delicate art. To try to do so by utilizing only two or three questions which are poorly worded, and without paying attention to the complex social and political world in which these opinions are held is, in my opinion, simply misleading, and makes no real contribution to our understanding of a particular issue."

Despite all this, however, the NCC was impressed enough with the mileage it got from the Gallup survey to hook into an Angus Reid omnibus poll in January 1989, asking pretty much the same question: "As you may or may not know, many Canadian workers are required by law to pay dues to unions. Do you think a union should or should not be allowed to use union dues to support a political party which a worker may not personally support?" Again, 84 percent said unions should not use union dues in this way, while only 12 percent said they should.

NCC boss David Somerville said, "Big unions funnel millions of dollars in workers' forced union dues to the NDP but only a small minority of these workers vote NDP. This is an outrageous violation of their freedoms of conscience, speech, and association. If unions want to get involved in politicking, let them do so with money voluntarily donated for that purpose."

It may indeed be all of that. But a badly designed question, sponsored and written by a group with a direct interest in the matter at hand, hardly constitutes scientific proof. Which is perhaps why, given Gallup's performance in this survey, the court didn't pay much attention to it.

The use of public-opinion polling in court cases raises another serious question: in dealing strictly with matters of law, why should it matter what the most popular view is? Polls perennially show majority support for capital punishment for murderers, for example, and if the courts were compelled to uphold popular sentiment, rather than the law as written, they'd be hanging killers instead of sending them to jail.

In April 1989, this question was raised by the lawyer for a thirty-four-year-old woman who was sentenced to jail for nine months by

Quebec court judge Gerard Charron because she did not protect her daughter from her husband's sexual assaults. Evidence showed that the assaults began in 1977, when the girl was six, and continued at a rate of two or three a week until the man underwent a religious "rebirth" in 1981. The mother often took her daughter to the bedroom, where the girl was assaulted by her father. The victim has since been hospitalized for suicidal tendencies.

Names cannot be used, to protect the daughter, but the thirty-five-year-old husband was given three years in jail for the assaults. Both parents had pleaded guilty to sexual assault.

In sentencing the mother, however, Judge Charron referred to a newspaper article submitted by crown attorney Gerard Larocque about a poll by the Montreal firm of Leger and Leger that said 86 percent of Quebec residents think sentences for sex offenders are not long enough.

"[The public] probably is right because, in the end, they make the decision," Charron said. "We [judges] are nothing but representatives of society."

The increasing use of polling in the courts is not directly related to political polling, but there is a causal connection between the two. In mid-1989, for example, after various polls showed public outrage over lenient sentences handed out for grievous crimes by youths, both politicians and court officials began talking about changes in the Young Offenders Act to make it easier, in cases involving serious crimes, to try youths in adult court.

Polling has had an impact on many other issues that affect both the courts and the politicians. Drunk-driving laws, for example, were only toughened at the political level after polls showed the politicians that the public was demanding harsher sentences. Judges differ from politicians, of course, in that they are not supposed to be influenced by external factors, but it's difficult to believe that judges are not at least subtly influenced by the clamour over poll results and the public reaction to them in matters directly affecting the court.

Crimes such as wife-beating, for example, have always existed, but it hasn't been until recently, when public-opinion polls have shown widespread disgust at the practice, that the courts have begun to deal more harshly with wife-beaters, sentencing them to fines and in some cases jail terms, rather than telling them to be good boys and sending them home.

Indeed, since polls wield so much influence over the lawmakers in our society, it would be naive to assume they go unnoticed by those who enforce the law, including judges, crown attorneys, and the police. Judge Charron's remark that judges are "nothing but representatives of society" clearly represents a direct link among the pollsters who gather the public opinion; the politicians who act, at least partially, as a result of it; and the courts that ultimately judge the specific cases.

It is unlikely that the mother of the sexually abused Quebec girl would have been jailed for her part in the sordid affair had the issue not become as salient to Canadians as it has in recent times. Part of the reason for this, of course, is the pressure from poll results showing politicians and judges that the public is fed up with what it sees as liberal sentencing.

Two probation officers had interviewed the woman and recommended she be given community work because she had made progress toward rehabilitation. Her lawyer, Jean-Charles Desjardins, said a public-opinion poll should not influence his client's sentence, that "the courts should not be influenced by the public clamour."

Fact is, the more the politicians are influenced by that clamour, the more likely it is that courts, like it or not, will follow suit. If politicians believe, upon reading the polls, that the public wants tougher laws, you can bet they'll introduce them. And whatever defence lawyers think of it, their opinion won't have much impact on a representative sample.

14

Poll Abuse

On October 18, 1988, *Vancouver Sun* columnist Vaughn Palmer, in a main front-page story, reported on a private poll that said more than 50 percent of British Columbians wanted their Social Credit premier Bill Vander Zalm to quit.

What's more, two-thirds of those polled thought the Socreds should call a leadership convention.

It's a classic case of the use of polling — by political operatives, pollsters, and journalists — not as a helpful tool, but as a partisan weapon, a blunt instrument designed to bludgeon a political enemy while maintaining a comfortable anonymity behind a screen of scientific objectivity.

The poll was conveniently released just two days before 1,100 Socred delegates would meet in Penticton to exercise their own judgment about Vander Zalm's controversial leadership.

Palmer, a strong critic of the premier, reported only that the mystery poll "was paid for by a group of B.C. businessmen who say they are concerned about the Social Credit party fortunes under Vander Zalm. The *Vancouver Sun* obtained the poll on condition that it not name those who were involved."

He added that these businessmen were not involved in another recent secret poll taken by people wanting to revive the moribund B.C. Liberal Party.

The same day, Palmer's political column quoted, anonymously, a Vander Zalm critic detailing Socred opposition to the premier, riding by riding, concluding that up to 420 Socred delegates could vote against their own leader at the convention.

As it turned out, Vander Zalm easily won a vote of confidence, 1,060 to 75, albeit in a show-of-hands vote after an attempt to have a secret ballot was soundly defeated 837 to 367. Even when Vander Zalm did get an overwhelming endorsement, the *Sun's* headline was, "Jury Still Out On Vander Zalm Saddened McCarthy Says," a reference to former Socred cabinet minister Grace McCarthy, no friend of the premier's.

In his follow-up story on October 19, also the main front-page article, Palmer reported Vander Zalm dismissing a poll that suggests he's "hated" by British Columbians. He also reported the $70,000 poll was conducted by Martin Goldfarb on behalf of "a group of Vancouver businessmen."

Actually, the poll did not find that British Columbians "hated" Vander Zalm. They certainly expressed strong reservations, but they were not asked if they hated him. That was Goldfarb's own word in his written summation, no doubt pleasing to his clients, but unsubstantiated by his numbers.

In its October 19 editorial, headlined, "Poll-axed Premier Must Face Truth," on the eve of the Socred convention, the *Sun* encouraged delegates to boot out Vander Zalm, offering just one fleeting reference to the underhanded nature of the poll.

As often happens in these affairs, Vander Zalm's supporters rushed into the fray with a poll of their own, reported sight unseen by Canadian Press (which has a strict policy against doing that sort of thing), indicating that 70 percent of British Columbians wanted Vander Zalm to stay after all.

Obviously, both polls couldn't be right. And they weren't. Goldfarb's was biased, and the CP-reported poll, conducted by United Communications Research Inc., was taken out of context. "If the other side can leak, we can leak too," an unidentified source told CP.

Two days later, Les Storey, president of United Communications, fumed that publication of his poll was "blatant manipulation of public opinion" and should not have happened. He said the same thing about the Goldfarb poll. "I do not think polls that are unattributed should receive any publicity." In an interview with the author, Storey said his poll did in fact show Vander Zalm in serious political difficulty, but whoever leaked the poll to CP fed the results of one or two out of 150 questions, the only ones where the premier got any positive response at all. "It was extraordinarily abusive. . . .

These things have to be done in context. Sure, a majority didn't want him to quit. They wanted to vote him out themselves."

To this day, no major media organization in British Columbia has reported who paid for the secret Goldfarb poll, although it was an open secret among journalists and editors alike that Socred businessman Peter Brown was certainly one of the group. This upset journalist-researcher Adrian du Plessis so much that, in late March, he published his own newsletter, called *Imprint*, in which the front-page story was headlined, "Peter Brown: Nosing In The Media."

Brown, nicknamed "The Rabbit" or "Mr. VSE," owns Canarim Investment Corp., which underwrites about half of all the new shares issued on the Vancouver Stock Exchange. He is chairman of the University of British Columbia board of governors, was chairman of the B.C. Enterprise Corp. and vice-chairman of Expo 86. In 1986 he considered running for the Socred leadership but decided against it when a poll showed Vander Zalm would win. A close friend of former premier Bill Bennett, Brown is a supporter of the party old guard who were displaced by Vander Zalm. There is little doubt he'd like to see one of them replace Vander Zalm to avoid an NDP defeat.

Brown is perhaps the most influential man in British Columbia. He was the centre of some unwelcome attention himself during much of 1988 when his name came up often in a sensational stock-fraud trial where Vancouver stock promoters David Ward and Edward Carter were hit for $17 million in damages to a Texas mutual fund. Brown was not a defendant in the Carter–Ward case, but testimony indicated he made about $470,000 in a three-month period early in 1985, trading Carter–Ward stocks. Brown says he "blew the whistle" on the operation, but in one point in the trial, after evidence showing Brown, Ward, and Carter were partners in a brokerage account identified as "Troika," Ward's former secretary testified that Brown received a $120,000 cheque for "introducing a group of investors to David Ward and Edward Carter." That prompted Madame Justice Mary Southin of the B.C. Supreme Court to say, "It doesn't appear to bear any natural resemblance to decent human behaviour." Brown filed a petition in the court, asking for an opportunity to defend himself, but it was ultimately denied. In April, Brown agreed to pay a $96,000 fine, the largest ever imposed on a brokerage in B.C., for failing to verify claims in a simplified prospectus for a 1986 share offering for a firm called Banco Resources Ltd. In addition, Brown returned his firm's $340,000 underwriting fee.

Despite Brown's importance in the scheme of things in that province, however, the media maintained a studious silence about his role in the Goldfarb poll. In a January 12, 1989, interview, Goldfarb did not deny that Brown was the man who organized the poll, but said, "The media has a responsibility not to publish polls that arrive on their desk unless they know who did it and what the criteria for the poll was. We did a poll . . . a first-class poll. . . . I had no idea the poll was going to end up in the press. . . . The fact is, the media should check. Somebody should phone and say, 'Did you do this poll?' Nobody did." Palmer says he did.

On March 1, a hostile Brown told the author the poll "has nothing to do with me." Asked if he was one of the businessmen who paid for it, Brown said, "Well, if I was, I wouldn't discuss it anyway. But no, I'm not." But after du Plessis published his newsletter accusing Brown of being behind the whole exercise, the Vancouver stock-broker telephoned the author at home to say he had been involved after all. "But I didn't commission it or initiate it. . . . I didn't give it to the media. I made a small contribution, less than 10 percent of the cost. . . . I thought it was research. It makes a huge difference in my business whether we have a Socred government or an NDP government. We knew the party was in trouble, we just wanted to see how bad it was. But it wasn't done for political purposes initially. When you've got eight or nine guys subscribing to a poll, you can't control them all. Once it was leaked, that's a different story. I suppose it did become political."

In his interview with du Plessis, incidentally, Goldfarb suggested Brown's role was larger than that, but claimed he was unaware of Brown's prominent role in B.C. business and politics. "He's another human being who retained us, and paid us, and we were glad to do the poll for him," Goldfarb said. That's hard to believe. Goldfarb had been doing business for years in B.C. and was such a good friend of Bennett he considered writing a book about him. It seems to be stretching credulity to suggest that, with his knowledge of the province, Brown was just another client looking for an apolitical poll.

British Columbia, while zanier than many parts of the country, certainly has no monopoly on the abuse of public-opinion polls. Nor is it always confined to powerful back-room boys.

In August 1981, the eight premiers fighting Pierre Trudeau's constitutional-reform bill released a Gallup poll that they claimed backed their position. Alberta's Peter Lougheed, on behalf of the premiers, urged Trudeau to scrap his plan and negotiate a new deal, even if the Supreme Court upheld its legality. But the poll asked a series of motherhood questions — such as, should an amending formula be made by Canadians? or should federal-provincial meetings be held in order to try to reach an agreement? The poll did not ask for an opinion on the substance of the package, or the proposed charter of rights. It was simply a public-relations ploy by the premiers, an attempt to use a poll to give a false impression, or at least an unsubstantiated impression, that they were on the side of the angels.

On January 20, 1983, news of a mysteriously sponsored Gallup poll appeared on the front pages of newspapers across the country announcing that if the Liberals had John Turner as their leader he would defeat the Conservatives under Joe Clark. The poll, delivered to the Toronto head office of Canadian Press in a plain brown envelope, came one week before Clark had to face a leadership test of his own at the Winnipeg convention.

Gallup acknowledged it had done a poll for a "private Canadian group," but, typical of pollsters, assumed no responsibility for it other than to say that the numbers were correct. An editorial in the *Victoria Times-Colonist* was critical of Gallup's position. "It is disappointing to see the respected Gallup organization being associated with such a shabby exercise. Those who commission public opinion polls are often less concerned with public information than political manipulation. If the poll results are to be made public, Gallup should insist on full disclosure and identification. Failure to do so may well discredit the pollsters, along with the shadowy people whose anonymity they are protecting."

Clearly, the poll was specifically designed to hurt Clark at the convention and perhaps it achieved its purpose. Clark won 66 percent of the vote, a figure he felt wasn't enough to secure his authority, and he subsequently called a leadership convention. The 66 percent result was certainly all the proof Tory MP Elmer MacKay needed, saying it showed Clark was perceived "like the dog food that won't sell." After Mulroney won the leadership, it was MacKay who stepped aside in Central Nova to give his new leader a seat in 1983. In the 1984 election, when Mulroney ran in Quebec, MacKay returned to his former seat. He has been in Mulroney's cabinet ever since.

The same poll also asked respondents about their attitudes toward other potential Tory federal leaders: Bill Davis, Peter Lougheed, David Crombie, Brian Mulroney, and Edmonton businessman Peter Pocklington. Pocklington, in fact, was publicly rumoured to be the man behind the poll, although that has not been confirmed.

The shenanigans with polls at the 1983 Tory convention were perhaps more brutal than the abuse of polls in the party's 1976 leadership convention, but one "poll" then did contribute substantially to a famous Canadian political truism.

Having lost to Trudeau twice, Bob Stanfield decided he'd had enough of politics and was stepping down, setting up the Tory convention for late February 1976. There were twelve candidates. Brian Mulroney finished third, and Joe Clark came up the middle to defeat Claude Wagner.

But one of the most enduring products of that convention was something called the "Flora Syndrome," a widely known Canadian political phenomenon that has come to mean the difference between public and private support for political leadership candidates. What is not commonly known, however, is that the "Flora Syndrome" is the result of a poll. Or, to be more precise, a phantom poll concocted by long-time Tory back-room boy Eddie Goodman and former New Brunswick premier Richard Hatfield, both key men in Flora MacDonald's failed leadership bid.

Before the first ballot on February 22, Flora wasn't seen by the media as a major contender for the job. It turned out she wasn't. Hatfield says she never really did have that much support, but everybody thought she did because they were whispering in reporters' ears about a poll that showed her with a good chance of winning. The idea, of course, was to overcome the reluctance among delegates who liked her, but felt a woman couldn't win. Instead, it heightened expectations to unrealistic levels, and spawned the "Flora Syndrome" as an explanation for her unexpectedly poor showing.

In his autobiographical book *Life of the Party*, Goodman wrote, "We had scrutineers at every polling booth to check on the number of Flora buttons that were worn into the booth. More people were wearing Flora buttons than were wearing the buttons of any other candidate, a total of 283. Unfortunately, when the vote was held, Flora finished sixth, with only 214 votes."

Hatfield now says, "Part of the so-called Flora Syndrome came about as a result of a poll not taken, but made up by Eddie Goodman, which I saw and used along with him and others during that leadership campaign. There was no poll taken, but people were publishing our results, and the expectation of her doing much better than she did was raised."

Goodman had done this sort of thing before. In his book, Goodman mentions a "poll" he and a colleague devised late in the 1968 "Trudeaumania" campaign, hoping to help Stanfield, based on "some rather superficial inquiries . . . in the most optimistic areas," published by Confederation Publishing, a company owned by the Tory party, purportedly showing the Tories doing better than they had in the last published Gallup. "No one had expected the poll to be believed," wrote Goodman. "I had not tried to camouflage the fact that it was taken totally under the auspices of the Conservatives. . . . The main purpose of the exercise . . . was to slow down the media's reporting of polls and perhaps make them question their accuracy."

The Tories, of course, have no monopoly on poll abuse. In 1982, then Multiculturalism minister Jim Fleming was trying to hype interest in a conference on race relations and the law, so he released the result of a Gallup poll that he said showed one-third of the 2,000 respondents supported the idea of an all-white society. Fleming said racism often increased during tough economic times, adding that the poll indicated we have "some serious problems."

One of those serious problems was the blatant abuse of polling data by politicians, Fleming in this case. A close examination of that poll shows that a substantial majority of Canadians surveyed by Gallup welcomed a multi-racial society. Asked if they favoured maintaining "a fairly open immigration policy with few limitations," 65 percent said yes, and only 16 percent were in general disagreement. Only 12 percent favoured cutting off all non-white immigration, while 71 percent disagreed with that suggestion.

Of the thirteen questions, only one elicited a negative response: "I would limit non-white immigration and those who were let in would have to prove themselves before they were entitled to government-supported services." Fifty-eight percent agreed. But it's a double-barrelled question. Were they agreeing to limit non-white immigration or did they want people to have to prove themselves before receiving government assistance? Since 65 percent said in response to a previous question they favoured an open immigration policy, it seems clear respondents were more concerned with people sponging off the system than they were with skin colour.

Still, as a result of Fleming's sensational statements, a front-page *Toronto Star* story began: "Canada has no intention of restricting immigration by race, in spite of the racist feelings of some Canadians, Multiculturalism Minister Jim Fleming says. 'It would be incredible if any of us started seriously considering restricting people by race,' Fleming told a news conference." It certainly would. First, nobody had asked for such race restrictions, and second, the poll showed the overwhelming majority of Canadians wouldn't approve of them.

But Fleming had achieved his purpose. He generated considerable news coverage and portrayed himself and the Liberals as the dauntless defenders of Canada's rapidly growing visible-minority community. Whether the exercise did anything to encourage racial harmony is another question.

The Liberals were playing polling games again a week before the 1988 Nova Scotia provincial election, when the *Lighthouse Log* in Bridgewater carried news of a poll that put the Liberals slightly ahead in Lunenberg West and Lunenberg Centre, two traditionally strong Tory ridings. The poll was organized by John MacDonald, described in the story as vice-principal of the Park View Education Centre. It was a project for about eighteen gifted Grade 8 graduates chosen for their marks each year in a program called "Stretch for Excellence."

MacDonald told the paper that, in Lunenberg West, forty-eight people responded, of which twenty, or 41.7 percent, supported Liberal Jack Logan, while seventeen, or 35.4 percent, favoured Tory Marie Dechman. Lunenberg Centre had just twenty-four respondents, eleven, or 45.8 percent, favouring the Liberals, and eight, or 33 percent, the Tories. MacDonald also polled Lunenberg East, but said that eleven respondents were not a valid sample.

As for Lunenberg West, however, MacDonald said forty-eight replies compare favourably to those garnered province-wide by Omnifacts Research Ltd. of Dartmouth, which surveys forty to eighty people in a constituency. "I would think there's some validity" to the Lunenberg West results. "It's an indication," he said.

Unfortunately, what the story didn't say is that MacDonald, in addition to being the school's vice-principal and head of the summer program, was a senior member of Liberal candidate Jack Logan's campaign team in Lunenberg West. MacDonald says the project was done "strictly as an academic exercise. I've always been interested in polls and I called Omnifacts to ask them how to conduct one. They were quite helpful. We devised an instrument with five or six questions, and had a practice session before we made the calls," telephoning every fiftieth number in the local phonebook. Asked if it wasn't seen as partisan, given his role as public-relations chairman for the Liberal candidate, MacDonald said, "It probably was, but it wasn't meant to be. I'm convinced we were winning at the time but that late Reid poll turned it against us. We would have won without that."

Perhaps, but local school-board chairman Jane Odergard wasn't impressed. She calls the poll "an error in judgment on MacDonald's part. He may have done it in all good conscience, but the fact he was involved in the campaign didn't wash. I was quite annoyed at the time, although I had to be careful what I said because I'm a known Tory. A person tends to get caught up in political fervor in the middle of the campaign.... I had some problems with his [MacDonald's] professionalism in using children in that way."

As things turned out, the Tories won both Lunenberg West and Centre, although not by much. Tory Marie Dechman, deputy-speaker of the Nova Scotia legislature, said she "wasn't personally offended by students being involved, but I think they [polls] should be done properly, under polling guidelines. Polls, of course, are supposed to be anonymous, random samples, but we know of a couple of cases where the callers knew the person's name and called them by it.... I think the fact that MacDonald was so active for the Liberals put him in a very bad light doing the poll. The appearance is bad. I would think if our communications and advertising director had gone to the school and asked to borrow twenty students to do a poll, they'd say, no way."

The Liberals won another pre-election poll in Lunenberg County, this one called "Magnolia's Burger Poll" after a thirty-seat restaurant in Lunenberg where co-owner Nancy Lohnes, a political-science major, offered customers a chance to buy a Tory, Liberal, or New Democratic hamburger. The NDP finished second; the Tories, third. "We even had a few for Dukakis," she said, from some American tourists, "and a few well-known Liberals and Tories are in here every second day, having a burger."

In neighbouring New Brunswick, one week before the November

21 federal election, reporters in Saint John were summoned to a press conference at the headquarters of Liberal candidate Joe Boyce where a poll by Delta Opinion Research of Fredericton showed Boyce leading Conservative cabinet minister Gerald Merrithew by eight points. At the time, Gallup had the Liberals leading the Conservatives 44 to 39 in Atlantic Canada, and Environics had a virtual tie in the region. (The Atlantic breakdown in the national polls has a margin of error of about plus or minus eight points.)

Mike Brown, a Saint John insurance salesman who was Boyce's acting campaign manager, said the poll was conducted Saturday, November 12, and asked five hundred Saint John voters who they would support. He said the exact results couldn't be released "for strategy purposes." Then again, maybe they didn't want to be too exact because there is no such company as Delta Opinion Research. According to University of New Brunswick history professor Art Doyle, it's a name used by New Brunswick Liberals on an ad-hoc basis. "Delta is simply in-home. It's not professional, although we try to be scientific. Normally it would never get quoted, and some people got annoyed when they quoted it."

In any event, after the poll was announced the radio stations, in particular, immediately reported the "news" that, according to the Delta poll, Boyce was beating Merrithew. Mark Tunney, a reporter for the *Saint John Evening Times-Globe*, was skeptical. He didn't write a story for that day's paper. Instead, Tunney sniffed around and wrote a story the next day, putting the findings in a dubious light. "The parties do internal stuff all the time," says Tunney, "but calling it a poll gives it a kind of official ring, which it doesn't deserve. It was a late-morning press conference to hit the noon broadcast news."

Rene Cormier, Merrithew's press secretary, says, "When we first heard it we said, 'Oh, my god, this is going to hurt.' It put us on edge, for a few hours anyway. The radio stations broadcast the numbers, but they did follow-up stories on Delta later. Still, it can hurt you a bit I suppose if people are putting out false information."

Brown concedes the poll was conducted by Liberal-party workers and volunteers, but he still speaks as if it's a real company. "Delta tells us the procedure to follow," he says. "It's an outfit in Fredericton. No, it's not listed. I forget who the principals are. It was a legitimate poll. I didn't want to get sucked into something so we'd be kidding ourselves." Brown says they got responses from five hundred people. Asked about the media coverage of the poll, Brown says, "We were very discouraged over the fact they implied it was rigged. It wasn't. We were told by Delta this is how you handle it." Boyce lost to Merrithew by about 2,000 votes. Maybe with some help from a real pollster, he might have gone over the top.

Across the Northumberland Strait and down to the east side of Prince Edward Island, businessman Gene Murphy was working in his general store on the main street of Montague last March, when some old friends came in and said, "I hear you're running for the Liberals." That was the first Murphy had heard of it. He had always gone out of his way to avoid any partisan activities with either the Liberals or the Tories.

Jim MacNeill, editor of the *Eastern Graphic*, explains, "Businessmen in a town like this can get themselves into difficulty with this sort of thing. Some people will deal with him if he belongs to one party, and others won't."

Murphy and some other people complained to MacNeill that someone had been calling local people with a list of four names, including Murphy's, asking if they'd vote Liberal in the next provincial election if any of those men carried the party banner. Murphy was furious. "It's frustrating. I don't know who took the poll, nobody will say, so there's no way for me to register my anger at the unauthorized use of my name. It's just not right. Nobody asked me if they could use my name. If I want to proclaim a particular party allegiance, that's one thing. But for somebody to presume a particular allegiance on my behalf, without my knowledge, that's outrageous."

MacNeill wrote a small item in his column entitled, "What Nerve," in which he blamed the P.E.I. Liberal Party, even though they weren't admitting to it. He says that one thing which really surprised him was "the one making the call was difficult to understand because he had a heavy French accent. It surprised me they would have somebody with an accent calling here."

It also surprised Glenda Duncan, executive director of the P.E.I. Liberal Party. "How do you know it's a Liberal poll?" she asked. "I'm not aware that it's a Liberal poll. We don't know who did it. It could be the PCs. Have you asked them?" At which point she volunteered the name and phone number of her Tory counterpart, then added, "He'll tell you it's a Liberal poll."

Provincial ridings in P.E.I. have two members, councillors and assemblymen, and both members for Third Kings at the time were

Tories. "They haven't been in the best of health," says Duncan. "Maybe the Tories are looking around for potential candidates." She says she hasn't seen a bill for a poll come across her desk. "Maybe the premier's office did it. The premier [Joe Ghiz] is always polling as any modern political party must do or they wouldn't stay in power. Maybe the government did it." Asked if that wouldn't be mixing government business and party business, she said, "That's the way it is in P.E.I. This island is so small too that if you start polling it doesn't take long to get out. If you get called in Toronto, you likely don't go out and tell your neighbour, but here you do. It gets election fever in the air, just the fact a poll is being taken."

Percy Downe, the premier's executive assistant, didn't hesitate a moment when told the query was being made for a book in the fall. "The poll was done for the Liberal Party of P.E.I. Glenda hasn't seen the bill yet because we haven't received the bill. . . . We want to know if people see potential candidates as people they'd want to elect. This is part of an ongoing process. We've done various ridings. Names come to the party. The local riding officials often mention certain people." Murphy says the local Liberal president phoned to say he had nothing to do with the poll.

Downe said the poll was done by "a national firm," but he couldn't name the firm. Asked if it was Decima, he laughed. Asked if it was Goldfarb, he said, "I can't say."

Downe thinks, however, that Murphy should be honoured not angered at being included. "It shows he's well liked by all sides, a successful businessman, well respected. I can understand why he's upset, I suppose, but he should look on it as a compliment as to how well he's thought of in the area."

He doesn't.

Newfoundland Tory leader Tom Rideout is another man who wasn't complimenting his pollster — Decima's Allan Gregg — on April 20, 1989, after suffering the ignominy of becoming Canada's shortest-reigning premier because he called an election based on a Gregg poll giving him a 51 to 30 percent lead over Clyde Wells and his provincial Liberals just three weeks before election day. Rideout, overseeing the end of a seventeen-year Tory dynasty, quipped sardonically to reporters that the Decima poll must have been "the twentieth time," a reference to the standard claim made by pollsters that their numbers are within certain margins of error nineteen out of twenty times.

Rideout will undoubtedly always regret having viewed the Decima poll as a reliable precursor of events, thus repeating the mistakes made by John Turner in 1984, who'd found both Gallup and Goldfarb irresistibly encouraging, and Ontario's Frank Miller in 1986, who'd been assured by Gregg he enjoyed an insurmountable lead over Liberal David Peterson. All three men lost their jobs. All three chose to go to the electorate quickly, tossing away the opportunity to strengthen their leadership presence through political action, simply because their polls, always inflated by convention publicity, gave them a temporary surge of support.

Granted, campaign events can alter pre-writ perceptions, but in Newfoundland, where the campaign is just three weeks long, and despite some unfriendly acts from Rideout's federal Tory cousins on the Canada–France fishing treaty, the Hibernia offshore oil-development delay, and Unemployment Insurance reform, Decima's twenty-one-point Tory lead does not seem credible in retrospect.

Gregg wasn't the only pollster who missed the boat in the Newfoundland election. Two others taken late in that campaign also gave the losing Tories a comfortable lead. An Omnifacts poll commissioned by the Tories and reported in the April 15 *St. John's Evening Telegram*, five days before the vote, gave Rideout an eleven-point lead over the Liberals, while a poll by Research Associates (RASE) published the next day in the *Sunday Express* gave the Tories a tidy six-point edge, 50 to 43.9.

The Tories had gone into the election holding thirty-four of the fifty-two legislative seats, with the Liberals far behind, with fourteen. The NDP had two, and there were two vacancies. When the fog had cleared election night, the Liberals had won thirty-one seats; the Tories, twenty-one; even though the Tories marginally out-polled their opponents province-wide, 48 to 47 percent of the vote, another reminder that in a parliamentary system the popular vote is only indirectly relevant to the election outcome, making seat projections based on global-survey numbers precarious at best.

Veteran Newfoundland Liberal MP George Baker says taking polls on the sea-tossed island province is particularly risky "because Newfoundlanders consider their vote a very private matter, so they're not going to tell some stranger over the phone who they're voting for."

One senior Newfoundland Liberal admits, however, that even

though the party was confident it was winning, based on their intelligence reports from around the province, they were worried that the two late-campaign polls showing the Tories winning would hurt their chances.

On the Sunday before the election, after the RASE poll put the Tories six points ahead, Wells took time out from campaigning in Renews on the south shore to discuss the polling situation with his aides.

One Liberal who took part in the ensuing events said, "Clyde was inundated with requests on the Sunday to respond to the polls. He was saying, 'We didn't get a goddamn poll done, but we're going to get some people on the phone and do one.' Then an aide said, 'Does it make any difference?' and everybody agreed it didn't, so we just decided to make one up."

About 7:00 that evening, four senior Liberal officials, two from Gander and two from St. John's, spent about fifteen minutes on a conference call, deciding what the Liberal "poll" would say. "There was no poll," says the Liberal insider. "In fact, we were into an awful argument about whether it should show us way ahead or show us in a tight battle with the Tories. We were convinced we were going to win, but we wanted to invent a poll just to balance things out in case too many people believed the published polls."

The main front-page story in the Monday, April 17, *Evening Telegram*, just four days before the vote, was headlined, "Poll Politics: Who Has The Momentum?" The news story explained, "Now the Liberals have added their own poll," reporting that a survey released by the party that morning gave them a 3.5 percent edge, 49.1 to 45.6, over the Tories. It said 421 Newfoundlanders were surveyed by telephone the night before by "research professionals within the Liberal campaign organization," supplemented with data provided by an unnamed "major national polling organization." The poll also asked if conditions in Newfoundland warranted the replacement of the Tory government, and 56.9 percent said "yes," 27.74 said "no," and 15.3 percent didn't know.

"The whole thing was bullshit," says the insider. "The figures were just pulled out of the air. Clyde knew about it. We told him it was concocted when we gave him the numbers. Hell, as it turned out, we were a lot closer than the so-called legitimate polls anyway. At least we picked the right winner."

15

Massaging the Message

On Monday, October 3, 1988, the *Globe and Mail* featured a major, front-page story by its Ottawa bureau chief Christopher Waddell on the election prospects of Prime Minister Brian Mulroney, capturing the tone of the media's poll-driven election coverage, setting the stage for a campaign that would see not only more media polling than ever, but the use of poll results as justification for muddying the traditional line between straight news and opinion.

The *Globe* wouldn't be the only media outlet guilty of excessive flattery in its coverage of the Tory campaign and blatant bias against, first, the Liberals and, then, both opposition parties. Nearly every major media operation in the country approached the campaign as if the only contest was for second, between the Liberals and the NDP, with the Tories cruising easily to another majority victory. The *Toronto Star*, Canada's largest-circulation newspaper, went against the grain but turned out to be just as biased in favour of the Liberals, mainly because of its editorial conviction that free trade was an abomination. But the *Globe*, Canada's self-styled "national newspaper," was equally fervent in promoting free trade and used the myriad campaign polls to push the point.

"With opinion polls suggesting the Progressive Conservatives could win a majority of seats in the federal election," wrote Waddell, in the *Globe*'s first edition after the election had been called, "the Tories know that one of their major tasks will be to gain at least grudging respect from Canadians for Prime Minister Brian Mulroney."

A kicker headline over the story shouted, "New Polls Boost Tory Hopes," and presumably, judging by what followed, the hopes of *Globe* management as well.

At the time, the latest *Globe*–Environics poll had the Tories at 37 percent of decided voters, the Liberals at 33, and the NDP at 25, nowhere near enough support to win a majority government. The story did not mention that, however. In fact, the only specific reference to the *Globe*'s own poll was to point out that Mulroney had been gaining ground on Ed Broadbent in terms of being the best candidate for prime minister.

This approach to the election was standard across the country in both print and broadcast journalism. When more polls emerged within that first week, showing the Tories higher — although still below majority numbers — one can only speculate on the impact this nation-wide outpouring of flattering Tory coverage had on the results of those polls.

In its first post-writ edition, *Maclean's* magazine featured a cover picture of a smiling Brian Mulroney, and again the theme was that the Tories were heading for easy victory, and John Turner and the Liberals would be lucky even to finish second, ahead of the NDP. Indeed, a story headline read, "Turner's Future Likely At Stake; Latest Poll Puts The NDP Second." It featured a colour picture of a smiling, relaxed Broadbent, sitting in a park-like setting, his white shirt open at the neck, a red sweater casually tossed over his shoulders, with the cutline, "Broadbent, the 'happy campaigner.'"

This same picture, of an election result predetermined by polls, emerged on the TV networks and most radio stations as well, despite the decidedly spotty record of campaign pollsters, past and present. In almost any other area, journalists tend to be skeptical, practitioners of the classic I'm-from-Missouri-show-me attitude. But polls are routinely regurgitated as fact, taken at face value, with journalists showing little interest, and even less knowledge, in exposing the shortcomings of survey techniques.

To a large extent, polls, rather than complementing experience and personal judgment, have replaced them in journalists, just as they have in politicians. Journalists constantly attack politicians for governing by polls, for lacking the guts to lead in the face of computerized data, while they themselves can't wait to rush off to the closest word processor in their breathless eagerness to tell the voters how they're going to vote long before the polling booths open.

Somewhere along the line, it's impossible to say where, exactly, pollsters have been elevated from being people who told us, approximately, what public opinion was, to clairvoyants, modern-day authors of Sibylline books whose numbers possess the mystical qualities of being able to divine the future with far more precision than they could ever define the past. Pollsters have achieved this status, have become the Merlins of the court, thanks largely to the reverential reportage of their efforts in the media. Not all journalists, of course, have been consumed by this new political theology, but most have, certainly to the point of allowing pollsters to become far and away the major determinants of how the 1988 federal election was covered.

Journalists will blithely report the pronouncements of "name" pollsters regardless of how much or how often they contradict themselves. Angus Reid, for example, was widely quoted between the two elections as predicting, with considerable certainty and flair, a minority Liberal government, a minority NDP government, the death of the Liberal party, and a Tory government to boot. Anyone in another field with this sort of track-record would be justifiably ignored or ridiculed, but the every utterance of pollsters becomes true wisdom — they have numbers, after all — and journalists suffer a collective amnesia in not reminding readers, viewers, and listeners of the excesses of past predictions from the same pollster. All this is a wonderful thing for the pollsters. But it makes for poor journalism, and short-changes the public.

Winnipeg Liberal MP David Walker, a former pollster himself, says, "The media too often takes these guys at face value. They don't even demand to see the questions. They're all partisan; Gregg, Goldfarb, Reid, all of them have their own axes to grind, just as everybody does. The media wouldn't do this in other areas. Why do they accept polls without a critical look?"

And *Globe* columnist Jeffrey Simpson, writing in the March 1987 edition of *Policy Options*, argued, "Just as love is often wasted on the young, so polls are often wasted on the media. The substantial increase in the number of pollsters has been matched only by the explosion in the number of journalists reporting them. Many journalists, including those who write about political matters, are unschooled in Canadian history, in polling methodology, in an understanding of any part of the country but their own. Yet the beguiling simplicity and easy accessibility of polling data embolden all journalists to become instant pundits, or worse still, experts. They can pontificate on the meaning of this, the likely outcome of that, the significance of everything, on the basis of a few stark numbers."

In July 1983, Tory pollster Allan Gregg blasted the media as 'hideous consumers of research. The media use them for predicting events, and polls are not good at telling you what is going to happen." Gregg, of course, does that sort of thing himself, and, what's more, is adept at whispering selective data in a reporter's ear and watching it come out as informed, insider journalism.

In a post-election survey of 1988 media coverage, the conservative Fraser Institute analysed CTV, CBC television, the *Globe*, and CBC radio, and concluded that polling horse-race stories represented only 10 percent of election coverage, 15 percent on CTV. They also argued that the coverage of Mulroney "tended to be negative and extensive." This bizarre finding was based, however, on the Institute's own data showing that 45 percent of this "negative" coverage was simple reportage of quotes from the other two leaders. In terms of issues, free trade led the way, with 1,115 references, followed by the debate (441), the economy (300), and the polls (268).

But even when polls are not mentioned in a story, they have a dramatic impact on the coverage. Turner's early attempt to drum up media interest in his forty-point platform, for example, failed primarily because at that point the media had decided, based on the polls, that Turner had no chance of implementing his program anyway. Mulroney, and to a lesser extent Broadbent, enjoyed predominantly positive coverage before the debate, the toughest criticism of the prime minister being that he was campaigning in a bubble.

After the debate, coverage changed dramatically, but only after the polls showed that Turner had a chance after all and Broadbent — whose poll standings had inspired journalists, and him, to romanticize about a two-party system — suddenly became the odd-guy out himself.

The Canadian Daily Newspaper Publishers Association has guidelines on polling coverage, observed more in the breach than in the observance. In any event, newspapers publishing polls are encouraged to include the name of the sponsor, the polling firm, precise question wording, sample size, error margin, interview methods (i.e., phone, in-home, or mail), and dates of the interviews. The *Globe* and CBC were relatively conscientious in reporting methodology — although they wavered badly on reporting regional breakdowns — but the bulk of the media continues at best to pay lip service to these guidelines.

The CBC opened the campaign by announcing it would not highlight the horse-race aspect of each individual poll. Instead, it showed a range of party-preference standings on a graph (unfortunately the graph was incomprehensible). CBC coverage adhered pretty much to this policy except when its own polls were announced. Then it ran big advertisements in the newspapers, even held a media lock-up, and allowed the poll to dominate coverage for at least the evening the poll was released.

When the *Globe*'s Environics poll had the Tories winning handily, it was the main front-page story. After the debate, when their poll had the Liberals ahead, the poll story was down-graded to just above the front-page fold, and even that only after a bitter dispute within the newsroom in which senior management wanted to play the story even lower. By the same token, when the *Globe*-Environics poll showed the free trade deal "gaining favor" — 44 percent in favour, 42 opposed — that too was on the front page. Later in the campaign, when their own poll showed support slipping, the *Globe* put the story on an inside page.

The main, front-page headline in the October 12 *Globe* read, "Tories Jump Up To Wide Lead In Polls As NDP Bumps Liberals To Third." That poll contained some data that was ten days old by the time the *Globe* published it, an eternity in the middle of an election campaign. Same thing with the CBC's first poll, aired on a special election edition of "Sunday Report" on October 16. Peter Mansbridge assured viewers that the Tories were headed for a majority if there were no radical opinion changes "between now and election day." Some of the "now" he was speaking of, however, was nine days old. For its part, the *Toronto Star* announced at the campaign outset that it would give front-page prominence to the Gallup polls it was paying for, although that resolve disappeared in the rabidly anti-free trade newspaper when Angus Reid's post-debate poll showed the Liberals had pulled ahead of the Tories, largely on the strength of Turner's remarkable attack on Mulroney's free-trade position.

Southam columnist Don McGillivray, a long-time advocate of the cautious use of polls by journalists, wrote that the dates when questions were asked are like the "best before" dates on groceries. "They

tell you how stale the merchandise is." This significant point is usually ignored, as the media routinely report the numbers as if they were
collected the day they are being published. They aren't. And given
the ups and downs of the last campaign, a delay of even four or five
days can make a dramatic difference in just precisely where public
opinion is.

The number of pre-debate campaign polls placing the Liberals
third provides a textbook example of how even some of Canada's
most experienced journalists give undue authority to polling. Peter
C. Newman, commenting in his October 24 *Maclean's* column on the
recent *Globe*-Environics poll putting the Liberals third, wrote,
"Unless this trend is reversed by November 21 — and that seems
unlikely because the longer Liberal Leader John Turner campaigns,
the lower he falls in public opinion ratings — a new coalition of
political forces is about to take power in Ottawa. As a third party, the
Liberals would eventually vanish as an ameliorating and socially
aware influence on Canada."

Newman went on to tell of a private dinner conversation among
Angus Reid, Jean Chrétien, and Manitoba Liberal leader Sharon
Carstairs about a week before the election was called, in which
Chrétien said a Tory majority and the collapse of the Liberals to third
would be disastrous. "Reid, who probably understands the Canadian
political scene better than anyone," wrote Newman, "shrugged and
casually predicted that both of these cataclysmic events were in the
cards." Newman, incidentally, might have pointed out to his readers,
particularly during the campaign, that he is under contract as
Mulroney's official biographer and has become fast friends with the
prime minister.

On the same day, Link Byfield, publisher of the pro-Tory *Western
Report*, writing a column based on the same Environics poll, could
not contain his glee at the prospect. Cautioning readers that the
"Liberals, admittedly, aren't dead yet," Byfield also wrote, "As we
watch John Turner's campaign die a lingering death, we may well be
witnessing the final collapse of Canada's once-invincible middle-
ground party. The prospect is enticing. The party which plundered
the West eight years ago is about to be skewered and shaken like a rat
on a pitchfork." Much of that smugness seemed to have vanished by
the November 14 issue, when the magazine worked itself into a frenzy
over Turner's come-back, running a front-page drawing of Turner,
his teeth bared like Dracula's fangs, with the headline, "The Politics
of FEAR."

In the meantime, the *Globe* was doing its bit to ensure a third-place Liberal finish with an October 20, front-page article by Waddell headlined, "Grit Demise A Tarnished Dream: Collapse Of Liberals Could Cut NDP Gains." The story basically took the Liberal death-rattle as a given, and even suggested that Broadbent's musings a week earlier of a two-party system (which turned out to be a dreadful error by the NDP leader) might have been a deliberate tactic "to stem falling support for the beleaguered Grits" because it is easier for them to win seats by sneaking up the middle when the Tories and Liberals split the vote. At the time this story was published, the NDP was just three points ahead of the Liberals in the Environics poll and one point ahead in Gallup, both well within margins of error, far too close to be considered meaningful, let alone absolute.

In late October, a computer analysis in the *Vancouver Sun* of the latest Angus Reid poll putting the Liberals and Tories tied at 35 percent each of decided voters, concluded that the Liberals "would win Vancouver Quadra, Vancouver Centre and North Vancouver if they take their current momentum into the polls November 21." With a national sample of 1,502, that worked out to 173 from British Columbia, fewer than 6 in any single riding, only 3 in the huge Vancouver Centre riding.

The *Sun*, of course, desperately wanted to turn a national poll into a local poll, but with such minute sampling it's not only absurd, it's irresponsible. Breaking out British Columbia by itself leads to huge margins of error, but going the next step and applying the results of a national poll to an individual riding shouldn't be done. Unfortunately, it's not an uncommon media practice. Even the *Sun* belatedly recognized the madness of their computer analysis and published a subsequent story clarifying the situation, but not before other media across the country got excited by the prospects of Liberal Tex Enemark defeating NDP national president Johanna den Hertog and former Socred leadership candidate Kim Campbell, who was representing the Tories. After the post-debate Liberal surge, some newspapers included Enemark's name as a sure-fire cabinet minister in a Liberal government. As it turned out, Enemark finished a distant third, behind Campbell, the winner, and den Hertog.

Winnipeg pollster Greg Mason says media polls "tend to be quick and dirty. They tend not to be financed well. Polling firms often do them, not for the purposes of revealing knowledge, but for straightforward marketing purposes . . . to become a household name. I will not say we've been completely impervious to that kind of motivation. A front-page story in which your poll is identified is worth a hell of a lot more advertising than you could possibly pay for. But it does tend to be less rigorous. It's not because you're taking it any less seriously, it's because the media tend to be notoriously cheap. They absolutely gasp when they hear some of the prices. National political polls run upwards of $70,000."

For its two polls, the CBC spent $167,000; the *Globe* paid Environics about $40,000 for three campaign polls; the *Star* paid Gallup about $10,000 for eight polls; CTV paid Insight about $70,000; Baton paid Goldfarb $20,000 for campaign polling; and Southam paid Angus Reid about $40,000 for three campaign polls. Only the CBC paid full market value. When *Maclean's* magazine began its deal for yearly state-of-the-nation polls with Allan Gregg, they paid less than $5,000 for a poll that was worth about $70,000 commercially, and part of the deal was the magazine would run pictures of Decima personnel along with the data.

The whole exercise raises serious ethical questions about the media accepting cut-rate professional services in return for company advertising. *Globe* reporters, for example, were told not to accept Aeroplan points on the campaign (even though the media pay heavily for the campaign seats) yet the newspaper thought nothing of paying Environics about one-quarter of what their polling work was worth commercially.

The other issue media polling raises is the whole matter of the media going from reporting the news to manufacturing it themselves. Public-opinion polls are not news in the sense that other campaign activities, such as speeches or announcements, are. But polling "news" is generated by the media themselves, not by external events that the media are covering.

Many U.S. newspapers and TV networks have designated beat reporters to specialize in polls so they'll be in a position to understand the meaning and methodology and not be snowed under by a fast-talking pollster. Many newspapers and TV networks in the United States have also joined forces to do joint polls, rather than each media outlet having its own.

Canadian Facts president Donald Monk says another shortcoming in the media's coverage of polls is "the tendency to make too much of a very small difference. You know, you hear the news saying the latest poll shows Conservatives have gone down by one point. Now I think that's really ridiculous. Nobody knows really whether they've gone down by one point or up by one point. That's too close to call." In addition, says Monk, rather than concentrate on a single poll, it's the trend over time that is really important, although during an election campaign that often gets lost.

cbc's Ottawa bureau chief Elly Alboim, a fierce advocate of media polling, says, "There's no doubt we [media] over-polled," but he is angry that much of the media polling was of "indifferent quality, in some case bad quality." The cbc had planned to do just one survey, "but then the world changed" after the debate and it did another one. The cbc, like the *Globe*, has a policy where it will not commission its own polls within ten days of the election, although both report other media polls during that period. Alboim disagrees with the policy. "I don't agree with the ten-day ban. It's an editorial tool like any other editorial tool and you suddenly tie one hand behind your back and say we are no longer going to commit journalism in this field."

Alboim says the ban caused serious problems in the presentation of the cbc's final poll because it had to be shown as part of the national-news package on a Thursday night rather than having the entire hour-long "Sunday Report" special devoted to it. "I think we ran nineteen out of twenty-two minutes on polls, which I'm afraid is wrong and we knew it," he says. "None of us was very happy with that.... We could have done a much fuller explanation of our conclusions, but it would have taken four or five minutes and we didn't have it."

Indeed, Martin Goldfarb said, when he watched the way the poll was presented, "There's no way based on what they showed that they could have come to the conclusion they did [a Tory minority]. On that day, Mansbridge presented the material with the Liberals ahead in Atlantic Canada, ahead in Quebec, and ahead in Ontario. There's no way you could come to that conclusion based on that data. It may be that the data they had said that, but they didn't show how they got to a Tory minority. I think that's irresponsible."

Alboim, who along with Arnold Amber has been in charge of the cbc polling for twelve years, says, "I don't do it for a living, but I'm good enough to be able to draw up a questionnaire. I'm good enough, in conjunction with other people, to do analysis." Unlike other media outlets, in fact, the cbc simply hires a professional polling firm (in the last election it was Canadian Facts) to do the field-work. The CBC essentially provides the questions and does the analysis. "We want control on methodology," says Alboim. "We would never allow our pollster to make the analytical judgments based on the numbers."

Alboim acknowledges "a lot of us head for these polls because they're an easy news pop. It's nice to say a CBC poll says this, or a *Globe* poll says that, and get the reverberating coverage in the other media. You enter the big leagues by having your own.... I've been very persistent all along on polling. I must confess there is an element of competitiveness there ... but more, polls give our reporters an evidentiary base on which to rest their conclusions ... and because the parties do so much polling, in order to understand them strategically and tactically, it's important to see why they're headed certain places and doing certain things when polling is the substreet on which they made decisions. It's also important for the quality and nature of our coverage.... Once we discovered through polling the astonishing illiteracy rate on free trade, it really did reposition our coverage. We did much more substantive, detailed reporting on the issue. We devoted two hours of 'Sunday Report.'" (Actually, Alboim could have bought the September 14 *Toronto Star* for 35 cents and learned that, according to a Decima poll, 72 percent of those inter- viewed said they didn't understand the free-trade deal.)

The CBC also attempted to show how a focus group works, but time constraints allowed only little snippets of a session to be shown from time to time, prompting Conservative campaign official John Tory to quip, "My reaction when I saw the CBC's focus groups was that Mansbridge had better keep his day job. It just didn't work."

Alboim is so into polling that in mid-campaign he called then *Globe* managing editor Geoffrey Stevens to complain about an Environics poll. "He told me they're the experts, we just publish this. I told him they publish it so they have ultimate responsibility for the content. He said no, this is an area of expertise we contract out. Well, it's a different view."

Another oddity with Alboim is his contiguous relationship with pollsters, a circumstance that, depending on your point of view, either makes him a valuable asset in CBC political coverage or places the normal journalistic notion of detached-observer status in jeop- ardy. Michael Adams of Environics says that, when Alboim called him on a regular basis, he seemed to know what the party numbers were. And Liberal campaign director John Webster said in a telephone interview with the author that Alboim tried to make a deal with him at the beginning of the campaign, but he wasn't interested.

"Elly came to see me at the beginning of the campaign and said, 'You show me yours, and I'll show you mine,'" said Webster. "I said no. He said he'd had this deal with [Michael] Kirby, so I told him to go and see Kirby then. Elly thinks he's a pollster. I don't think he is. He looked at me as the new kid on the block. He wanted to see if I would drop my pants, but I wouldn't. I told him I wasn't in the business of trading information, so he went and made his deal with Kirby."

Alboim flatly denies he made any deals with anybody, although he admits he did have regular access to the polling numbers from the three major parties. "I'm not going to be disingenuous and tell you I didn't have a very good sense during the campaign what the three parties' numbers were, but I'm not alone in that. I think you could find a number of reporters in this town who had them."

Alboim says the night the screwy Gallup showed the Liberals miles ahead of the Tories, reporter Wendy Mesley ended her report by saying the Gallup numbers don't correspond with the numbers from the three political parties. "That obviously implies we knew something about the numbers the parties had," he says. "But I didn't make any deal to trade numbers. . . . I'm concerned people would say that. The only briefing I gave was of the CBC poll the day it was published. . . . We provide them [the parties] with a detailed breakdown as a courtesy; that's all."

Alboim says he met with Webster twice during the campaign, once right at the beginning, "and there isn't any doubt that we discussed polling. I said I would like to be able to call him during the campaign and see how things were going. Either he misunderstood, or misinterpreted that . . . or he's angry about that [mid-campaign Turner coup] story. I was just trying to establish a relationship with the new kid on the block, that's all. . . . I have a technocratic interest in the subject of polling that other guys in our business don't have. Over the years you build up contacts and trusts in this business, and of course you talk to these people. But it doesn't extend to any formal relationship. That would be despicable. It would put me in an intolerable position of conflict."

Jack Fleischman, a former long-term CTV producer who came back on contract to run CTV's coverage of the 1988 campaign happened to bring his client Michael Marzolini along with him. CTV had been using

Thompson and Lightstone with considerable success, "but they're more into marketing, very touchy-feely stuff," says Fleischman. "It takes a strange mix of instinct and care for detail to make polling work. Marzolini did a good job. No media organization had ever commissioned a rolling poll before, but it's a terrific asset in our coverage.... You see the politicians playing to their strengths and avoiding the weaknesses. Instead of a snapshot of the campaign, it's a motion picture. Even with the violent changes in this election, we were there. Twelve hours after the debate, we were in the field. We knew what had happened."

Fleischman says the cbc spent a lot of money needlessly and polled double and triple ctv's samples. "That's a questionable thing to do. Once you've hit the magic 1,000, the only way to improve the veracity of what you've got is by asking the right questions, not by asking more people. The fact is, cbc was behind us every time. That has a lot to do with the instrument. It's one thing to be a good reporter, as Elly [Alboim] is. It's another thing to be a good pollster. Listen, Elly is a friend of mine, but he shouldn't ought to have done it the way he did.

"We had a professional building our questions. We'd suggest the issues, but we were not only using his telephones, we were using his talent as well.

"Potentially, there's nothing more powerful than information you can cull from opinion polls," says Fleischman. "You can sense people's emotions from the numbers, sense what they sense, what they fear. You can see their dreams and sense the difference between their dreams and the reality. You can see that from polling, and parties use polling to try to bridge that gap.... Too bad cbc and ctv do polling only in election campaigns. They should be doing it all the time. Why shouldn't the public know what it thinks? The government certainly does."

After the leaders' debates, of course, the polls showed a sudden Liberal surge and that too affected the subsequent media coverage. Certainly the cbc and others continued to report the reaction of the leaders to the many polls (Turner would say he doesn't react to them; Mulroney would say he'd always said elections are tough; and Broadbent would say the party had never been in better shape). But just as the ndp passing the Liberals had led to journalistic excesses, so too did the Liberal jump to the top. *Ottawa Citizen* columnist Marjorie Nichols, a thorough and effective critic of polling, got a bit carried away herself November 3 in a column headlined, "Mulroney

Goofed When He Called This Election," and ending with the line, "a fall election was a dumb idea." Didn't turn out that way.

Around the same time, panic set in at those newspapers committed to the free-trade deal and hence, to the Tories winning the election. Much was made of the impact of the Liberal lead on the stock exchange, with major stories reporting that the Tory collapse in the polls had led to a drop in the dollar. Since the polls were also showing support for the free-trade deal was also waning, the *Globe*, hoping to jolt Canadians back to their senses, republished six pro–free trade editorials on the op-ed page on the same day, an unprecedented action that clearly demonstrated not only the newspaper's passion for the deal, but just how far it was prepared to go to promote the cause. Had this promotion been confined to the editorial pages, of course, that would be acceptable. But, alas, it spilled over into the news pages and coloured the paper's campaign coverage from start to finish.

The *Calgary Herald* got so sick of the media's use of public-opinion polls that it ran an editorial on November 11, saying: "Intended to be a snapshot of public opinion, polls too often lead public opinion by the nose. Candidates, the electorate and yes, the media, are to blame. This form of witchcraft is fine as far as it goes, which during a heated campaign is always too far." The day before, the main, front-page story in the *Herald* was headlined, "Polls Point To Cliff-hanger"; the story was on the latest Reid and Environics polls.

Also on Remembrance Day, the *Globe*, remembering how much its business audience wanted the Tories to win, ran a series of stories designed to help that process, including an Environics poll with blazing headlines saying, Canadians "Want To Renegotiate, Not Rip Up Trade Deal," all the better to downplay the poll's major finding that 52 percent were now opposed to the deal and only 39 in favour. The *Globe* also ran a story by reporter Ross Howard telling how Tory "strategists have narrowed their focus to a final seven-day effort to rebuild their campaign for a majority government on November 21." There was no story detailing Liberal plans to maintain their momentum for the final week.

On November 19, the pro-Tory *Toronto Sun* ran a full-page story by their then Ottawa columnist Joe O'Donnell based on an "unscientific" poll of 100 voters in the hotly contested Toronto St. Paul's riding, headlined, "Swing Riding Turns To Tory." The *Sun* "poll" found 50 percent voting for Tory minister Barbara McDougall, 38 percent for Liberal Aideen Nicholson, and 12 percent for New Democrat Diane Bull. The story contained a large picture of

McDougall and a picture of a woman that the *Sun* identified as Nicholson, but wasn't. The *Sun*, in fact, had spoken with at least two pollsters — Insight and Carleton's Alan Frizell — about doing campaign polls but decided against it because of the cost. Instead, it sent O'Donnell out to talk to 100 voters in a swing riding that has about 80,000 eligible voters.

On election night itself, Insight called the 43–32–20 vote breakdown dead on with its last poll. Gallup sampled an unprecedented 4,067 Canadians but still missed, although it did make it under its margin of error.

Still, Don Monk says, "By and large it's not very difficult to get the election result right two days before an election. Most people have made up their mind at that time. It's basically the easiest call there is."

Angus Reid says pollsters upset some of the media elite because they undercut their traditional role as pundits. "It makes me puke sometimes to sit back and listen to what some of these media guys say," says Reid. "We have all of the so-called media experts, this little group of fifteen people who think they run the kind of intelligentsia from the media standpoint, who like to wax away about what they think moves the Canadian people."

Editor John Honderich of the *Toronto Star*, one of eight newspapers that used Gallup regularly, says he still has "serious concerns" about the one post-debate poll. "The figures looked startling when they came in, but Gallup has had a good reputation for a long period of time so you decide to stick with it or not. We've done a postmortem on the campaign. Having one's own poll seems to have become part of the competitive framework of the media, and apart from the rogue poll, I think there was general satisfaction."

Southam's Ottawa general manager Doug Fischer calls Reid "the *Toronto Sun* of polling, sort of the tits-and-ass of polling. He certainly has a better record than Gallup, but these guys gang up on him. . . . He has a tendency to shoot his mouth off, so the polling fraternity doesn't like this kind of headline-making." Fischer said Reid makes money from the secondary rights to the polling, which he sells in his quarterly report. As a matter of principle, Southam applies through Access to Information for every government poll. "Look at the polling those guys do, then they've got the nerve to criticize the media for polling. What do they want us to do? We plan to continue."

Former *Globe* managing editor Geoffrey Stevens says, "One of the biggest errors in polling is the interpretation by reporters who don't know how to read them. We insisted the people who do polling write the results." Stevens says he ordered the mid-campaign Environics poll to be downplayed before he even knew what it said. "We wanted to be careful about our play and placement polls, so we're not playing it as if it were the revealed truth. It's not."

Baton boss Doug Bassett says, bluntly, media polls are "a good way to sell newspapers. . . . I use them more for internal things, like what do people think of Sandy Rinaldo now that she's working on 'Night Beat News,' or what do they think of the new set I spent hundreds of thousands on. . . ."

Baton political editor Tom Clark says, "We're not going to see the end of media polling, but there's a growing public reaction against them. It was a counter-productive exercise in the end. There were so many polls the results just lost their impact."

Back in May 1974, Jean-François Bertrand, a Laval University communications professor and son of a former Quebec premier, argued that the media had a responsibility to make more use of polling. "Political parties are going to use polls more and more to find out the party's standing and public opinion on issues and ideas so they can manipulate the public their propaganda is aimed at," he said. "Because of this the mass media must fulfil its function of informing the public."

For all the shortcomings, they've certainly done that.

16

To Ban or Not to Ban

On January 13, 1989, having lost her bid to join her husband Joe Clark and form the first husband-wife team in House of Commons history, Maureen McTeer said there should be "no published polls" during election campaigns.

McTeer, a guest on the PBS TV show "The Editors," said, "I find them [polls] very negative. I find that it distracts people from discussing the issues . . . if in fact we are going to have a situation where we don't somehow control or provide a framework for the information that comes out of polls, that they do become more destructive than beneficial. . . . I have travelled a fair amount in this country and I have never met anyone who has been polled."

Thus, McTeer joined a lengthy chorus of politicians who want to see an end to published polls during election campaigns. Not an end to polling, mind you. McTeer herself commissioned her own constituency poll during her unsuccessful bid for a Commons seat.

Most politicians who call for a ban on public polling share two characteristics: they, or their party, either just lost an election or are behind in the polls; and they want to retain the right to conduct their own private polls.

Still, duplicity has certainly never stopped politicians from moving ahead, and it could be that the only thing stopping a publishing ban is that, as things stand, it would likely not meet the free-speech requirements of the Charter of Rights and Freedoms.

Many countries, unencumbered by charters, already do impose various restrictions upon polling and its publication. France, the United Kingdom, Luxemburg, Malta, Portugal, Spain, Brazil,

Venezuela, and South Africa, all restrict the publication of polling —
from the day before the election in the U.K., to seven days before in
France, forty-two days before in South Africa, and ninety days
before in Portugal. In West Germany, polling firms have long practised a self-imposed restriction on publishing election forecasts during
the last week of a campaign, and in Indonesia a survey permit from
the government, practically impossible to get, is required before a
poll can be taken. In Korea, voter-preference polls simply aren't
allowed, and in such countries as Libya, Iran, Iraq, and Syria no
surveys of any kind are taken. In Saudi Arabia, Jordan, Oman,
Sudan, Kuwait, Bahrein, and Egypt, commercial market-research
surveys are taken, usually with an official government permit required, but no public political polling is done.

Japan, however, is as poll-crazy as North America, with two major
polling associations consisting not only of dozens of polling companies but of representatives of the major media outlets as well. Polls
are also commonplace during Italian elections but often not very
good since, about 40 percent of Italians do not own a telephone,
making telephone samples less than representative. None the less,
that doesn't stop the media from splashing the results all over the
front pages whenever another polling firm wants to make a name for
itself.

In the Soviet Union, there are about fifty full-time pollsters working for the Soviet Institute of Sociological Research, one of a growing
number of public-opinion research organizations to have appeared
during the last few years of Mikhail Gorbachev's glasnost, activities
that would have been unthinkable not many years ago. The Soviet
State Committee planned to conduct ten major polls during 1989
alone, dealing with public attitudes toward such problems as crime,
alcoholism, drug addiction, and pollution. Even Gallup is now allowed into the Soviet Union to conduct market research and measure
consumer demand.

Pollster Angus Reid was moved to write a four-page article about
his business after a trip to China where the China Social Survey (css),
established in 1986, is the most prominent of a growing number of
market-research organizations formed under that country's struc-
tural and economic reforms. css has carried out more than twenty
studies, ranging from how Beijing residents feel about new packaging
for bean-curd milk to their views on reforms presented by party chief
Zhao Ziyang at the Chinese Communist Party's 13th Congress. (That

poll, incidentally, gained international prominence because it showed a significant minority was opposed to the changes, a major departure from these events where the media reports total unanimity to party policies.)

Albert Einstein once offered the following advice to a young man who was uncertain about his career: "Become a public opinion pollster. There you will never be unemployed. We know, after all, that people are ruled by being told tall stories — so the rulers must constantly test and see what they can get away with."

One thing the Liberal government of British Columbia didn't want people to get away with in the late 1930s was publishing public-opinion polls during election campaigns, so they made it illegal, a law that stood until the Social Credit government dropped the ban in 1982 after deciding it was too difficult to enforce, particularly under the new Charter of Rights and Freedoms. The B.C. law did spawn the famous Hamburger Poll, the brain-child in 1964 of restaurateur John Dys who decided to offer burgers named after the political leaders of the day and monitor the sales in his Frying Dutchman restaurants.

The poll, which was clearly illegal, generally showed results of within 10 percent of the actual vote during the early years. But as publicity snowballed, the politicians took a more active role in influencing the outcome of the poll. During the 1972 campaign, with an aging W.A.C. Bennett losing to the NDP after twenty years in power, the Socreds tried to buy the poll but Dys insisted they would have to take delivery of burgers or the results wouldn't count. Three days before the election, cooks began filling the Socred order at 5:00 a.m., and trucks were used to deliver more than 3,000 hamburgers to welfare organizations and party workers, giving the Socreds the lead in the poll. On election night, having been reduced to ten seats in the landslide NDP win, Bennett, with tears in his eyes, said, "We won the poll but we lost the election."

Bennett, of course, is not the first political leader to have won the poll (even the real ones) and lost the election, nor was he alone in expressing strong reservations about them.

In October 1973, Quebec premier Robert Bourassa openly talked about banning polls during the dying days of election campaigns, despite the publication of a CROP poll showing his Liberals well ahead of the Parti Québécois. Bourassa said polls, especially late in campaigns, may have "an unfair influence" on the electorate. In October

1974, Robert Stanfield blamed the "bandwagon effect" of polls for propelling the Liberals to a majority government, and called for a ban on campaign polls.

Two years later, MPS from all parties on the Commons elections committee gave support to two conservative private members' bills promoting a ban. One of those bills was written by Nova Scotia Tory Bob Coates, a former Tory-party president who was the first cabinet minister to resign under the Mulroney regime in the wake of news stories that he and some aides had spent some time in a sleazy, West German strip club. Over the years, Coates was a persistent champion of banning polls, presenting half a dozen bills to Parliament, all of which received general support but ultimately got nowhere.

A 1977 Gallup found that 57 percent of respondents said pre-election polls should not be banned, while 32 percent said they should be. The next year, Ontario's Bill Davis made a move to ban election polls in that province. He had said after the 1975 election — where he had been trailing the Liberals in the polls but still managed to win a bare minority — that "there have to be some controls. You can alter the democratic process if you aren't careful. They [polls] do have some effect and they can be — manipulated, isn't the right word — but you can have figures that vary from what can be the case."

In April 1978, all three parties in the Ontario legislature approved a non-binding private member's resolution that said the government should consider legislation to prohibit during campaigns "the publication or broadcasting of all public opinion polls that purport to indicate the standing of any leader, candidate or party or the status of any issue in the election." About the same time, Conservative MP Dean Whiteway introduced his private member's bill in the Commons, which would have allowed polls to be published, but only if the publication included such information as who took the poll, how many people were asked, and exactly what the questions were.

In 1979, a group of Quebec professors released a study entitled *Political Surveys and Survey Policies in Quebec*, arguing that polls should be outlawed during the final week of a campaign. At other times, they said, published polls should include precise information as to how the poll was conducted, and the methodology and findings should be deposited in the National Assembly library to be available for public scrutiny.

During the 1980 election, with polls giving the Liberals a 17.1-point lead shortly before the election, then prime minister Joe Clark said on an open-line radio program in Charlottetown that the CBC poll (conducted by Carleton's journalism school) was "out of step" and that, indeed, election polls should be prohibited because they are misleading and influence voters. In June 1980, New Brunswick premier Richard Hatfield told a meeting of broadcasters that, if it were up to him, polls would be banned. "I'm totally and completely opposed to them because they are starting to corrupt our political system." And in October 1980, Pierre Trudeau said he would support legislation making it illegal for governments in Canada to conduct public-opinion polling. At the time, Trudeau was under fire from the opposition for refusing to release dozens of publicly financed polls carried out by his government. At one point, Trudeau said, "Quite frankly, I do not give a damn about polls and I do not take polls. I would be perfectly happy to support any move or any legislation making polling at the federal and provincial levels completely illegal."

Again in 1982, MPs from all three parties supported a bill by Coates to ban election polls, but the hour set aside for the private member's bill was talked out before a vote could be taken, effectively killing the bill.

In June 1986, Tory House leader Ray Hnatyshyn introduced a white paper that recommended forcing newspapers and broadcasters to publish "full and unvarnished" details about their polls, including details of the size of the sample, how the poll was conducted, the questions asked, and who sponsored and paid for the poll. Two years earlier, when the Tories hit record highs in the Gallup, there was no talk of restricting the process, but at the time Hnatyshyn introduced his white paper Mulroney's Tories were suffering a prolonged slide in all of the published polls.

An Environics poll on the white-paper suggestions, published in that company's *Focus Canada* report, showed 53 percent of respondents agreed with the suggestions, while 41 percent disagreed. Media reaction, however, was almost universally negative, as the government was accused of trying to muzzle and/or censor the media. Southam columnist Don McGillivray compared it to the infamous Depression-era Alberta Act attempting to tell newspapers what they might publish. That bill, An Act to Ensure the Publication of Accurate News and Information, was ultimately declared beyond the powers of the province in a Supreme Court decision that said,

"There must be untrammelled publication of the news and political opinions of the political parties contending for ascendancy."

The issue heated up again after deputy prime minister Don Mazankowski tabled amendments to the federal-election law just before the 1987 summer break, calling for fines of up to $5,000 for individual journalists and $25,000 for newspapers or broadcast companies for breaking the following law: "The results of every commissioned opinion poll in relation to a candidate or registered party that are printed, or broadcast by printed or electronic media must, in each printing or at the time of the broadcast, be accompanied by the disclosure of a. the name and address of the person or organization that conducted the inquiry; b. the size of the sample; c. the dates of the first and last completed interviews; d. the name and address of the person or organization who paid for the conduct of the opinion poll; e. the margin of error if calculable; and f. the exact wording of each question the answers to which led to the results so printed or broadcast." The law would apply at all times, not just during election campaigns.

Both the Canadian Daily Newspaper Publishers Association (which studiously ignores the mass disregard of its own somewhat similar guidelines) and the Canadian Association of Broadcasters threatened to launch a constitutional challenge, calling the law "scandalous" and an infringement on freedom of the press.

None of this threatened political action would be necessary if the media practised the social responsibility they claim to treasure. While there were a few obvious problems with the amendments as worded — would passing references to polls in newspaper columns be required to carry all the other information, for example? — the overall impact of the legislation, ultimately allowed to die a quiet death, would be to force more responsible reporting of polling data and spare us from much of the shoddy and nonsensical stuff that passes for "scientific" surveys. But social responsibility is not particularly what feeds the media, for all their claims to the contrary. What sells, to varying degrees, is crime, underwear, and outrage, and if a poll helps readers, listeners, and viewers to peek up the collective skirts of society then it will be "news" regardless of how the titillating view was obtained. If the media cared as much as they claim, they would not countenance the polling quickies, the down-and-dirty surveys performed by pollsters whose own interest, like that of the media outlet that is using their cut-rate services, is self-promotion, plain and simple.

The broadcast media, in particular, complain that a requirement to include methodological details would make it impossible for them to report polls. Many radio stations, for example, devote about three minutes to an entire newscast, so adding thirty seconds to explain a poll would be too much of an imposition. But would it really? Broadcasters are already regulated by the CRTC, which imposes considerable restrictions and obligations upon them. Surely it is not unreasonable to expect a radio station, particularly during election campaigns, to perhaps play one less record an hour in exchange for offering its listeners more complete understanding of a public-opinion poll. And if it is too much for a particular station, it could simply exercise its option of not reporting the story, a choice every media outlet makes several times a day as a result of normal space and time limitations.

Pollsters who do market-research surveys for corporate clients, and get paid accordingly, would never skip as many methodological basics as the media pollsters do. To them, a call-back is important because it retains the integrity of the random sample to the highest possible degree. To a pollster turning around a survey in two days, proper call-backs represent two significant obstacles: time, which they don't have in order to meet media deadlines; and money, which the media, despite their wealth, refuse to pay. In the United States, for example, at least major media outlets have the decency to combine forces and pay the freight for more precise polling. In Canada, we have a polling industry with no enforceable standards and a media industry that, even if it gave a damn, is plagued by such massive ignorance of the limitations of polling that it wouldn't much matter. The media and media pollsters have become co-conspirators in an exercise to promote themselves — either to sell more polls or to sell more papers — while at the same time hoodwinking the public into believing the numbers presented are not only absolute, but are equivalent to Moses delivering the tablets to the Children of Israel. How often have you read or heard the big "news" of the latest poll that the Tories have dropped two points, or the Liberals have gained three, or whatever, information that means absolutely nothing, given the vagaries of the polling craft, particularly the low-cost media polls? If the same polling firm polled the same people on the same day with the same questions, it would get minor variations in the results, yet the media continue to get excited about meaningless shifts and compare different polls taken at different times using different techniques. Rather than being used as an imperfect guide to follow trends, polls are presented as the key to open the door into the collective will of Canadians. The media, in fact, give polls more weight than pollsters do. That's because pollsters understand their business. The media, with few exceptions, don't.

No other group in society gets the relatively free ride from media scrutiny that pollsters enjoy. This surely is in part because the two crafts are sharing the same bed, a self-inflicted conflict-of-interest the media wouldn't tolerate under any other circumstances. If a newspaper or TV station hires a pollster, the results of the pollster's work, by definition, are big news for that newspaper or TV station, not subject to normal journalistic scrutiny. Was it really a front-page story when the fourth or fifth poll in the last campaign came out, showing the Tories well in front? No, at least not by the usual editorial yardstick. But it becomes the main story because it is the *Globe*'s poll, or the CBC's poll, or whatever. It is less to do with news value and much more to do with promotional value for both the pollster and the media outlet.

It is equally remarkable to see so many journalists being conned by the partisan political pollsters, naively accepting little snippets of inside stuff as if both Allan Gregg and Martin Goldfarb have no particular axes to grind or propaganda to push, but are interested solely in the selfless promotion of truth, justice, and the Canadian way.

For all that, however, those who would ban public-opinion polling, or at least the publishing of polling, cannot be separated from those who would burn books they didn't like. The very people who claim to be sacrificing their private lives for the sake of public democracy would deny the public access to the same information — actually, it's usually not as good — as they themselves have access to. It is a remarkably elitist view of the public, which basically says that we, the insiders, are mature enough to handle this information — and use it to exercise our power over you — but you, the mythical average Canadian, are too stupid to understand and too susceptible to being unduly influenced by the published polls.

Many people are too stupid to understand them. So what? They're too stupid to understand many things — although not so stupid as to misunderstand the hypocrisy of those politicians who would censor public access while retaining private access.

There are four traditional arguments used for banning public-opinion polls, particularly during election campaigns: they unduly influence the electoral process; they invade the privacy of respondents; they oversimplify the issues and thus undermine the democratic process; and they are unreliable.

All of these arguments are substantially correct. But then, polls are not the only instruments that could be accused of the same things. Politicians and the media, for example, are guilty of the same short-comings, but we hear no talk of banning them.

Of course polls influence elections, although some pollsters hotly deny it. Right after the last election, Environics published a poll on polls that found 13 percent of respondents admitting they were in-fluenced by the polls. Other pollsters have shown both higher and lower numbers, despite the fact there is a tendency for people not to want to admit they didn't make up their own minds but were swayed by external factors. But political advertising influences voters too, and newspaper columns, and television commentary, and front-page news stories, and the physical appearance of candidates — just ask Joe Clark about that.

Certainly polls have a tendency to reduce election campaigns to a horse race. Again, so what? Horse races have a certain following just as solemn literary readings do. And they do make cowards of politi-cians, generating a reluctance for decision-making on issues that does not serve us well.

But the strength of a democracy is that people are entitled to vote for whatever reason they freely choose, no matter how shallow or how sound it is. In those few moments when the voter is marking an X on the ballot, he or she has the same say in the configuration of the system as the prime minister has. It doesn't last, of course; but it's there for a fleeting moment, and those who would ban polls would strip the voter of one of many influences that go into the numbers the chief electoral officer tallies on election night.

In a perfect society, we would have properly conducted polls, scrupulously reported by responsible media. We are not perfect. We are good enough, however, or should be, to expect something better than we've been getting by way of polls and their reportage. If we do not get that, then, alas, we will ultimately reap the harvest of our own irresponsibility. If pollsters themselves, and their media publicists, don't clean up their own act, politicians will. Count on it. After all, properly conducted public-opinion polling represents a threat to the primacy of politicians and their advisers. To the extent that published polls do reflect public opinion, they infringe on the closeted wisdom of the power elite, giving the general public at least some information it wouldn't otherwise be privy to. The most enduring characteristic of power is exclusivity, whether it's exclusivity of tanks, money, ideas, or knowledge. Those who have it wish not only to profit by it, but above all, to keep it as much to themselves as possible.

The strength of published public-opinion polls is that the knowledge they provide, however flawed, undercuts the exclusivity of the power elite.

The weakness of them is they are often so badly done and so poorly reported. That is where the challenge lies for both the polling firms and the journalists; to voluntarily nurse the system back to health before the politicians impose a cure that, inevitably, will be more serious than the disease itself.

Let us end, as we began, with a poll. A 1986 Gallup found that 22 percent of Canadians asked felt civilization will be in ruins by the year 2005. This was up sharply from the 8 percent in 1960 who felt we wouldn't see 1980. While these views were no doubt solemnly offered and dutifully reported, how would anybody know what to expect in twenty years? Still, if the dooms-dayers are correct, this could be the ultimate exit poll, and disputes over correct methodology and honest reporting would lose their urgency. Until then, however, we should consider both.

Index